Deconstructing Durkheim

A post-post-structuralist critique

Jennifer M. Lehmann

London and New York

First published in 1993
by Routledge
11 New Fetter Lane, London EC4P 4EE

Simultaneously published in the USA and Canada
by Routledge
29 West 35th Street, New York, NY 10001

New in paperback 1995

Typeset in Linotron Baskerville by
J&L Composition Ltd, Filey, North Yorkshire
Printed and bound in Great Britain by
Mackays of Chatham PLC, Chatham, Kent

British Library Cataloguing in Publication Data
A catalogue record for this book is available from the British Library.

Library of Congress Cataloging in Publication Data
Lehmann, Jennifer M., 1956–
    Deconstructing Durkheim: a post-post-structuralist critique /
Jennifer M. Lehmann.
        p.   cm.
    Includes bibliographical references and index.
    1. Durkheimian school of sociology.   2. Sociology–Philosophy.
    3. Deconstruction.   I. Title.
    HM22.F79L44   1993
    301'.01–dc20
    92–28815
    CIP

ISBN 0–415–07039–2 (hbk)
ISBN 0–415–12374–7 (pbk)

This book is dedicated to my father, Wesley A. Lehmann (1920–92), who asked me how many pages I had written every week until the first manuscript was finished, and how many pages I had eliminated every week until the final manuscript was finished.

Contents

Acknowledgements

This text would not have been written without Ben Agger at SUNY/Buffalo. I owe Ben the irredeemable debt of what is now about twelve years of hard mentoring – unflagging support and encouragement in the face of twelve years of adversity in one form or another. Ben and I are not theoretical twins, but he is my greatest intellectual inspiration. He has continually nurtured, sustained and challenged me throughout my academic career. This text would not be a book without Chris Rojek at Routledge. I owe Chris the invaluable debt of having faith in this project, and communicating that faith to me, when I was experiencing a 'lapse in faith'. In addition to Chris, I would like to thank Anne Gee, Katy Wimhurst, Jo Thurm, and Hugo de Klee for their trustworthy and meticulous care of my manuscript during the production process. I would especially like to thank the reviewers, anonymous or otherwise, who helped make this a better book.

From my SUNY days I would like to thank, in addition to Ben: Beth Anne Shelton and Lionel Lewis for their generous, superlative and practical help; those 'fellow' students who braved graduate school with me and are still my long-distance companions, especially Mitu Hirshman, Peter Murphy, and the Bazargan family; the faculty from other departments who inspired and instructed me, especially Molefi Asante, Brian Henderson, Bruce Jenkins at SUNY; and Stanley Aronowitz, at the CUNY Graduate Center. I would also like to look back even further, to Michigan, and my friendships which began there and have endured many years; I single out: Cindy Lamberts-Anderson, Arne Anderson, Inge LaFleur, Tony Catanese, Chuck Dedic, and Sue Seymour.

This project was begun at SUNY, but it was completed at the

University of Nebraska. There is no more hospitable and collegial academic environment in the world than the Sociology Department at the University of Nebraska, which manages to combine productivity with humility and amiability. I would like to thank *all* of my colleagues there, and especially Lynn White, Helen Moore, Paul Amato and David Brinkerhoff. They are true friends as well as perfect co-workers. Alan Booth, now at Penn State, has been a role model and has helped me in many ways, all of them gracious. I must also acknowledge those students in the department – undergraduate and graduate – who constantly contribute to my intellectual growth and development. I have many friendly colleagues and collegial friends outside of the Sociology Department, most notably Sonia Partridge in Clinical Psychology, Moira Ferguson in the English Department, Bill Regier and Nancy Rosen at the University Press, and, collectively, the Women's Studies Faculty.

Finally, I would like to thank my family: Mildred N. Lehmann, Wesley A. Lehmann and Jonathan W. Lehmann. It is ultimately for them that I do what I do.

Introduction
Durkheim/deconstruction/structuralism

DECONSTRUCTION

Who now reads Durkheim?[1] Why do we still read and debate about Durkheim (and Marx), more than one hundred years after they wrote and debated about capitalism? The answer, I think, is that capitalism, and its discontents – along with the poor – are still with us. Durkheim, in my view, wrote the consummate and quintessential statement of capitalist ideology, including the formula for the salvation of capitalism through reform, as opposed to the destruction of capitalism through reaction or revolution. Durkheim presciently and eloquently articulated the dominant philosophy of our own – not his – day, the philosophy of late or state capitalism, which I call neo-liberalism.

This is/not a deconstruction of Durkheim. For what is deconstruction? Definition is antithetical to the 'spirit' (if not 'the' letter) of 'deconstruction', which militates against thingness, presence, identification. However, this work is simultaneously an intervention in Durkheim's work, and in the work of deconstruction. Thus, logically and/or arbitrarily, 'it' 'is' a deconstruction, in the following 'senses' of that word, the following identities of that 'name'.

First, it represents a certain 'style' of reading. It pursues a strategy of close, textual/subtextual/countertextual, symptomatic, 'writerly' reading. It is a reading which works against the grain of Durkheim's writing. It looks for contradictions, ambiguities, and aporia rather than coherence, clarity, and plenitude. It doesn't seek, or find, closure or essence in Durkheim's text. It doesn't seek, or find, some 'one true meaning', the perfect objective embodiment of Durkheim's subjective intention.

Second, this reading/writing operates on the assumption that there 'is' an object which can be called the classical, metaphysical, humanist, philosophical episteme. It attempts to locate Durkheim's work in relation to this philosophical terrain, and to some extent it situates his work – however groundbreaking, radical, 'seminal' (Durkheim, after all, can claim paternity of sociology) it was – within this epistemological structure. Durkheim's work is the site of philosophical humanism, at an ontological as well as an epistemological level.

Durkheim falls within the humanist camp, first because he deploys an ontology of collective subjectivism. For Durkheim, 'society' is a living, conscious being. His organicism combines materialism (collective organism/biology) and idealism (collective consciousness/psychology) to portray society as an anthropomorphic/andromorphic subject replete with body and soul, *corps* and *esprit*. In other words, Durkheim's organicism is a metaphor only in the sense that all theory is metaphorical. Durkheim's organicism is to be taken literally. The social subject is the ultimate unity, the pinnacle of nature, incorporating individual human subjects – bodies and minds – as its complex elements. Durkheim ascribes to the collective entity both the voluntarism of consciousness and the determinism of nature, as well as the evolution common to all life.

Durkheim's epistemology, like his ontology, is based on collective subjectivism. The 'subject' of knowledge, like the 'subject' of reality, is society. Durkheim's organicism, in which society appears as both a physical and mental entity, conditions his view of knowledge, which combines collective empiricism with collective rationalism. The social subject perceives reality better than the individual subject does; and the social subject processes its perceptions, transforming concrete, specific and temporal things into abstract, universal and eternal concepts, categories and relations – an activity of which the individual subject is altogether incapable. Thus Durkheim believes that the corporeal and mental collective entity knows reality both perceptually and conceptually; and that this knowledge is both unproblematic and cumulative. Durkheim's epistemology is an epistemology of enlightenment.

Third, this reading/writing operates on the assumption that there 'is' an object which can be called a 'break' – a radical rupture, a difference, or an alternative – with respect to the previous object – the classical, metaphysical, humanist, philosophical episteme. Correspondingly, it attempts to locate Durkheim's work in relation to this new, 'other' philosophical terrain. To some extent it situates his work – however conventional, conservative, 'terminal' (to the extent that the birth of sociology contains the 'seeds' of the death of man) it was – within this alternative epistemological structure. Durkheim's work is the site of philosophical anti-humanism, at an ontological as well as an epistemological level.

Durkheim falls within the anti-humanist camp, first because he deploys an ontology of individual anti-subjectivism. Durkheim's foundational organicism implicitly necessitates collective subjectivism, but also necessarily implies social determinism. Social determinism, in Durkheim's time as in our own, is a radical, unpalatable threat to individualistic liberal humanism. Durkheim poses social determinism, not only as an absolute, but also as both negative (destructive, controlling) and positive (creative, constitutive), with respect to individual 'subjects'. Thus, he not only scandalized his contemporaries (and continues to scandalize us, and ours), he also anticipated the later scandals of both structuralism and post-structuralism.

Durkheim's epistemology, like his ontology, is based on individual anti-subjectivism. Again, his collective subjectivism is the theoretical wedge he employs to break with individual subjectivism, as individual subjectivism had served as a wedge to break with metaphysical fatalism and skepticism. Durkheim maintains that the individual is an inferior subject of knowledge; and that individual empiricism is an inferior form of knowledge. Thus, he makes an ideology/science distinction which places doctrines of individual self-determination, voluntarism, and idealism on the side of ideology. They are derived from the misleading, subjective misrecognition of reality, the direct experience and sensations of concrete, isolated individuals. Collective knowledge, on the other hand, is inherently scientific, necessarily rationalistic and deterministic. It is clear that Durkheim's theory of social determinism and his sociological theory of knowledge are mutually complementary, and equally anti-individualist as well as (collective) subjectivist.

CRITICAL STRUCTURALISM

Conversely, with respect to what follows, logically and/or arbitrarily, 'it' 'is' *not* a deconstruction. It is not a deconstruction because it assumes that the radical break with metaphysical humanism occurs with modernism and some form of 'structuralism' – not with 'post-modernism' or post-structuralism. It posits the existence of two, alternative, epistemes, and relates Durkheim's theory to each of them. By contrast, according to deconstruction, the only radical departure from the discursive structure of humanistic philosophy 'is' deconstruction 'itself', a skeptical, undermining, decentering, anti-foundational, processual critique of absolutely everything (including the very concept 'thing' and the declarative nexus 'it' 'is' underlying thought, language, ontology, and science), as part and parcel of the metaphysics of presence. Deconstruction is posed as the most radical escape from conventional philosophy, as somehow outside of it, as not just another ontology and epistemology, but as, putatively, the absence or end of ontology and epistemology.[2]

The present work represents a form of structural and structuralist analysis, and not a work of deconstruction, for the following reasons. First, while it pushes Durkheim's text, to find subtexts, conflicting texts, and absences in the text, it also seeks to determine – to ascertain – the preponderant, predominant, and dominant 'meaning' of the text. It seeks to finitely reconstruct the structure or problematic of Durkheimian theory, rather than to infinitely open up absolute play, textuality, writerliness, contradiction, ambiguity, indeterminacy, or undecidability. Further, it takes a stance with respect to Durkheim's stance, a positioned opposition to Durkheim's position. Specifically, it opposes Durkheim's sociological naturalism – his structural functionalist, organicist and evolutionary ontology; his positivist, empiricist, unproblematized epistemology – with a critical form of structuralist theory and practice.[3] At the same time, it supports those tendencies in Durkheimian theory which represent radical anti-humanism (anticipating structuralist ontology and epistemology): social determinism and material rationalism.

Thus, in the second place, this reading is not a deconstruction because it is a reading from a particular point of view (as opposed to deconstruction), and from an alternative point of view (as opposed to Durkheimianism). This point of view, critical structuralism, represents a radical, third position, in relation to Durkheim's philosophical conservatism and political neo-liberalism, and deconstruction's philosophical nihilism and political anarchism. Unlike deconstruction, critical structuralism suggests that social structures do in fact exist and determine individual behavior, both negatively and positively. Further, social structures are intelligible, social science is possible. Unlike Durkheimian structural functionalism, critical structuralism views these structures as social rather than natural, as structures rather than organisms, and as questionable and mutable rather than necessary and beneficial. Further, knowledge of social structures is problematic and political.

Third, this is not a work of deconstruction because deconstruction does not recognize a 'third position'. It only allows that there is a vast epistemological illusion – the Western, metaphysical, philosophical, humanist episteme – which encompasses all thought – with a sole, external, escape or exception: deconstruction itself, which actually 'is not'. Thus deconstruction, without a differentiated analysis of structuralism, or an analysis of its own relationship to structuralism, would assert that structuralism – including critical structuralism – represents not an *alternative* to 'the episteme' (which contains all apparent alternatives), but the *apotheosis* of Western metaphysics. Deconstruction conflates all theory, except itself, into one vast relatively homogeneous epistemological structure.

Post-structuralism reduces all pre-post-structuralist thought to one misguided 'episteme'. It is thereby able to avoid the difficulties of disentangling naturalism and structuralism; organicist holism and dialectical materialism; expressive totality and structure-in-dominance; structural functionalism and critical structuralism; Durkheimianism and Marxism; pro-capitalism and anti-capitalism; positivism and material rationalism; an epistemology of problematic, political production and an epistemology of unproblematic, apolitical perception, etc. Thus, besides being philosophically negative (anti-ontological, anti-epistemological) instead of explicitly philosophical, deconstruction tends to be philosophical instead of explicitly social or political.

Deconstruction rejects everything, both sides of every opposition – philosophical, theoretical or political – as well as opposition, hierarchy, and dichotomy itself – and therefore it rejects nothing. It neither chooses for or against, refusing to recognize *difference* because it generalizes, pluralizes, and trivializes difference into meaninglessness. Furthermore, it rejects opposition, hierarchy, and dichotomy exclusively at the philosophical level – ideationally rather than materially. Of course, deconstruction rejects the dichotomy ideal/material, as well as idealism/materialism.

Deconstruction doesn't posit that there is nothing but discourse, nothing but ideas. Rather, deconstruction posits that there is *no* difference between the world and the text because there is *only* difference: the world is like a text; the world is a text; the world is textual. And there is no 'outside the text': opposites are the same, all oppositions are equal, 'there is only difference'. Marxism and Durkheimianism, socialism and capitalism (as well as Marxism and socialism, Durkheimianism and capitalism, theory and practice, politics and philosophy, ideology and science, text and world) co-exist as differences among an infinity of differences . . . and as *identities*, within the great world/text, the great totality, the singular ontological, epistemological formation: 'the episteme'.

Critical structuralism is located between Durkheim and deconstruction. It represents a break with subjectivism – collective as well as individual – naturalism, organicism, idealism, essentialism, individualism, voluntarism, mysticism, positivism, empiricism, etc. – in short, all of the 'metaphysical' ideologies of pre-structuralist theory. Yet critical structuralism does not 'go all the way' to become post-structuralism.

Ontologically, critical structuralism retains the concept of structure – as relational rather than substantial, as complex and contradictory rather than expressive, as specifically social rather than natural, as differentially deleterious rather than beneficial, as mutable rather than necessary, as social structure rather than organism. Epistemologically, critical structuralism retains the concept of science – as production rather than perception, as problematic rather than automatic, as political rather than neutral or objective. Knowledge is an approximate model of structural reality. It is distinguished from ideology by a recognition of the existence of determinative structures, and a criticism of specific social structures, as opposed to either the defense of any structures which exist, or the denial of the existence of any structures.

The present work opposes the tendencies in Durkheim's theory to a naturalist epistemology of positivism and a naturalist ontology of organicism, as philosophically conservative. To this extent, it is in agreement with deconstruction. However, it supports the tendencies in Durkheim's theory to an epistemology of material rationalism and an ontology of social determinism, as 'radical' breaks with classical philosophy, and as anticipations of structuralist philosophy. To this extent, it departs from deconstruction. Above all, the present work represents a third, an Other position, between the pre-structuralism of Durkheim and the post-structuralism of deconstruction.

Actually, this third position, opposed to pre-structuralism on the one hand, and post-structuralism on the other, could also represent a point of conjuncture between structuralism and deconstruction. I have discussed elsewhere the way in which structuralism must be rigorously distinguished from pre-structuralism or structural functionalism; as well as the way in which deconstruction can be viewed as less anti-structuralist than is generally supposed, according to Derrida himself.[4] Certainly structuralism and deconstruction share many common positions – notably anti-subjectivism – and a common 'foundation' in Saussure. Certainly deconstruction can recognize the existence of *structures* – both 'textual' and 'real'. Certainly structuralism can recognize the desirability, and the possibility, of *deconstructing* specific structures – in texts, in reality, and in the relation between 'texts' and 'reality'. I have called this conjuncture critical structuralism. Another way of describing the conjuncture of structuralism and deconstruction, as well as the orientation of the present work, is the rubric of cultural studies.[5]

DURKHEIM'S POLITICAL ECONOMY AND IDEOLOGY

Assuming a certain contrast between deconstruction and structuralism, the present work is more oriented toward deconstruction, in the following sense: it concentrates on a philosophical rather than a directly political analysis of Durkheim's work. It seems necessary, therefore, to at least suggest the general outline of a political reading of Durkheim.

In the first place, the question of the 'proper name' for the politics of Durkheim's theory continues to haunt his interpreters.

He is alternately called a conservative and a liberal, a reformer and a radical, a capitalist and a socialist. The most recent trends are to recognize the enormous complexity of Durkheim's work, as well as to probe and explore the more critical and radical tendencies within his theoretical labyrinth. My own answer to this question follows.

Philosophically, Durkheim's theory is conservative, due to its foundation in naturalism. Durkheim's naturalism produces ontological organicism, entailing a positive – structural, functional and evolutionary – analysis of the collective organism or subject, 'society'. It produces epistemological positivism, entailing a de-politicized and non-problematized view of knowledge as the evolutionary enlightenment of the collective organism or subject, the increasingly perfect self-knowledge of 'society'. Conversely, Durkheim's work manifests 'radical' philosophical tendencies, notably the ontological and epistemological anti-subjectivism of social determinism and material rationalism.

Politically, Durkheim's theory epitomizes the dual philosophy of the dual social systems, capitalism and patriarchy. In relation to men, economy and society, Durkheim is a liberal 'of sorts'. He advocates the maintenance, as well as the simultaneously individualizing and socializing reform, of capitalism. Durkheim's liberalism is thus a combination of 'conservatism' and 'reformism' with respect to capitalism. On the other hand, in relation to women, children and the family, which Durkheim locates 'outside' of society, he is a traditional conservative. He advocates the maintenance or the return to patriarchy in the private or domestic sphere, where women and children should remain sequestered.

The male, public, social, political and economic sphere, is what Durkheim means when he says 'society'. Thus 'society' actually includes a minority of individuals in a given geographical area: women and children are excluded, asocial, outside of society. Durkheim focuses on 'society' in this sense, on one sphere of a dichotomy. In relation to this isolated hemisphere, 'society', Durkheim is a neo-liberal. As opposed to the 'conservative' or 'reactionary' position contemporary with Durkheim, he does not advocate a return to feudalism or traditionalism. As opposed to the classic liberalism contemporary with Durkheim, he does not advocate utilitarian, laissez-faire, reductive individualism and economism, either as a scientific principle or as a political objective. As opposed to the radicalism contemporary with Durkheim, he does not advocate a revolutionary transformation of capitalism into socialism.

Durkheim supports the maintenance of private ownership of the means of production and the class division, owners/workers. Collective ownership is communistic and thus ostensibly primitive. Marxism allegedly combines this primitive collectivism with classic liberal economism and Durkheim opposes it. He supports an individualization in relation to feudalism: he favors individual mobility and equal opportunity (a 'spontaneous' division of labor) as opposed to castes (a 'forced' division of labor). He supports a socialization in relation to pure, early, laissez-faire capitalism: he favors intermediate bodies (corporations), to integrate and regulate individuals (social cells) within occupational groups (social organs); and a strong state, to integrate and regulate the whole collective society (the social organism). Durkheim calls himself a socialist. In reality he stands for the reform of capitalism; he is a neo-liberal.

DURKHEIM AND DIFFERENCE

Durkheim does not discuss the differences of race, class and sex (or sexuality).[6] Consistent with his organicism, he focuses instead on the differences individuals (cells) and occupations (organs), and their relation to the unified totality, society (the differentiated but holistic organism). Furthermore, his discussion of individuals, occupations, and society, refers exclusively to men. Women are outside of society and therefore not part of his object of study.

With respect to race, Durkheim's views are consistent with his neo-liberal sociologism. He refutes racialism as an anachronistic survival of feudal castes, of primitive or traditional biological and social structures. Durkheim maintains that modern society resolves race into discrete individuals, and replaces heredity with the social acquisition of skills. Therefore, he argues against race as a method of categorizing people or allocating occupations, advocating a racially blind system of equal opportunity and individual mobility. However, theorizing the evolutionary eradication of race through the twin movements of individualization and socialization is both optimistic and assimilationist. Durkheim too easily dismisses race, as an irrelevant social category; and racism, as false consciousness.[7]

Durkheim's views of class are, in a sense, similar to his views of race. Again, Durkheim is consistent with his neo-liberal sociologism. Class (or caste) systems are archaic social structures reflecting earlier, more biological, human groups and dispositions. With the erosion of race by individuation on the one hand, and socialization on the other, Durkheim expects the system of class or caste, since it is founded on race, to resolve itself into discrete individuals on the one hand, and the collectivity of discrete individuals on the other. Individuals and society are intermediated by the occupational groups into which individuals are allocated depending on their native ability and social acquisition of skills.

Class in modern society is merely a division of labor, a distribution of differentiated individuals into the appropriate specialized functions, a meritocratic reflection of their individual aptitudes. Class in the Marxist sense, differential relations to the means of production (ownership and non-ownership), is reduced by Durkheim to occupational differentiation and specialization. Some individuals occupy the specialized function, 'employer'; others occupy the specialized function, 'employee'. Durkheim advocates corporations, to organize the individual cells and occupational organs of society; and a strong state, to organize the individual cells and occupational organs into a complex collective organism, 'society'. Marxist socialism, which is based on a social ontology of class structure, is therefore incorrect, theoretically; and anti-social and divisive, politically. Durkheim too easily dismisses class, as an irrelevant social category; and socialism, as false consciousness.

In relation to women, Durkheim is inconsistent, with respect to his neo-liberalism and his sociologism alike. Durkheim believes that women, unlike men, form a unified, undifferentiated group or caste. Therefore, he takes the conservative, patriarchal position that they should monolithically specialize in one singular type of labor. Further, Durkheim believes that women, unlike men, are essentially asocial in nature. Therefore, he takes the conservative, patriarchal position that they should monolithically specialize in domestic labor, and remain in the home, ostensibly outside of society, where they belong. Durkheim invokes group attributes and biological determinism when he discusses women, as opposed to the individual attributes and social determinism he imputes to men. His dual theory of human nature, in which the structures of women and men *are* differentiated, into natural (inferior, less human) female structures and social (superior, more human) male structures, leads him to a dual theory of human labor, in which the functions of women and men *should be* specialized, into natural reproduction and social production. Feminism is theoretically incorrect, based on an inaccurate assumption of sexual similarity and equality; and politically anti-social and divisive. Durkheim too easily emphasizes sex, as a basic natural/social category; and too easily dismisses feminism, as false consciousness.

Following Durkheim, I haven't written explicitly about his political/economic/ideological positions, and his theorizations of difference here, although I have elsewhere.[8] Following Durkheim, I haven't written about the second sphere, the sphere of women, concentrating instead on his 'general' theory of 'individuals' (men) in 'society' (the public sphere). Further, I haven't written explicitly about the relations between structural functionalism (pre-structuralism), critical structuralism, and deconstruction (post-structuralism), although I have elsewhere.[9] These are different matters, and they must be deferred. What I have written about here is the underlying philosophical structure of Durkheim's social theory, rather than the political implications of his philosophy, his science, his ideology. In my view, however, philosophy, politics, science and ideology, are inextricably interconnected, within that overdetermined epistemological structure-in-contradiction called 'theory'.

Part I

Durkheim's social ontology

Chapter 1

The 'structure' of individuals

SOCIAL STRUCTURE AS ORGANISM

To understand Durkheim's social ontology, it is necessary to scrutinize his conception of social 'structure'. The most important factor in his thought here, as elsewhere, is his fundamental organicism.[1] The organic analogy, the comparison of society to an organism, is so pervasive in his work as to become inconspicuous, or taken for granted, like any permeating presence. His terminology provides overwhelming evidence of this practice. The phrases 'social body' and 'social organism' appear habitually, innumerably. 'Morphology' and 'physiology' are routine *social* concepts for Durkheim, as are 'structure' and 'function'; 'health' and 'pathology'. And he is quite conscious of this aspect of his theoretical framework. The 'essential concepts' from 'other fields of knowledge', 'such as those of species, organ, function, health and morbidity, appear in sociology under entirely new aspects'.[2] This organicist metaphor qua social theory is crucial to Durkheim's vision of social 'structure'. In fact, in a sense, this *is* his vision of social structure.

A society, like an organism, is a supracomplex totality of complex elements. In the organism, these elements are organs, and *their* component elements, cells. Durkheim, while he occasionally mixes his metaphor, generally depicts society as an organism composed of institutions, which he compares to organs; and individuals, which he compares to cells. The most important systematic alternative to this schema is the comparison of occupations, rather than institutions, to organs. However, there are other, more confusing exceptions. For example, he often refers to individuals as 'atoms' rather than 'cells'. On the other hand, he sometimes implicitly conceives of them as 'organs', particularly when he is discussing organic solidarity, or the interdependence of individuals based on their division of labor. Yet it is the model of individuals=cells and institutions=organs; and its major variation, in which individuals=cells and occupations= organs, which predominate.

The individual is to society what the cell is to the organism: 'What is one man less to society? What does one lost cell mean to the organism?'[3] Both the cell and the individual are simultaneously a totality, in relation to their own elements; and an element, in relation to the larger totality which they form in combination. Simple, inanimate molecules combine to produce complex, animate cells, which in turn are only themselves parts of even more complex wholes. How much more complex is society, whose elements are individual human beings. These social 'cells' are themselves the most complex combinations of natural elements in existence, and the totality they form is almost incomprehensible in its dimensions. In fact, there is an ascending ontological order of complexity, with society naturally at its apex. The physicochemical world provides the matter which combines to form the biological world; and this provides the basic matter of its most elaborate product, the psychological world of the human being. The physicochemical, biological and psychological human being, in turn, is not the ultimate in complexity nor the ultimate level at which causality resides, but merely an element itself in the social conglomeration. Social phenomena are 'distinguishable' from the lower levels 'only by a greater complexity'.[4] Yet despite the 'extreme complexity' of 'social facts' or 'social things', they are neither 'inhospitable to science' nor reducible to 'their elemental conditions, either psychic or organic'.[5] In the same way that an organism cannot be understood by analysis of its cells, but must be analyzed in all its complexity, so society cannot be understood by analysis of its individual human elements, regardless of the extreme complexity of these elements, to say nothing of their compound product. 'Therefore, if the psychologist and the biologist correctly regard the phenomena of their study as well founded merely through the fact of their connection with a combination of elements of the next lower order, why should it not be the same in sociology?'[6]

Between the individual 'cells' and their complex unity, the 'social organism', there is an intermediate level, a complex unity

situated or 'intercalated' between two complex unities. This is
the social unit analogous to the organ in the biological organism.
Durkheim conceives of this, as mentioned, in several ways. His
most vivid metaphors are of social institutions conceived of as
social organs. He concentrates on the institutions of morality
(particularly religion), the state, and the economy. These he
depicts repeatedly as the 'heart', the 'brain' and the 'viscera' of
society, respectively. This schema is equivalent to the concept of
'institutional specialization'.

Specialized occupations are equally treated by Durkheim as
organs in the social body, without apparent regard for the
conceptual difficulties this usage engenders. The problem for
Durkheim is a more practical one. He is concerned with the
nature of the relations among the various occupations, just as
he is concerned with the nature of the relations among the
specialized individual elements, and among the specialized institutional elements. For the 'organization' of society, which is how
he refers to occupational specialization, is a new phenomenon.
Societies were originally simple undifferentiated units. They
were composed of 'masses', 'amorphous or without structure'.
The first 'political' or compound societies were themselves
composed not of diverse occupations, but of 'a number of
elementary societies' and were thus not 'organized' but 'poly-
segmental'. It is only more advanced 'political societies' which
are composed of other 'secondary groups', particularly the
'professional groups' or occupations.[7] Thus, a second sense of
organic solidarity would be the relations, real or ideal, obtaining among the diverse occupations which form modern society
as diverse organs form advanced organisms. 'All the functions
of society are social, as all the functions of the organism are
organic.'[8]

There is a second way in which Durkheim's organicism
informs his conception of social 'structure'. He conceives of any
given society as an organism; that much is obvious. But more
than this, he can only conceive of *different* societies, different
social structures, as different types of organisms. Therefore he
is led by the logic of his own theory to posit two basic social
structures (or 'types' or 'species'), located at either end of a
continuum of social evolution, and corresponding to two basic
organismic categories, located at either end of a continuum of
biological evolution; simple, or segmental ('mechanical'); and

complex, or differentiated ('organic').[9] The first of these two social types, so-called 'inferior societies', are compared to 'mono-cellular organisms' while the second, 'elevated societies', are compared to 'organisms of higher type'. 'Primitive' societies are like 'protozoans'. The first 'social type' is a 'veritable social protoplasm', which forms simple segments or aggregates. These in turn combine in repetition 'analogous to the rings of an earthworm'.[10] That which differentiates societies is 'differences in types of association' of their elements, like the 'differences . . . between the lower and higher organisms, between highly organized living things and protoplasm, between the latter and the inorganic molecules of which it is composed'.[11] Durkheim goes so far as to claim that this typology of societies is not merely metaphorical. He contends that societies literally undergo the same evolution as biological organisms, as this evolution is part of a universal natural law:

> the law of the division of labor applies to organisms as to societies . . . the more specialized the functions of the organism, the greater its development . . . It is . . . a phenomenon of general biology whose conditions must be sought in the essential properties of organized matter. The division of labor in society appears to be no more than a particular form of this general process; and societies, in conforming to that law, seem to be yielding to a movement that was born before them, and that similarly governs the entire world.[12]

Durkheim defines 'social evolution' as a 'double movement' wherein segmental organization is gradually supplanted by 'occupational organization' until 'our whole social and political organization will have a base exclusively, or almost exclusively, occupational'. He goes on to say that:
'The same law holds of biological development . . . lower animals are formed of similar segments . . . at the lowest rung of the ladder, the elements are not only alike, they are still in homo-geneous composition'. These organisms are 'colonies' and the individuality of the colony, including its 'structural plan' and its form of solidarity, is 'identical with that of societies that we have termed segmental'. The colonial type 'disappears as we go up in the scale of organisms', 'even as the segmental type becomes effaced as we advance in the scale of social evolution'. Colonies give way to earthworms, which give way to molluscs

and eventually vertebrates. At this point the 'analogies' are between the animal type and 'organic societies': 'In the one case as in the other, the structure derives from the division of labor and its solidarity'.[13] There are, then, two types of social structure, one of which is merely a developed form of the other. There is 'a social structure of a determined nature to which mechanical solidarity corresponds'. It is characterized by 'a system of segments homogeneous and similar to each other'. On the other hand, there is 'the structure of societies where organic solidarity is preponderant'. These 'are constituted, not by a repetition of similar, homogeneous segments, but by a system of different organs each of which has a special role, and which are themselves formed of differentiated parts'. These 'social elements' are 'not of the same nature' and are 'not arranged in the same manner'. They are not simply 'juxtaposed' nor 'entwined' but are 'co-ordinated and subordinated one to another around the same central organ'.[14]

THE COLLECTIVE BODY

'Structure', thus conceived, is not the ultimate, ulterior causal factor for Durkheim. Structure, in the organicist sense, is the shape or morphology of the social body. It has two basic variants: simple and complex. These variants themselves are produced by underlying 'conditions of existence', the 'internal milieu' of the organism. Structure is thus not 'absolute', but rather is itself determined by a substructure upon which it rests. There is a deeper level of 'anatomic or morphological' social facts. The 'substratum of collective life' is, primarily, 'the number and nature of the elementary parts of which society is composed'.[15] It is 'the number of social elements and the way in which they are grouped and distributed'.[16] The 'content' of the 'social substratum' is, 'first of all, the total mass of the population in its numerical size and density'.[17] The formula that the division of labor is the result of population 'volume and density' can thus be understood as a causal relation between substructure and structure.

> The division of labor varies in direct ratio with the volume and density of societies, and, if it progresses in a continuous manner in the course of social development, it is because societies become regularly denser and generally more voluminous.[18]

This pattern has the force of a 'law', according to which 'the growth and condensation of societies . . . *necessitate* a greater division of labor . . . it is its determining cause'. Furthermore, this law is another which is considered by Durkheim to be universal, applying equally to natural organisms and social bodies. Thus,

> We shall not be astonished by the importance attached to the numerical factor if we notice the very capital role it plays in the history of organisms . . . As the constitutive parts of the animal are more numerous, their relations are no longer the same, the conditions of social life are changed, and it is these changes which, in turn, determine both the division of labor, polymorphism, and the concentration of vital forces and their greater energy. The growth of organic substance is, then, the fact which dominates all zoological development. It is not surprising that social development is submitted to the same law.[19]

The mechanism through which the substratum, the quantity of elements, determines the structure, the quality of the whole, is presented in several ways. Sometimes emphasis is placed on the nature of the relations among the individual elements. Individuals who are numerous and interconnected either through physical proximity or the means of transportation and communication, should have more frequent interaction with each other. This intensity of social intercourse, or 'moral density', transforms society, producing a greater 'vitality' along with the division of labor and 'civilization'. On the other hand, the increase in numbers creates 'pressure' or competition for scarce resources. In this view, the division of labor is the result of disequilibrium and conflict brought about by the change in population size. It intervenes as 'a mellowed denouement' of 'the struggle for existence'.[20]

Regardless of the mechanism, it is curious that Durkheim regards social elements, individuals, as having causal precedence in relation to the structure of the whole. Society 'has no other substratum' than the individuals which form it.[21] 'Society has for its substratum the mass of associated individuals.'[22] This can be more readily understood in the light of the fact that Durkheim conceives of society as a *collectivity*, of the social body as a *collective body*. There is a 'collective reality', a 'collective entity', a 'collective being' which emerges from the combination of individuals and this is the 'thing' which Durkheim indicates when he uses the term 'society'. The unity of associated individuals is *the* social fact for Durkheim; it *is* society.

The 'association of individuals' is used interchangeably with 'society', as it identifies the same concept. Thus, Durkheim can say that 'as the association is formed it gives birth to phenomena which do not derive directly from the nature of the associated elements'.[23] Or that there remains, beyond the individual, 'only a single, empirically observable moral being, that which individuals form by their association – that is, society'.[24] Elsewhere, he says that 'every aggregate of individuals who are in continuous contact form a society', which he compares to the individual animal formed by a 'continuity of tissue'.[25] In addition to 'association', he also uses the terms 'plurality' and 'synthesis' of individuals or elements. And of course he frequently uses the term 'group'. 'Outside or beyond individuals there is nothing other than groups formed by the union of individuals, that is to say, societies.'[26] 'Social life has various manifestations . . . All of them . . . have this in common: They emanate from a group, simple or complex; the group is their substratum'.[27] And in *Suicide* he argues that 'the group formed by associated individuals has a reality'.[28] It is the group which produces collective states, as much as it is the group in which they exist. In fact, 'human groups have a way of thinking, of feeling, and of living differing from that of their members when they think, feel, and live as isolates'.[29]

Durkheim often points out the functions which assemblies or gatherings have for society. But beyond this, an actual, physical collectivity is for him a *model* of society. When individuals are in direct contact with each other, they form a new, collective entity; a 'moral being', a real group, a small-scale society. This double meaning of the assembly, as a vital element of society as well as its image, emerges most clearly in *The Elementary Forms*, where Durkheim frequently has occasion to discuss religious gatherings. Typically, he says that the practice of the cult has the effect of recreating the 'moral being' upon which individuals are dependent and which is in turn dependent on them. 'Now this being does exist: it is society.'[30] Gatherings and assemblies are like materially and morally dense societies; societies are like large assemblies. In fact, 'societies . . . are only permanent and organized crowds'.[31]

A similar if not more striking model of society on a small scale can be inferred in Durkheim's treatment of sexual intercourse. The 'sexual act' is 'a communion'.

> Through this communion, the two persons united become one; the units which originally circumscribed each of them are first displaced and later transferred. A new personality is born, enveloping and embracing the other two. Should this fusion become critical and the new unity thus constituted become lasting . . . there are no longer two distinct, separate people, but one.[32]

The sexual act is an extreme form of sociability, in that 'there is no act which creates such strong bonds between human beings. It has an associative, and consequently moral power without compare.'[33]

The significance of all this is that for Durkheim society is a very *concrete* object. It is a substantive, a tangible reality. It *is* the group or collectivity itself. It is formed of real, concrete individuals. It is transcendent in relation to these real, concrete individuals. It dominates them. But it is not a different sort of reality. It is not merely *like* a body . . . it *is* a body. It is a living being of ultimate complexity, as it is composed of other living beings. But it is *not* an abstract, determinative set of roles or functions or relations, which individuals occupy as functionaries or 'supports'. It is not an impersonal system into which individuals are placed, like interchangeable parts. It does not precede and succeed individuals. It *is* individuals. This is the meaning of the 'collective body'.[34]

THE COLLECTIVE MIND

The social body thus has two aspects: its substratum, the quantity of individuals which collectively form it; and its structure, the simple or complex quality of the organism they form. Just as an individual organism is the material base for an individual mind, so the collective body, in its dual aspects, is the material base for a collective mind, which can be viewed as the social superstructure.[35] References to the collective mind are ubiquitous in Durkheim's work, and appear in many guises. There is the 'popular consciousness' or 'conscience', the 'moral conscience of nations', the 'public mind', the 'psychic life of society', 'public opinion', the 'mentality of groups', etc., as well as the 'collective mind' per se, and its most well-known appellation, the 'collective consciousness'. While the collective mind arises out of the collective body, its most immediate components are the individual minds which constitute it through their association.

The group psyche is of the same nature as the individual psyche, but has a different substratum, society and all of the minds it contains; and is therefore of a different order. It cannot be reduced to the individual minds which comprise it any more than the social body can be reduced to individuals. 'From the actions and reactions between its [society's] individuals arises an entirely new mental life'.[36] 'When individual minds are not isolated but enter into close relation with and work upon each other, from their synthesis arises a new kind of psychic life . . . This is a world not only more intense but also qualitatively different.'[37] The 'collective consciousness is the highest form of the psychic life, since it is a consciousness of consciousnesses'.[38] If the individual 'representational life' is characterized by *spirituality*', then the social form of this life is 'defined by its *hyperspirituality* . . . All the constituent attributes of mental life are found in it, but elevated to a very much higher power and in such a manner as to constitute something entirely new'.[39]

Consistent with the notion that the social mind is collective, is the proposition that the products or contents of the social mind are collective elaborations. An 'association of living minds becomes the field of action of phenomena *sui generis* which these minds could not have produced by the strength of their nature alone'.[40] Thus 'collective representations' are 'exterior to individual minds' and derive from 'the association of minds'. Individual minds and mental phenomena enter into combination and are transformed; as in a chemical synthesis which transforms its elements. 'Since this synthesis is the work of the whole, its sphere is the whole.'[41] Collective representations are 'the result of an immense co-operation', wherein 'a multitude of minds have associated, united and combined their ideas and sentiments . . . A special intellectual activity is therefore concentrated in them which is infinitely richer and complexer than that of the individual.'[42] Social 'ideals', or 'ideas and sentiments that are elaborated by a collectivity' are 'the effects of that singularly creative and fertile psychic operation . . . by which a plurality of individual consciousnesses enter into communion and are fused into a common consciousness'.[43]

The content of the collective psyche is centered around two poles. There is an intellectual content, or collective thought; and a normative content, or collective morality. These are not clearly delineated in Durkheim's work, and this is part of the reason for the confusion over the translation of the French *'conscience collective'*. *'Conscience'* has two meanings in French. The primary definition is equivalent to the English 'consciousness', a concept for which there is no other term in French. The secondary definition is equivalent to the English 'conscience'. Durkheim clearly meant the term to designate a collective psychology encompassing consciousness as well as conscience. However, focus on the ideal, as opposed to the ideational, aspect of the collective mind; as well as the apparent accuracy of using an English word with the same spelling, has led some translators to the usage, collective 'conscience'. This is a very misleading limitation of *'conscience collective'* to only one of its two dimensions, the moral dimension.[44]

This collective mind or consciousness is considered by Durkheim to be the most important aspect of society. At times, he even speaks as if it actually *were* society, as if society were fundamentally a mental phenomenon or entity. Sometimes this tendency appears in a picture of society as a collection of ideas.[45] Thus in *Sociology and Philosophy*, society is defined as 'above all a composition of ideas, beliefs and sentiments of all sorts . . . Foremost of these ideas is the moral ideal which is its principal *raison d'etre*'.[46] And the 'principal social phenomena' (religion, morality, law, economics and aesthetics) are said to be 'nothing more than systems of values and hence of ideals'.[47] In *Suicide*, the 'social environment' is described as being 'fundamentally one of common ideas, beliefs, customs and tendencies'.[48] Social life is 'made up of representations'.[49] In *Rules* this is stated even more emphatically: 'social life is constituted wholly of collective "representations"'.[50] Social facts are *things*, but not 'material things'. 'To allow . . . that social facts must be treated as things, it is not necessary to maintain that social life consists of other than "representations"'.[51]

Other times, society is presented as a collection of consciousnesses. It is 'communion of mind and wills' which is 'a first condition of any social life'.[52] Social phenomena 'have as a substratum' the consciousness 'formed by all the individual consciousnesses in union and combination'.[53] In *The Elementary Forms*, the clan is said to be formed by 'individual consciousnesses' in association.[54] Society is defined as 'a synthesis of human consciousnesses'.[55] Society has unequalled creative power because it is composed of 'vast syntheses of complete consciousnesses'.[56] In *Rules* Durkheim says that, collectively, individual consciousnesses produce a social being.

> These consciousnesses must be combined in a certain way; social life results from this combination and is, consequently, explained by it. Individual minds, forming groups by mingling and fusing, give birth to a being, psychological if you will, but constituting a psychological individuality of a new sort.[57]

This psychological conception of society as a set of ideas and/or minds forces Durkheim to reestablish the distinction which he insists upon, that between sociology and psychology. He admits that sociology *is* in fact a psychology, but a psychology of the collective mind rather than the individual mind. To distinguish between these two related but separate fields, the term 'psychology' will continue to stand for the study of the individual; while sociology will refer to the study of the (psychological) processes of the collective. Sociology 'principally consists in' the study or the science of 'public opinion'.[58] 'Sociology moves from the beginning in the field of ideals ... The ideal is in fact its particular field of study.' 'Collective psychology is sociology, quite simply'; while 'psychology' per se denotes 'individual psychology'.[59] In the preface to the second edition of *Rules*, Durkheim refers to 'social psychology', the science of 'the laws of collective thinking'. Durkheim has 'no objection to calling sociology a variety of psychology, if we carefully add that social psychology has its own laws which are not those of individual psychology'.[60]

This position, that society is co-extensive with the group mind, reduced to the collective consciousness, is an extreme within Durkheim's thought. What is more general is his insistence on the absolute importance of the mental and moral aspects of society. First, he proposes that they constitute a realm with reality, specificity, and relative autonomy. The collective consciousness actually exists. And it is not reducible to the individual consciousnesses which comprise it. Collective psychology is not reducible to individual psychology in the same way that individual psychology is not reducible to its biological substratum. The complex cannot be understood in terms of the simple, the whole cannot be understood in terms of the parts, higher forms cannot be understood in terms of lower forms. In this way, the 'basic matter of the social consciousness' is closely related to its substratum, 'the number of social elements and the way in which they are grouped and distributed'. However,

> once a basic number of representations has been thus created, they become . . . partially autonomous realities with their own way of life. They have the power to attract and repel each other and to form amongst themselves various syntheses, which are determined by their natural affinities and not by the condition of their matrix. As a consequence, the new representations born of these syntheses have the same nature; they are immediately caused by other collective representations and not by this or that characteristic of the social structure.[61]

Ultimately, this real and relatively independent collective consciousness emerges as, if not the *only* social reality, the *most important* social reality. For it is here that Durkheim locates the determinative, causal force in his sociological scheme.

The 'ideal', meaning for Durkheim simultaneously the ideational and the moral, is the domain of social force. It is the site of the ideal, the collective consciousness of a society, which controls or determines individuals. The collective consciousness, composed of individual consciousnesses, nonetheless transcends and dominates them once it is formed. And through individual consciousnesses, it directs individual behavior. This is the actual mechanism of Durkheim's 'social determinism', its content or meaning. 'Social constraint' is the 'pressure . . . which the consciousness of a group exercises on the consciousnesses of its members'.[62] Society has 'moral ascendency' over its members, an authority which is based on the power which one 'moral being', the group, has over 'those other moral beings, its individual members'. This is due to 'the way in which the collective consciousness acts upon individual consciousnesses.' Thus 'social thought' has 'imperative authority'; it has 'efficacy', because of 'the power which it has over our minds'.[63]

The collective consciousness works through the individual

consciousness, and affects the individual will. Collective 'ideas and sentiments' have an 'ascendancy and an authority' as 'moral forces that dominate and sustain' individuals. 'When these ideals move our wills, we feel that we are being led, directed, and carried along by singular energies that do not come from us but are imposed on us from the outside.'[64] The 'ideal' has 'its own reality and nature'. It 'looms impersonally above the individual wills that it moves'.[65] It is the will which transforms the ideal into something else. The ideal must have 'a force capable of swaying our wills' because '[o]ur wills alone can make it a living reality. . . . this force must ultimately be translated in terms of muscular movement'.[66] 'Muscular movement' or behavior is the determinate effect, the physical reality and materiality, the ultimate *product* of the collective mind. An ideal is 'a body of ideas that soar above the individual while vigorously stimulating certain behavior'.[67] Collective representations shape the content of the individual mind, which in turn is responsible for individual behavior.

> Our whole social environment seems to us to be filled with forces which really exist only in our own minds . . . Yet the powers which are thus conferred, though purely ideal, act as though they were real; they determine the conduct of men with the same degree of necessity as physical forces.[68]

Thus, on the one hand, social forces are ideal. A 'representation' is 'not simply a mere image of reality, an inert shadow projected by things upon us, but it is a force which raises around itself a turbulence of organic and psychical activity'.[69] Social authority is moral authority and moral authority is 'a psychic reality, a higher and richer conscience than our own . . . a mental being higher than ourselves from which our mental powers emanate'.[70] It is 'an interior and profound fact which is wholly ideal'. The norm 'has an efficacy coming solely from its psychical properties'. Collective forces are 'entirely psychical; they are made up of objectified ideas and sentiments'.[71] On the other hand, they have the same power as physical forces. The 'social states of mind' are exterior to individuals and coercive, and therefore stand in the same relation to the individual as physical forces. Ideals are collective forces, or 'natural but at the same time moral forces, comparable to the other forces of the universe'.[72] Collective sentiment 'is a force quite as real and active as the forces that fill the physical world'.[73] Social life is a set of 'moral milieus' which surround the individual. They are determinative over the individual mind as physical milieus are determinative over organisms. Humans must submit to both sets of forces, and the only factor which distinguishes one from the other is that 'the reality, the coercive force, to which we submit our bodies, and the reality to which we submit our wills' have different sources; the one derives from facts of physical nature, the other consists in social facts.[74]

The collective consciousness determines thought and thereby behavior; this much is clear in Durkheim's work. But the collective consciousness exists on a continuum, with two possible variants. And Durkheim moves between these variants in a sometimes confusing manner. The collective consciousness can be extremely 'diffuse', on the one hand. Or, on the other hand, it can be definite and 'crystallized'. At the one end of this polarity are public opinion, public sentiment, public morality, etc. At the other end are explicit moral and legal regulations. Durkheim attributes the power of social determinism to all of these concepts, and he tends to use them interchangeably. But he is unambiguous about their relationship with respect to each other. It is the diffuse collective consciousness which is the foundation of a society's rules. The rules are a crystallization *of* the diffuse collective consciousness, which gives them their support and their force. Beyond the 'maxim', there are 'collective sentiments, the condition of public opinion that renders effective the rules'.[75] Social 'regulation . . . rests in a state of opinion'.[76] The clearest statement of this theory is in *Suicide*, where Durkheim frequently discusses the direct causality of diffuse social 'moods', 'currents', and sentiments on behavior and rates of behavior. There are, of course, 'definite formulae into which the dogmas of faith are precipitated', and 'legal precepts' which 'become fixed externally in a consecrated form'. But 'not all social consciousness achieves such externalization and materialization . . . not all of morality is formulated in clear precepts. The greater part is diffused'. And the former, the precepts,

> merely express a whole sub-jacent life of which they partake; they spring from it but do not supplant it. Beneath all these maxims are actual, living sentiments, summed up by these

formulae but only as in a superficial envelope. The formulae would awake no echo if they did not correspond to definite emotions and impressions scattered throughout society. If, then, we ascribe a kind of reality to them, we do not dream of supposing them to be the whole of moral reality. That would be to take the sign for the thing signified. A sign is certainly something; it is not a kind of supererogatory epiphenomenon ... But after all it is only a sign.[77]

Thus Durkheim, who came under attack for the alleged 'materialism' of his social facts, is actually much more susceptible to the charge of idealism.[78] He refuses to posit mental and moral reality as 'absolute', in other words as unfounded in any other, natural reality. He grounds it in the collective entity which he claims is real and natural, society. But once determined itself, the collective consciousness and its representations become to some extent self-determining. Even within the collective consciousness, the more material aspect is determined by the more ideal, the rule by the thought. And, crucially, the collective mind – including both its mental and moral aspects, and both the spirit and the letter of public morality – are, for Durkheim, *the social determinants* of individual thought and behavior. He himself is aware of the fact that this position is an idealist one. He writes:

> Thus there is one division of nature where the formula of idealism is applicable almost to the letter: this is the social kingdom. Here more than anywhere else, the idea is the reality ... here the part of matter is reduced to a minimum.[79]

THE COLLECTIVE SUBJECT

Durkheim's assumption of a social organism, or collective body; and a social mind, or collective consciousness; is striking enough – when it is not ignored or denied (or suppressed in translation). But another of his theoretical underpinnings, again so pervasive as to inure the reader to its presence, is even more unsettling. And that is his anthropomorphic tendency. He views the collective body and mind in a particular relation of unity, as constituting a real, objective *entity*.[80] Society is to him a vast, complex, superior, living *being*:

we take it as evident that social life depends upon its material foundation and bears its mark, just as the mental life of an individual depends upon his nervous system and in fact his whole organism. But collective consciousness is something more than a mere epiphenomenon of its morphological basis, just as individual consciousness is something more than a simple efflorescence of the nervous system.[81]

And again in *Sociology and Philosophy*:

society was presented as a system of organs and functions, maintaining itself against outside forces of destruction just like a physical organism whose entire life consists in appropriate reactions to external stimuli. Society is, however, more than this, for it is the centre of a moral life ... of which the strength and independence have not always been fully recognized ... To see society only as an organized body of vital functions is to diminish it, for this body has a soul, which is the composition of collective ideals.[82]

This social 'soul', the 'ideal', the 'totality of ideas', 'animates this concrete and living body ... society'.[83]

Durkheim realizes that his personification of society is relatively unthinkable. But he counters that 'it is natural that any being having superhuman powers should baffle man's intelligence'.[84] It is ironic that Durkheim is widely known for his theory that 'God' is really society. But he believed, equally, that society is really God.

I know of only one being that possesses a richer and more complex moral reality than our own, and that is the collective being ... there is another being which could play the same part, and that is the Divinity. Between God and society lies the choice ... I myself am quite indifferent to this choice, since I see in the Divinity only society transfigured and symbolically expressed.[85]

Durkheim uses many terms to express this concept, society as a superhuman being, which he employs throughout his work. The most frequent are 'being' ('être'), and many variations on it, including 'collective being' and 'social being' ('être collectif', 'être social'); as well as 'personality' and 'collective personality' ('personnalité', 'personnalité collective'). Individuality ('individualité') and psychic individuality ('individualité psychique') are common. Even 'social ego' ('le moi social') appears, though not commonly.

There are many descriptions of this 'person' which society is conceived to be. In *Suicide* the collective being is noted for its nature or character, and its 'moods', which express themselves in group tendencies, or social rates of behavior. The 'coenaesthesia' which exists in 'collective existences' as well as in individuals, gives its 'effects' 'the same personality and stability'.[86] The suicide rate is 'a distinctive trait of each collective personality'.[87] In *Rules* there is a 'being, psychological if you will' which results from the combination of a plurality of 'organico-psychological' beings. This being constitutes 'a psychological individuality of a new sort'. It is 'in the nature of this collective individuality . . . that we must seek the immediate and determining causes of the facts appearing therein'.[88] The 'conditions in which the social group in its totality is placed' produce certain 'collective representations, emotions, and tendencies',[89] which are themselves productive of social thought and behavior, and which are distinguished from individual thoughts and tendencies by their collective nature. The social being is essentially like an individual being, except that, because it is formed from individual beings, it is infinitely more complex. The social being is 'richer, more complex, and more permanent than the individual being'.[90] It is, therefore, 'a nature *sui generis*', 'a new form of existence'.[91] In the *Elementary Forms*, society is 'a reality *sui generis*; it has its own peculiar characteristics, which are not found elsewhere and which are not met with again in the same form in all the rest of the universe'. The collective representations which express it are the results of a 'special intellectual activity . . . which is infinitely richer and complexer than that of the individual'.[92] Society 'has a nature which is peculiar to itself and different from our individual nature'. Therefore, it 'pursues ends which are likewise special to it'.[93] Society is 'an individuality . . . which has its own personal physiognomy and its idiosyncrasies'.[94] Society is 'not a nominal being created by reason, but a system of active forces', a 'super-individual reality'.[95] In *Moral Education*, society is a living, conscious and sentient being; with its own identity, its own consciousness, its own personal temperament. 'Outside and above the conscious being that I am, outside and above the conscious beings that other human individuals are, there is nothing else, except the conscious being that society is.' Society is the object of all moral behavior, and in that capacity it must

> constitute a being *sui generis* which has its own special nature, distinct from its members, and its own personality, different from individual personalities. In a word, there must exist, in the full sense of the term, a social being.[96]

The fact that it is the object of morality, combined with the fact that for Durkheim an object of morality must be an actual entity, constitutes for him a 'practical' proof of a conception already proved 'in theory': 'that conception of society as a being distinct from the individuals which compose it'. Moral action is that which is directed toward 'a superior being'. And beyond the individual there is only 'one single empirically observable moral being . . . society'.[97] Humanity itself, unlike particular nations, cannot serve as this object of morality, because it is not a 'constituted society'. 'It is not a social organism with its own consciousness, its individuality, its organization.'[98] Society is a 'collective being'; a 'vast' and 'complex' 'personality'; 'a being which has superhuman powers'; a 'concrete and living being'; a 'directly observed being'. It is a 'real and concrete thing'.[99]

In addition to descriptions of its nature, the social being is described in its activity. Individuals in combination form 'a psychical existence of a new species, which consequently has its own manner of thinking and feeling'.[100] Social facts are not 'psychological', meaning that they are not individual. But they are 'mental', since 'they all consist of ways of thinking or behaving'. The 'group' 'thinks, feels, and acts'.[101] Human 'groups have a way of thinking, of feeling, and of living differing from that of their members when they think, feel, and live as isolates'. Society is a 'psychic being that has its own particular way of thought, feeling and action'.[102] It is 'the aggregate in its totality' which 'thinks, feels, wishes'.[103] All 'functional phenomena of the social order are psychological in the sense that all constitute a way of thinking or acting'. There is this difference: 'collective ideas and actions' are different from individual ideas and actions, in that they are *collective*.[104]

It is clear that Durkheim conceives of society as a *collective subject*, as a real and distinct entity which thinks and acts. In fact, he even uses the term subject ('sujet'). It is not always translated as such. Note, for example, the following passages in *Sociology and Philosophy*. First, the term 'personality' is omitted. Durkheim says that society must be considered 'as a personality', distinct from 'individual personalities'.[105] This is translated with the statement that society must be considered 'as being qualitatively different from the individual beings that compose it'.[106] Then, further, Durkheim refers to society as a 'conscious subject', 'the subject *sui generis*', 'the collective subject', the 'one subject which possesses a moral reality richer and more complex than ours . . . the collectivity'.[107] 'Subject' ('sujet') is translated as 'conscious beings'; 'the *sui generis* collective being'; 'the collective personality'; and 'one being', respectively.[108] In *Rules*, the translation is precise, in the following passage:

> The group differs from the individual in its constitution, and the things that affect it are therefore of a different nature. Representations or concepts that reflect neither the same objects nor the same *subjects* cannot be traced to the same causes.[109]

In *Elementary Forms*, Durkheim reiterates this conception of the collective subject and its specific objects.

> If society is something universal in relation to the individual, it is nonetheless an individuality itself, which has its own personal physiognomy and its idiosyncrasies; it is a particular *subject* and consequently particularizes whatever it thinks of. Therefore collective representations also contain subjective elements.[110]

The 'world expressed by the entire system of concepts is the one that society regards', and 'such an object can be embraced only by *a subject which contains all the individual subjects within it*'.[111]

THE TOTAL 'STRUCTURE'

Durkheim's understanding of society, then, is that it is a collective subject, which has been reconstructed from its constituent systems (collective body, collective mind) above. It can be analyzed back down into its subsystems, in order to recreate Durkheim's model, this time as an entity viewed not in its unity but in its composition, its component interrelated structures. Durkheim's model can actually be looked at as a variation of the substructure/

structure/superstructure model, with the proviso that it remains organicist, a model of a complex physical and psychical organism. The physical basis of this organism, the social body, has two aspects: substructure and structure. The substructure, or ultimate foundation, is, again, the number of elements, individuals, in interaction. This is population 'mass and density'. The structure rising out of this base is the pattern of interaction, the relations obtaining among these elements, their arrangement. This is the morphology of the social body, the social 'type'. The superstructure, or collective consciousness, arises out of this substructure/structure configuration which comprises the collective body. The collective consciousness includes both the social mentality and the social morality, and it also has two aspects: a diffuse aspect, on the one hand; and the crystallized forms of this diffuse mentality and morality, on the other. The superstructure is the realm of immediate effectivity. It is the collective consciousness which determines individual thought, and, via individual thought and will, individual behavior. This is how the 'ideal' becomes real or manifest, and how the social structure is reproduced. A vertical view of this overall structure would obviously place the substructure (number of organic or social elements) at the bottom; structure (organic or social morphology) next; and superstructure (social mind and morality) at the top, ascending from the diffuse consciousness, which forms a base, to its definite forms. It is this uppermost layer, in its diffuse and definite aspects, which regulates the behavior and relations of the individual elements, descending now from the individual mind and morality where they intervene, to the individual body where they are enacted. A horizontal view would be: substructure (quantity and density of elements) › structure (interrelation of elements) › diffuse superstructure (social consciousness) › crystalline superstructure (social consciousness) › individual mentality and morality › individual behavior.

This is a generalized or abstract model. But because of Durkheim's thorough and uncompromising organicism, this form only contains two possible contents. There are only two possible variants of size and density; two possible variants of structure; two possible variants of social mentality and morality; and therefore two possible types of individual consciousness and behavior. A small population produces a homogeneous, segmental social structure. A segmental social structure produces mechanical solidarity, with its entirely collective diffuse mentality and morality. This is crystallized in, among other things, repressive penal law. These are all embodied in the corresponding (homogeneous) thought and behavior of (identical) individuals. A large (materially dense), interacting (morally dense), population produces a heterogeneous, organized social structure through the mediation of the division of labor. A specialized social structure produces organic solidarity, with its partially individualized mentality and morality. This is crystallized in, among other things, restitutive civil law. These are all embodied in the (partially individualized) thought and behavior of (specialized) individuals. These are the only two social types or organisms conceivable to Durkheim, because there are only two types of biological organism: complex and simple; differentiated and undifferentiated.

Again in line with his organicism, Durkheim considers the relations of determination between each of these levels as inviolable. There is one and only one structure which corresponds to material and moral isolation; as there is one and only one structure which corresponds to material and moral density. Segmental social structure necessarily produces mechanical solidarity; as differentiated social structure necessarily produces organic solidarity. These forms of solidarity, sanctioned by public opinion, will automatically engender the appropriate thought and behavior in individuals, as social determinism proceeds from collective thought and morality to concrete individual action. Each lower level is conceived of as an internal 'environment' or 'milieu' or 'condition' to which the next level must adapt. Thus the relation which exists between levels is variously thought as 'expression', wherein a higher level 'expresses' the nature of a lower level; 'necessity', wherein a lower level 'necessarily' produces a certain form of the higher level; 'foundation', wherein the higher level is 'founded' in the lower level; 'adaptation', wherein the higher level is 'adapted' to the lower level; 'correspondence'; 'determination'; 'function'; et cetera. Health and normality prevail when these conditions obtain, when the various structures are in natural correspondence. The 'normal' is what 'generally' exists, and the 'generality' of a phenomenon is due to the fact that it is 'grounded in the nature of things'. The normal phenomenon is, 'most frequently', 'useful'; but at least 'necessarily implied in the nature of the being'.[112]

Pathology and crisis occur when the structures are out of alignment, notably in the period of transition between the two forms, during which inappropriate forms persist as 'survivals' or are eradicated but not yet replaced with the appropriate forms. The substructural systems have shifted inexorably; the social body has been reorganized as a differentiated structure under the pressure of its expanding mass. But the superstructural systems – the social mentality and morality, social 'norms' – are either obsolete, non-existent, or only partially formed. But as this is precisely a crisis of transition, Durkheim expects the organism to adjust eventually, and for a new condition of normalcy to emerge, in the shape of a completely complex social organism. The division of labor has been made 'necessary because of changes in the social environment'.[113] Now it remains for the upper levels, the levels for which the specialized structure is the 'environment', to adapt in their turn.

Durkheim often conflates the substructure and structure; and refers to the combined object as, alternately, the social structure per se; or the substratum, in relation to the superstructural levels. He performs the same operation on the various aspects and dimensions of the superstructure, referring to them in combination as 'social life', the social or collective consciousness, et cetera. This is perfectly consistent with his division of society into body and mind. This dual structure conception is evident, for example in *Sociology and Philosophy*: 'the basic matter of the social consciousness is in close relation with the number of social elements and the way in which they are grouped and distributed, etc. – that is to say, with the nature of the substratum'.[114] Or:

Society has for its substratum the mass of associated individuals. The system which they form by uniting together, and which varies according to their geographical disposition and the nature and number of their channels of communication, is the base from which social life is raised. The representations which form the network of social life arise from the relations between the individuals thus combined . . . The conception of the relationship which unites the social substratum and the social life is at every point analogous to that which undeniably exists between the physiological substratum and the psychic life of individuals.[115]

The 'ideal' varies in different groups, according to 'the nature of things'.[116] And in *Suicide*, Durkheim says that the 'mental system' of a people:

> depends really on the grouping and organization of social elements. Given a people composed of a certain number of individuals arranged in a certain way, we obtain a definite total of collective ideas and practices which remain constant so long as the conditions on which they depend are themselves the same. To be sure, the nature of the collective existence necessarily varies depending on whether its composite parts are more or less numerous, arranged on this or that plan, and so its ways of thinking and acting change; but the latter may be changed only by changing the collective existence itself and this cannot be done without modifying its anatomical constitution . . . [a] change in moral temperament thus betrayed bears witness to a profound change in our social structure.[117]

Social 'life' is 'natural' because it 'springs directly from the collective being'.[118] Social life 'depends upon its material foundation and bears its mark, just as the mental life of an individual depends upon his . . . whole organism'.[119]

Sometimes, within this dichotomy, Durkheim focuses on the nexus in which the social body (substructure and structure combined) produces the diffuse aspect of the social consciousness. Thus, for example, in *Suicide*, there are both general and particular collective 'states' (moral states, spiritual states, states of mind) and sentiments which are 'adapted' to general and particular social 'circumstances' and 'environments';[120] they come from 'the collective organization'.[121] The 'mood of societies', like the mood of an individual, 'reflects the state of the most fundamental part of the organism'.[122] It is natural that the discussion of diffuse states should occur in *Suicide*, since here Durkheim is discussing a behavioral manifestation (suicide) not of a socially sanctioned act, but of an officially condemned act. Suicides embody, not regulations, but vague feelings. They result from 'collective melancholy'. They 'express' the 'mood' of a people.

Much more prevalent is his discussion of the way in which the social body determines or produces a specific *morality*.[123] Morality is a part of the collective consciousness somewhere between vague, diffuse feelings and codified legal regulations. In 'normal' conditions, the diffuse social sentiments would spontaneously reflect the underlying social structure. The group ideally 'feels' the needs of the social structure, in the form of collective opinion.[124] These feelings would in turn be reflected and crystallized in the social morality, or moral rules of the society. And these would be more consciously reflected and crystallized in the actual legal codes. (And, again, this whole moral social consciousness would then be reproduced and embodied in individual thought and behavior.) But Durkheim is not as concerned with either the very diffuse or the very definite; he concentrates on the intermediate level, popular morality, where moral precepts are clear and general products of social consensus. They are neither vague nor are they written in stone.

In *The Division of Labor*, moral regulation 'rests in a state of opinion', and ultimately 'expresses ... social needs'.[125] The 'moral facts', 'rules of action' or 'ethics' of a society are based in social conditions, which, at a given time 'do not permit [their] being otherwise'. Alternatively, change in 'the structure of societies' necessitates change in its 'customs'.[126] There is a 'normal' morality for each society. Moral rules 'depend on the nature of social types'. Thus the normal morality 'evolves, as do societies themselves and all organisms'. A crisis occurs 'when the moral conscience of nations is not yet adapted to the changes which have been produced in the milieu'.[127] Each society or people 'has its morality which is determined by the conditions in which it lives'.[128] In Durkheim's contemporary society, 'certain of our duties are no longer founded in the reality of things'. This situation resulted in a 'breakdown', the only remedy for which was 'a new discipline'. Old 'traditions and practices ... no longer responding to present conditions of society can only live an artificial, false existence'.[129] The old social conditions were characterized by the resemblance of social elements and the relations ensuing from that resemblance. These relations were regulated by mechanical solidarity. The new social conditions were characterized by elements with specialized natures and relations, which could only be regulated by organic solidarity. Both types of regulation or solidarity 'correspond to the same social need, but satisfy the need differently, because the conditions of existence in the societies themselves differ'. Morality 'never varies except in relation to social conditions'.[130] The segmental 'structure' of society had been displaced by the division of labor. 'Accordingly, the morality which corresponds to this social type has regressed, but without another developing quickly enough to fill the ground that the first left vacant in our consciences.'[131] The 'moral conscience of nations' must adapt to the new structure. And indeed, 'opinion is steadily inclining towards making the division of labor an imperative rule of conduct, to present it as a duty'. The 'categorical imperative' of the 'moral conscience' had begun 'assuming the following form: *Make yourself usefully fulfil a determinate function*'.[132]

In the *Rules*, there are two aspects of morality, the variable and the fixed. 'The former correspond to the changing, the latter to the constant conditions of social life.'[133] Thus 'law and morality vary from one social type to the next' and also 'within the same type if the conditions of life are modified'.[134] Again, there are normal and pathological or 'morbid' phenomena. Normal phenomena are 'bound up with the conditions of existence of the species under consideration, either as a mechanically necessary effect of these conditions or as a means permitting the organisms to adapt themselves'. This state is disrupted during 'periods of transition' in the 'evolution' of the 'species'. Then the only 'normal type' is that 'from the previous condition', which 'no longer corresponds to the new conditions of existence'. This is exemplified by 'the present economic state of Europe, with the absence of organization characterizing it'.[135]

In *Sociology and Philosophy*, there is only one morality 'endorsed by the condition of society' at any given time. Therefore, '[t]o desire a morality other than that implied by the nature of society is to deny the latter'.[136] There are permanent moral principles, which are 'related to such or such essential and ever-present conditions of our social organization'. For example, 'the rights of the individual are so closely bound to the structure of the great European societies and our whole mentality that to deny them is to deny the most essential interests of society'.[137] The science of morals, which relates various moral systems to their social structural conditions,

> allows us to take up a position between the two divergent moralities, the one now existing and the one in the process

of becoming. It teaches us . . . that the first is related to an order which has disappeared or is disappearing, and that the new ideas on the contrary are related to recent changes in the conditions of collective existence and are made necessary by these changes . . . we cannot aspire to a morality other than that which is related to the state of our society . . . It is from society . . . that morality derives.[138]

This science can evaluate 'the present condition of moral opinion in its relation to the social reality which it should express'.[139]

In *Essays on Morals and Education*, morality is defined as:

a set of rules of conduct, of practical imperatives which have grown up historically under the influence of specific social necessities. All people of the same type have at all stages of their development a morality which results from the way they are organized and which expresses their mentality, just as the nervous system results from and conveys the nature of the living being.[140]

Thus: 'Each social type has its own particular moral discipline'. All 'moral institutions' are 'equally natural', as they are all 'founded in the nature of the societies which uphold them'. In addition to this moral relativism, there is a moral absolutism implied here, in that: 'There is only one particular morality that a society can have, given the way it is constituted'. It receives its morality 'with its very organization . . . when it receives life'.[141] Durkheim's aim is to discover 'what the social needs, the ideas and the collective sentiments are' from which moral precepts result, as well as 'how these sentiments, ideas and needs are connected with and derive from the nature of society'.[142] Moral maxims result from social conditions and states, and serve social ends. And yet, because society changes, morality must change too; 'it must change so as to fit in with the new conditions of social life'. The evolution of morality must be traced in conjunction with the evolution of society. The variations in moral rules must be considered in terms of the various social milieux. The history of morality follows the history of social types. Conversely, to 'separate the rule from the milieu is to separate it from the living springs from whence it flows'.[143] Every moral system is 'rational', for every moral system has its *raison d'être* in the society which produces it. On the other hand, an institution which has its 'justification in a given social system ... cannot be other than it is'.[144] The morality of a nation 'expresses its temperament, its mentality and the conditions in which it lives'.[145]

> The purpose of the morality practised by a people is to enable it to live: hence morality changes with societies. There is not just one morality but several and as many as there are social types. And as our societies change, so will our morality.[146]

The clearest and most succinct expression of this view of the relation between the social body and the social morality is found in *Moral Education*:

> the morality of each people is directly related to the social structure of the people practicing it ... given the general character of the morality observed in a given society ... one can infer the nature of that society, the elements of its structure and the way it is organized ... each social type has the morality necessary to it, just as each biological type has a nervous system that enables it to sustain itself. A moral system is built up by the same society whose structure is thus faithfully reflected in it.[147]

The laws of the moral order 'express the nature of the concrete reality that is society'. The unity of a moral system 'derives from that of the concrete being that serves as its foundation, the nature of which is expressed in morality ... society'.[148]

Again, morality is in the center of the continuum formed by the collective consciousness. It is necessitated by the specific configurations of the social body, but it is immediately founded in relatively amorphous social sentiments. It 'expresses' the social 'temperament' and 'mentality'. It 'results' from 'sentiments, ideas and needs' which themselves 'are connected with and derive from the nature of society'. It 'rests' in 'a state of opinion', which is itself the result of the group, the collectivity, society, 'feeling' its own needs. At the other end of the continuum is the crystallized expression of morality, formal law. The process by which the exigencies of the social structure are ultimately translated into moral and thence legal codes is presented in two different ways by Durkheim. On the one hand, he describes it as a matter of functional repetition and habit. The division of labor brings certain 'functions' or 'ways of definite action' in relation with each other. These ways of action are 'identically repeated in given circumstances, since they cling to general, constant conditions of social life'. Therefore,

> the relations which are formed among these functions cannot fail to partake of the same degree of fixity and regularity. There are certain ways of mutual reaction which, finding themselves very conformable to the nature of things, are repeated very often and become habits. Then these habits, becoming forceful, are transformed into rules of conduct . . . there is a certain sorting of rights and duties which is established by usage and becomes obligatory. The rule . . . expresses . . . the result of a given situation.[149]

Those modes of action which are 'most in accord with the nature of things' tend to 'repeat themselves with the same regularity'.[150] Certain 'manners of acting and thinking' acquire,

> by reason of their repetition, a certain rigidity which on its own account crystallizes them . . . They thus acquire a body, a tangible form, and constitute a reality in their own right . . . Such is the origin and nature of legal and moral rules . . . etc.[151]

However, this is not the explanation which predominates in the general *oeuvre*. The mechanism which Durkheim usually implies is the spontaneous correspondence between public opinion and social imperatives. The collective mind grows out of the collective body, and naturally knows its needs. Public opinion is to be respected as it is 'right'. Popular morality mandates the individual behavior appropriate to the given social structure. And once again, this relation only becomes problematic in periods of transition. Then public thought is out of synchrony with its structural foundation, and confused. But the condition is only temporary, as the natural relation between social structure and thought is one of expression and reflection. Moral precepts, and ultimately laws, are the outward forms of this 'diffused' morality of the automatically knowing, collective consciousness (or subconscious). As external manifestations, laws, proverbs, maxims, customs, et cetera, 'help us to go further in our analysis of the communal conscience to that substratum where these obscure and only half-conscious currents are elaborated'.[152] The 'main legal and moral precepts, immobilized in their sacrosanct forms' are opposed to 'a large collective life which is at liberty', 'currents' which are 'constantly mobile' and 'never crystallized in an objective form':

> these very precepts merely express a whole sub-adjacent life of which they partake; they spring from it but do not supplant it. Beneath all these maxims are actual, living sentiments, summed up by these formulae but only as in a superficial envelope. The formulae would awake no echo if they did not correspond to definite emotions and impressions scattered through society. If, then, we ascribe a kind of reality to them, we do not dream of supposing them to be the whole of moral reality. That would be to take the sign for the thing signified. A sign is certainly something; it is not a kind of supererogatory epiphenomenon . . . But after all it is only a sign.[153]

At the other end of the continuum, Durkheim is consistent. Law is the outermost 'materialization' and 'externalization' of the social consciousness. Moral precepts express the diffuse social consciousness, and law simply formalizes moral precepts. It is merely collective or public opinion 'organized'. 'In law the greater part of domestic morality, the morality of contract and obligation, all the ideas relating to the great fundamental duties, are translated and reflected'.[154] Law is the most concrete form of morality, but it is also the least real. Law rests on public morality, without which it would have no force. Customs form its 'substratum', from which it generally 'cannot be detached'.[155] By itself it is ineffective and cannot act on public opinion, as 'our moral sensitiveness will never be aroused by legislative measures'. And if it should enter into conflict with public opinion, it would lose. 'When the law forbids acts which public sentiment considers inoffensive, we are indignant with the law, not with the act it punishes.'[156]

Reconsidering Durkheim's image of society as an overall structure, composed of interlocking levels, reinforces the sense that he considered society to be an organism, a body and a mind united as an active subject. But it also produces the knowledge that he considered the internal unity in his subject to be a unity of *expression*. He considered the relations between the levels to be *expressive* relations. Thus the lowest level or substratum, population mass and density, is *expressed in* a certain social structure. This combination of elements in arrangement in turn provides the material substratum for the mental life of society. The collective consciousness, in its obscure and diffused form, *expresses* the needs of the organism in the form of vague moral sentiments. These sentiments then form a substratum in relation to the more defined moral precepts which *express* them. Finally, this collective morality is inscribed or *expressed* in legal codes. The entire collective consciousness – from vague underlying feelings, to explicit moral beliefs, to precise and official legal formulas – is *expressed* in its totality in the thought and then, ultimately, in the behavior of individuals.[157]

Chapter 2

The social determination of 'individuals'

For Durkheim, the individual/society relation is partially har-monious: this is its part/whole aspect. At the same time, it is primarily hostile: this is its aspect of conflict, wherein the individual and society are at war. Durkheim, from the ramparts of society, sees the individual as problematic for society. And he sees society as victorious over the individual, as dominating the individual. Finally, the individual/society relation is ultimately harmonious. Although at one level the individual and society are two opposing entities with two opposing interests, at another level it is in the *true* interest of the individual to be dominated by society, as domination is the means to transcendent elevation. Through society, the physical, animal individual becomes the mental and moral, the human, being, communing in and benefitting from civilization. It is for the individual's own good that society destroys it, to resurrect it again in a superior form. Death of the mortal flesh is necessary for a spiritual life everlasting.

Another way of conceptualizing the individual/society relation is the relation of determinism. There is clearly a deterministic tendency, a social determinism, in Durkheim's thought. In a cause/effect schema, it is society which has precedence. It is the whole which determines the nature and behavior of the parts. This is one of the more notorious, scandalous, elements of the *oeuvre* to be codified in Durkheim lore: Durkheim's deter-ministic position is not necessarily accepted as true, but it is unquestioningly accepted as Durkheim's position.[1] One of the ways in which Durkheim's work opens onto social determinism, opens the possibility of social determinism, is through his description of traditional society.

TOTAL SOCIALIZATION

Traditional, 'primitive', society is the society of mechanical solidarity, the society wherein the individual parts are unified through resemblance. It is the society where the collective consciousness is absolute, where there is only a collective 'type' or personality, in which the component individuals are completely fused, completely dissolved. A recurrent figure which Durkheim uses is absorption. (The French verb in Durkheim's text is, actually, *absorber*.) Traditional society entirely absorbs the individual. The independence of individuals in relation to the group is 'not a pristine fact', because 'originally the individual is absorbed in the group'. Where solidarity is based on resemblance, 'the individual personality is absorbed into the collective personality'. Totally collective society or 'communism' is characterized by a 'special cohesion which absorbs the individual in the group, the part in the whole'. In this type of society, social life is 'as absolute as possible', because 'nowhere is the individual more completely absorbed in the group'. The individual occupies little place and has little value in traditional society because it is 'almost completely absorbed' in the 'very highly integrated' group. In fact, Durkheim accuses 'lower societies' of a social integration which is 'too strong'; and, conversely, of an 'insufficient individuation'.[2]

Individuals are related to each other through similarity, which becomes identification: they are identical to one another; and they are merged in a singular, common, group identity. Collective society is characterized by 'conformity'. There is obviously conformity of conduct, but this 'only translates the conformity of thought'; 'intellectual and moral uniformity'. All particular consciousnesses 'conform' to the common consciousness, the 'psychic type of society'. The homogeneity of traditional society is composed not only of behavioral similarity and even 'organic likenesses' but, most importantly, of 'psychic likenesses'.

This psychic identity occurs, first, because in traditional society the environment and the relation to the environment are the same for all individuals of the group. Therefore, representations of the environment are both identical and collective. The individual 'states of consciousness . . . have the same character' because objects 'affect all consciences in the same way'. The result is a 'fusion' of individual impressions into 'collective impressions'. The same, common conditions of existence 'determine perfectly identical sentiments everywhere'. Everyone leads the same life and therefore 'everything', including occupations, ideas and feelings, is 'common to all'.

Secondly, in traditional, totally unified society, religion 'comprises all' and religious consciousnesses are 'identical . . . this identity is absolute'. Therefore, all individual consciousnesses are 'composed of practically the same elements'. Originality is not simply rare; it 'has no place'. The identity of consciousness, then, is conceived of as resulting from the identity of experience, and from the social state which this unity facilitates, the co-extensiveness of religion with society, and of religious society with the individual. In society constituted by mechanical solidarity, it is through this 'similitude of consciousnesses' that individuals are 'socialized'.[3]

The identity of individuals is so profound that they become 'indistinct' from each other and from the collectivity. (This is also a literal translation, of the French *indistinct*.) The individual, with no separate environment and therefore no differentiated nature or 'physiognomy', is 'indistinct from his companions'.[4] Further, the individual is 'not distinct from the group'. This is because the individual consciousness is 'scarcely distinct from the collective consciousness'.[5] The individual is totally submerged in the collectivity. The individual ego is 'not its own property'.[6] The individual consciousness is 'completely outside itself'.[7]

Society tightly or completely encloses (*enserrer*) the individual. Conversely, the individual, along with its counterparts, blends (*se confond*) into the unique, the collective personality. All consciousnesses are 'drawn into the same eddy', and the individual personality is nearly confounded (*se confond*) with the 'generic' personality.[8] Society is a 'continuous mass', and the individual personality is 'lost' in this mass.[9] In fact, at the height of mechanical solidarity, the collective consciousness 'exactly overlaps our entire consciousness and coincides with it at all points'.[10]

This complete identification of the individual and the collectivity, in which 'we are no longer ourselves but the collective being', means that the individual has neither identity nor autonomy. The individual does not belong to itself, the ego is not its own property, inasmuch as it is 'blended with something not itself' and also inasmuch as 'the goal of its conduct is exterior to itself'. The individual is one with society, and society totally, absolutely determines the individual's thought and behavior.[11] Mechanical solidarity joins individual 'social molecules' which 'have no actions of their own'. They are so determined that they are not even like the elements of an organism, but rather like elements of an inanimate object. Alternatively, the individual is to society like an object to a person, to its owner. It is 'a thing of which society disposes'.[12]

Another analogy is with despotic government. In collective society, as in despotism, the individual has 'no sphere of action proper to him'. However, a society's despotism is not coercive in the same way as a government's. First, social life is 'spontaneous'. The individual 'abdicates' its liberty 'spontaneously'. But more importantly, in totalitarian society, 'there is nothing to abdicate'.[13] In collective society, mechanical solidarity, the 'motives which govern conduct', as well as the 'actions that they inspire' are collective and impersonal. The individual's activity:

> is not really his. It is society, the race acting in and through him; he is only the intermediary through which they realize themselves. His liberty is only apparent and his personality borrowed.[14]

Durkheim is describing a total social determinism of the individual. His most radical formulation of this absolutism is that, in the collective type of society, under the unification of mechanical solidarity, the individual *does not exist*. He does not merely say that, originally, 'society is everything, the individual nothing', although he does say this. He says that in the fullness of mechanical solidarity, individuality is 'null' (*nulle*). When mechanical solidarity 'exercises its force', the personality 'vanishes'. In the absence of the individual personality, the collective personality is 'the only one which exists'.[15] Individuality is 'something which the society possesses'. In primitive society, the individual personality 'does not exist'.[16] It is not the case 'that it was suppressed or artificially repressed, but simply that at this moment of history, *it did not exist*'.[17]

DETERMINISM IN MODERN SOCIETY

Individuation

The individual emerges, acquires reality, a genuine existence, only in modern society.[18] It is disengaged from the inchoate amorphous mass, the single individual entity which is traditional society, only by the division of labor. This social watershed, in which the evolutionary process of specialization at some point reaches 'critical mass', and quantitative change becomes qualitative change, produces modern society and the individual in the same movement. Differentiated occupations simultaneously allow and demand differentiated individuals. Specialized functions both permit and require specialized functionaries.

The division of labor ultimately unites, as the unity of interdependence is stronger than the unity of resemblance. But it first divides. The individual is not a 'pristine', natural fact from which society emerges. Rather, it is a historical social product, possible only in a particular social context. 'Collective life is not born from individual life, but it is, on the contrary, the second which is born from the first.'[19] However, the individual *is* born. It is born in the lacuna of uniformity, in the space of difference. It is born as a part of a complex whole, an organ in a complex organism, or a cell of an organ in a complex organism. It is born into relative autonomy.

The individual exists, inasmuch as it is distinct and independent. Once it appears, as a cell in a complex organism, it is no longer a monocellular organism in a protozoan colony. It is no longer totally identical with other individuals. It is no longer totally identified with society. It acquires its independence at the expense of self-sufficiency, and its identity at the expense of the complete identity of the collective personality. The social organism becomes structured, organized, through specialization. Individuals become individuals through specialization, in structured society.

Whereas mechanical society implies the resemblance of individuals, organic society 'presumes their difference'. Traditional society is possible 'only in so far as the individual personality is absorbed into the collective personality'. Modern society is possible 'only if each one has a sphere of action which is peculiar to him; that is, a personality'. Activity becomes 'personal' to the extent that it becomes specialized. The collective consciousness must 'leave open a part' of the individual consciousness, 'in order that special functions may be established there'. Society no longer 'completely controls us' but 'leaves much more place open for the free play of our initiative'.[20]

The collective being is diminished as collective, common behavior is no longer the rule. It is diminished to the extent that specialized behavior and specialized beings multiply. The individual is still 'socialized', no longer through the absence of individuation, but through the interdependence resulting from the presence of individuation. The individual develops 'a physiognomy and a personal activity which distinguishes him from others'. Simultaneously, the individual is dependent upon others, and the social ensemble they form, 'in the same measure that he is distinguished from them'.[21] The 'personal individuality of social units' has been 'formed and enlarged', but without 'disintegrating' society because:

> It is not the absolute personality of the monad . . . but that of an organ or part of an organ having its determined function, but which cannot, without risking dissolution, separate itself from the rest of the organism.[22]

Negative determination: power, force, internalization

The relative autonomy of individuals, as cells/organs in an organism, is a difficult concept. On the one hand, Durkheim points to a genuine autonomy when he discusses the crises of transition: post-division of labor/pre-organic solidarity. Individuals have escaped society's influence. They are egoistic or overindividuated and anomic or underregulated. They have excessively separate identities and excessive freedom. On the other hand, Durkheim depicts 'society' in the abstract, society in general, modern society as well as traditional society, as deterministic. In modern society, individuals are not only restricted to a merely partial or limited autonomy, due to their position of interaction and interdependence with respect to other cells, organs, and the organism. They are *determined* by society.

The determinism of modern society is specific, entirely different from the determinism of traditional society. It is no longer determinism in the form of total absorption, the absence of the individual as a real entity. The individual and society and are no longer merged, co-extensive, *one*. From their primordial unity, society and the individual are *divided* into *two* separate beings. They are put into *relation* with each other. Durkheim describes this emergent individual/society relation as a relation of determination. Once the individual is crystallized and authentic, social determinism pits the old, collective being against the newly differentiated, nascent individual. It takes the form of social action *on* the individual, of social *forces*, of *cause/effect* relations, and of *constitution*.

Modern social determinism, which arises with the individuation of society, the breakdown of its perfect and total oneness as the singular social Subject, is the determinism of the social fact. Durkheim insists upon the reality of social phenomena, upon their status as 'facts', in order to insist upon their determination of individuals. He assumes that social phenomena, inasmuch as they are collective, are of infinitely greater power than their infinitesimal individual components. Therefore, the admission of their predominance, which he desires, is contained within the admission of their existence, which he explicitly and repeatedly advocates. The acceptance of social facts as real entails the acceptance of social facts as Durkheim defines them. Their essential, defining characteristics are that they are *external* and *coercive* vis-à-vis the individual.

First, social facts are 'things', things which are external to individuals. This externality primarily indicates the lack of power of individuals with respect to social facts. Social facts are *not* products of individuals. Social facts can only be products of other social facts. Individuals do not create social reality any more than cells create the corporal realities in which they find themselves. Society precedes and surrounds individuals as their matrix. The embryo does not engender the womb. Social facts are external in the sense that they 'reside exclusively in the very society itself which produces them, and not in its parts, i.e., its members'. They are external or irreducible to individuals 'just as the distinctive characteristics of life are external to the mineral substances composing the living being'.[23]

Society is the product of 'forces which, far from our having desired or contrived them, combine according to laws and forms of which we are ignorant'. The most important social fact, morality, is 'an expression of the social nature'. It therefore represents 'a dangerous illusion to imagine that morality is a personal artifact, under human control.[24] The individual 'finds' social facts, 'collective ways of acting or thinking', 'completely formed'. Further, 'he cannot evade or change them'. Social facts constitute an external or 'objective' reality, meaning that the individual subject 'did not create them'. Their 'source' is 'not in the individual'. Individuals may be unaware of the externality of social facts, in which case they become 'victims of the illusion of having . . . created that which actually forced itself from without'.

Social facts do not originate with individuals: 'No force can be engendered except by an antecedent force'. Neither can they be altered by individuals. Social facts are things, and 'the most important characteristic of a "thing" is the impossibility of its modification by a simple effort of the will'. It is the illusion of the 'omnipotence' of humans over society and social facts, the 'anthropocentric bias', which serves as Durkheim's bête noire, as the antithesis of and obstacle to social science.[25] The idea which 'radically impedes the constitution of social science' is that society is a 'human work', that it is like a humanly produced machine and not like a natural, self-producing organism. When society is rightfully conceived as an organism, individuals are, necessarily, rightly conceived as causally dependent cells.[26]

Even the collective efforts of individuals are, in actuality, impotent, in the face of society as a natural entity, a 'fact of nature'. Society is a 'natural product', a being with its own nature and laws. It operates according to 'internal necessity'. It has no need of intervention, which in any case is 'useless':

> all efforts by governments to modify societies according to their will are useless . . . nature . . . follows its own course alone, without the necessity of either aid or constraint, even supposing their possibility.[27]

Society's externality means that it is 'a reality which is no more our work than the external world'.[28] Social facts are independent of individuals.

Second, social facts are 'things', things which are coercive of individuals. This coerciveness primarily indicates the power of social facts with respect to individuals. Individuals *are* products of social facts. Social facts are things which are forces, which are effective and efficacious, which force. A frequent figure is that they *impose* both behavior and thought, as well as sentiments, on individuals. In Durkheim's words, they act on, coerce, dominate, control, compel, constrain, cause, govern, command, explain, create, predetermine . . . determine . . . individuals. Individuals, on the other hand, are seen as passive in relation to these active forces. Durkheim portrays individuals as receiving,

submitting, obeying, bowing, deferring, conforming . . . determined. Durkheim uses many metaphors for the social determinism of individuals, a theme which is ubiquitous in his work.
However, this plenitude of metaphors can be structured in
terms of three central nodal points around they tend to circulate.

(i) First is the figure of society as government or God, as Lord,
in its historically conflated meaning which is simultaneously
political and theological. The concomitant figure is of the
individual as serf or servant. This is the figure of Master/Slave.
Society is *sovereign*, the individual is *subject*. The duality which
they form is connected by a relation of *power*. This relation is
the relation of dominance/submission, of command/obedience,
of control, imposition, imperative. The social world is the world
of the ruler, imperious society, and the ruled, acquiescent
individuals. They are mediated by the political/theological construct, rule or commandment.

This modality of determinism operates as a result of the
superiority of society over individuals. Superiority means that
society, like God or government, is *above* the individual, and
greater than the individual: better than, vaster than, more
powerful than the individual. The superiority of society invests
it with authority. This authority, like governmental or divine
authority, is equally the product of society's superior force and
of society's moral transcendence. It is the product of both a
physical and a moral supremacy; it is both necessary and proper,
both inherent and legitimate. Constraint is the distinguishing
characteristic of social facts because 'the individual finds himself
in the presence of a force which is superior to him and before
which he bows'.

By virtue of its might, society automatically has the right
to control individuals. But since society is righteous, since
it represents the Good, its right to rule is recognized by
individuals. Thus the dual nature of society, that it dominates
and uplifts, that its ascendance includes both power and virtue,
bestows upon it the seigniorial quality of noblesse oblige, the
divine right of benevolent dictatorship which characterizes both
divinity and despotism. Individuals both fear and love society,
and both of these forms of attachment are effective; they bring
the individual before society in an authoritarian attitude,
an attitude of obedience. Social facts; institutions, collective

thought and behavior, exercise a 'double action' on individuals. They

> impose themselves upon us, but we cling to them; they compel us, and we love them; they constrain us and we find our welfare in our adherence to them and in this very constraint.[29]

The individual submits to society and to subordination through an awareness of 'his state of natural dependence and inferiority'. This awareness may take the form of the 'tangible and symbolic' representations of religion, or the 'adequate and definite' notions of science.[30] Society is the inspiration for religion, because

> a society has all that is necessary to arouse the sensation of the divine in minds, merely by the power that it has over them; for to its members it is what a god is to his worshippers. In fact, a god is, first of all, a being whom men think of as superior to themselves, and upon whom they feel that they depend . . . Now society also gives us the sensation of a perpetual dependence . . . it imperiously demands our aid. It requires that, forgetful of our own interest, we make ourselves its servitors, and it submits us to every sort of inconvenience, privation and sacrifice, without which social life would be impossible.[31]

Society exercises its power primarily in 'spiritual ways'. In fact, although physical constraint is the sign by which social facts are recognized, it is only 'the material apparent expression of an interior and profound fact which is wholly ideal: this is moral authority'. Because of this spiritual character of social pressure, 'it could not fail to give men the idea that outside themselves there exist one or several powers, both moral and, at the same time, efficacious, upon which they depend'. These invisible powers are naturally thought of as external to individuals, as gods, 'for these address them in a tone of command and sometimes order them to do violence to their most natural inclinations'. The religious believer is actually 'not deceived' in presuming 'the existence of a moral power upon which he depends' because 'that power exists, it is society'. Society, like God, is the 'great moral force' which both 'dominates' and 'sustains' individuals.[32]

But for all that society's authority is grounded in the fact that it is desired, respected, prestigious, it remains authority nonetheless. Humans accept a 'moral' rather than a physical bond; but it remains a bond. Humans are governed by a superior consciousness, but they are governed. The individual escapes the body's yoke, but 'is subject to that of society'.[33] The behaviors which society requires and which individuals resist, which involve 'sacrifice and privation' are effectively:

> forced on us by a power to which we have submitted . . . However willingly we obey the voice dictating this abnegation, we feel sure that its tone is imperative beyond that of instinct . . . it commands us and we obey.[34]

The essential characteristic of social phenomena is 'their power of exerting pressure on individual consciousnesses'. They possess the 'power of constraint' and 'control' individuals by 'force' and by 'weighing upon us more or less heavily'. Society represents an 'authority before which the individual bows' which 'governs' him and which is the product of 'social forces which transcend him'. It constitutes an 'external impulse to which he submits'.[35] Social rules have authority, an 'imperative character'. They reflect a 'compelling force to which we submit'. Together, these rules 'imperatively determine conduct'. Moral law 'is invested with an authority that imposes deference even upon reason'. It 'dominates' the 'whole nature', physical and mental, of the individual.[36]

Individuals may obey social rules consciously or unconsciously, voluntarily or passively. But in either case, they obey and conform; the rules remain 'imperative':

> on condition of having adequate knowledge of moral precepts, of their causes and of their functions, we are in a position to conform to them, but consciously and knowing why . . . [But] these latter do not on that account lose their imperative character. Because we know that there is something useful in that which is commanded, it follows not that we fail to obey but that we obey voluntarily.[37]

Social phenomena are by nature imposed, by nature they exert pressure on individuals. The pressure may go unnoticed, like 'the pressure of the atmosphere on our bodies'. However, 'unconscious or no, freely accepted or passively borne, social pressure is no less real'.

The 'characteristic feature of social phenomena' is 'this quality of imposing themselves on the individual'. Society presents 'directive impulses', to which individuals docilely or by constraint 'submit'.[38] Therefore, while society may be a divine, heroic dictator; the ultimately moral and venerable being, it does not thereby cease being a dictator. It may be the ideal, perfect tyrant, but it is a tyrant nonetheless. Durkheim uses the term 'despot'. Individuals will not be submissive, 'except to a collective despotism'. This is because they can only be 'dominated' by 'a force which is superior to them' and only the group (but any group) possesses such superiority.[39] Naturally, and necessarily, and inconspicuously, 'like the atmosphere that weighs on our shoulders': 'Every society is despotic'.[40]

(ii) Second is the figure of natural determinism. Society is a natural object and is governed, in the mechanical sense, by natural laws. Individuals in society are in turn governed, mechanically, by these natural/social laws. Society is conceived as a *thing*, which determines other *things*, its individual members. The relation between the social thing and the individual things is that of *cause and effect*. Social phenomena function as instincts, environments, or forces in relation to individuals, and they function with necessity. The social realm is on a higher plane, but remains an extension of the natural realm. The social world is more complex than the physical world, but not qualitatively different. The social whole and the individual part are mediated by *law* in its natural, scientific form.

In the first place, social rules regulate the parts of the social body, just as reflexes, nerves, *instincts*, regulate the parts of the physical organism. Rules of conduct are 'facts' equivalent to the 'reflexes of organic life'. As such, they constitute 'moulds in which activities must run'. These reflexes are social, and not biological, 'inscribed' in the law and customs of the larger organism rather than in the physical body of the individual. As such they do not 'determine the activity from within' the individual, but 'stimulate it from without'.[41]

Social life is 'subject to the same imperatives' as organic life. Both physical and social life require 'regulatory organs'. In the physical body, 'the nervous system has this function'. However, as human, social, mental life 'transcends the organism' individuals must be regulated by 'spiritual forces'. Moral rules are 'genuine forces' which 'contain and constrain' the will. They 'predetermine conduct'. It is the 'function' of moral rules 'to determine conduct, to fix it, to eliminate the element of individual arbitrariness'.[42] Through 'moral regulation', society:

> plays, as far as supra-organic life is concerned, the same role that instinct fills with respect to physical existence. It determines, and it rules what is left undetermined. The system of instincts is the discipline of the organism, just as moral discipline is the instinctive system of social life.[43]

In the second place, society forms an additional, supra-material *environment* for the individual. The individual must adapt to the social environment as well as to its organic and physical milieux. The human individual 'depends . . . upon three sorts of milieux: the organism, the external world, society'.[44] The physical milieu is the reality to which individuals submit their bodies. The moral milieu is 'the reality to which we submit our wills'. They are of a different nature, but: 'We must adapt ourselves to both'.[45] In fact, the individual must adapt to the social environment with the same necessity as to its organic and physical milieux: it must adapt socially 'to exist', 'to live'.

Society 'is a reality which is no more our work than the external world, and to which, consequently, we must submit in order to exist'. It is a reality *sui generis* to which the individual 'is held to adapt himself in order to live, just as to his physical environment'.[46] Humans:

> are not only in relations with the physical environment, but also with a social environment infinitely more extended, more stable and more active than the one whose influence animals undergo. To live they must adapt themselves to this.[47]

The social environment is conceived as something to which individuals *adapt*. It is also conceived as something which *causes* individual thought and behavior. The social milieu is not a 'first cause', an 'ultimate and absolute fact', because it is itself the result of other social causes. But it is a 'primary fact', general enough 'to explain a great number of other facts'. (These other facts include the 'special milieus' which are themselves determinative of social phenomena, but which are determined by the 'general milieu'.) The 'internal social milieu', the 'state of society' provides the aspect of 'causality' in social life: 'if we eliminate this type of cause, there are no concomitant conditions on which social phenomena can depend'.[48] To understand social facts, 'one must relate them to a particular social milieu, to a definite type of society; and it is in the constitutive characteristics of this type that one must search for the determining causes of the phenomenon under consideration'.[49]

Generally speaking, Durkheim understands that 'the major part of psychic phenomena' does not 'come' from organic causes but from another 'natural cause', 'the social milieu'.[50] In particular, Durkheim understands specific social behavior as *caused by* social environment.

> We shall try to determine the *productive causes* of suicide directly, without concerning ourselves with the forms they can assume in particular individuals. Disregarding the individual as such, his motives and ideas, we shall seek directly the states of various *social environments* (religious confessions, family, political society, occupational groups, etc.) in terms of which the variations of suicide occur. Only then returning to the individual, shall we study how these *general causes* become individualized so as to *produce* the homicidal *results* involved.[51]

In the third place, the image which Durkheim uses again and again is the image of social *forces*.[52] Society and its character, its characteristics; collective reality, including collective states and institutions, are 'real, living, active forces' which 'determine' and 'control' the individual, which are 'effective'.[53] Society is 'not a nominal being' but 'a system of active forces'. Once this is recognized, 'a new manner of explaining men becomes possible'.[54]

In one sense, these forces both supplement and supplant natural forces in the determination of human behavior. The 'bond' (*frein*) of human bondage is not physical but social. Humans are ruled by the law of the collective consciousness rather than that of the material environment. They are 'subject' to the 'yoke' of society rather than that of the body.[55] Humans are relatively independent of the organism and the physical environment but are to the same extent 'dependent on social causes'. For humans, 'social causes substitute themselves for organic causes'.[56]

In another sense, these social forces *are* natural forces. Durkheim credits Aristotle with presciently seeing in society 'a fact of nature'. Following Aristotle, Comte rightly perceived that 'social phenomena are natural facts'.[57] Durkheim follows suit, and regards the most important social phenomenon, morality, for example, 'as a system of natural phenomena'.[58] The social level is above, transcendent over, the rest of nature. However, Durkheim situates the social level *within* nature: society is the highest, most complex, all-inclusive plane of nature. But it is *of* nature. The social order is unique, in that it 'implies and includes within itself the other realms of nature'.[59] But its uniqueness is due to its position of supremacy on the hierarchical continuum of natural order/s.[60] It is not outside of this continuum.

Durkheim's 'sociological naturalism' mandates that social phenomena be considered a distinct and irreducible level of reality. Sociology must not explain social phenomena by phenomena of psychological (individual) or material nature. But it must not place them 'beyond the realm of nature'.[61] As the relative complexity of psychic facts does not place them 'outside of the world and of science', neither should social facts be excluded from nature and scientific analysis.[62] Facts of psychic life, for example, are explained by, derive from, social causes, rather than physical causes. But society is considered an equally 'natural cause': 'the social realm is not less natural than the organic realm'.[63]

Through his insistence that social reality is part of nature, Durkheim sets the stage for the more radical claim that social reality is *like* natural reality, that *social* forces are *like natural* forces. Durkheim's terminology is the terminology of the natural sciences: determinism, causality, necessity. Although individuals may fail to perceive them, there are 'reasons which have determined that we act and the nature of our action'.[64] Social things, social facts are not products of the will and cannot be modified by it. Rather, 'they determine it from without; they are like molds in which our actions are inevitably shaped. This necessity is often inescapable'.[65] Human behavior, when considered retrospectively, 'can be reduced to relationships of cause and effect'.[66]

The social world is like the physical world. Thus, humans may 'individualize' or personalize social beliefs and practices as they reflectively assimilate them. Thus it may be said that individuals 'receive' thought and behavior from without, but not 'passively or without modification'. However, this is only equivalent to the process wherein 'in reflecting on the physical world, each of us colors it after his own fashion, and different individuals adapt themselves differently to the same physical environment'.[67]

In the social world, as in the physical world, the only form of 'autonomy' humans can enjoy is knowledge. Natural science has 'liberated' humans from the physical world, through accurate *representation* (humans are 'autonomous' in that they do not have to refer directly to the objective realm, but may evoke it introspectively) and through accurate *comprehension* (humans are 'free' to adapt and conform to the natural order voluntarily). There is an 'order of things' which one can freely desire 'through an understanding of the cause'.[68] 'We liberate ourselves through understanding; there is no other means of liberation. Science is the wellspring of our autonomy.'

Furthermore, this is the only means of liberation in the social world.

> In the moral order there is room for the same autonomy; and there is place for no other. Since morality expresses the nature of society . . . individual reason can no more be the lawmaker for the moral world than that of the physical world . . . However, it is possible through science to get hold of this order, which the individual, *qua* individual, has not created and for which he has not deliberately wished. We can investigate the nature of these moral rules . . . We can investigate the reasons for their being, their immediate and more remote conditions. In a word, we can create a scientific study of the moral order.

Through a science of the moral order, humans can become its 'masters' in the same sense in which they are masters of the physical order. They can achieve an internal representation of this order, and they can achieve an understanding of its causes. To the extent that the moral order is 'founded in the nature of things – that is, in the nature of society', humans can then 'freely conform to it'. They can *not* wish for it to be 'other than is implied by the natural make-up of the reality that it expresses'. The ineluctable resignation before the social order which individuals must accept, their 'passivity', is 'at the same time activity, through the active part we take in deliberately desiring it. We desire it because we know the reason for its existence'. Individuals who understand why they are 'blind instruments' are 'free'. This is 'the only kind of autonomy to which we have any claim'. This is a very specific and specified autonomy: '*It does not imply that the human being, in any of his aspects, escapes the world and its laws.*'

Social forces are more than analogous to the forces of the physical world. They are the *same* as, they have as much reality and power as, physical forces. There is a 'parallelism' between 'other phenomena of nature' and 'social phenomena'. Both are 'real things' and as such have 'a definite nature that asserts control'. Thus the individual 'finds' collective ways of thinking and acting 'completely formed' and 'cannot evade or change them'.[69] Social forces are 'ideal', ideational, rather than material. But these ideal forces 'act as though they were real; they determine the conduct of men with the same degree of necessity as physical forces'.[70]

In fact ideal social forces are real. Collective tendencies or patterns are 'things', 'causes', 'forces *sui generis*', 'forces as real as cosmic forces, though of another sort'. The proof that the reality of collective tendencies 'is no less than that of cosmic forces' is 'demonstrated in the same way, by the uniformity of effects'. Social or moral forces are forces 'which cause us to act from without, like the physico-chemical forces to which we react'. Durkheim says that his conception 'merely adds to physical, chemical, biological and psychological forces, social forces which like these act upon men from without'.[71] The difference between the social and physical worlds is simply one of degree. Social phenomena are distinguished from biological and physico-chemical phenomena 'only by a greater complexity'.[72]

There is a general law which mandates that all natural phenomena work according to laws. Societies, as part of nature, must obey this general law. Societies 'are submitted to laws like all things'. All natural beings, 'from minerals to man', are subject to positive science; 'which is to say that everything occurs according to necessary laws'. It is the early economists whom Durkheim credits with the discovery that 'social laws are as necessary as physical laws'.[73]

Within society, there is a general 'law of moral mechanics', which is 'just as inevitable as the laws of physical mechanics'. It expresses the fact that the group, 'of necessity' tends to subordinate its members to itself. 'The parts are unable *not* to fall under its domination.' There is a social as well as a physical 'nature' against which individuals are helpless to rebel; 'such a revolt being futile and fruitless, whether attempted against the forces of the material world or those of the social world'. 'Nothing that we do can make the laws of things other than they are.'[74]

> Since the law of causality has been verified in the other realms of nature, and since it has progressively extended its authority from the physicochemical world to the biological, and from the latter to the psychological, we are justified in claiming that it is equally true of the social world.[75]

This is the sense, the full meaning, of Durkheim's statement that 'there are only differences of degree and form between the mineral realm and the thinking person'.[76]

Durkheim addresses the specificity of social determinism explicitly in several places. In *Suicide*, for example, he claims that his 'determinism' is actually reconciled with 'liberty'. This is because a social force:

> does not determine one individual rather than another. It exacts a definite number of certain kinds of actions, but not that they should be performed by this or that person. It may be granted that some people resist the force and that it has its way with others.[77]

This is another way of introducing the notion of complexity as the distinct property of social causality. Each social force encounters a multitude of individuals. It is able to 'have its way' with some of these individuals and not with others. Conversely, each person is subject to a multitude of forces. Some of these 'have their way', and others do not.

This conceptualization parallels the notion of overdetermination. It is a confluence of forces, outweighing a confluence of countervailing forces, which actually determines a given action. No single force has the power of a determinant. But action is not thereby delivered over to freedom and spontaneity. It is complexly determined. But it is determined. Durkheim's remarks about the reconciliation of determinism and liberty are found in the same passage as the following:

> Actually, our conception merely adds to physical, chemical, biological and psychological forces, social forces which like these act upon men from without. If the former do not preclude human freedom, the latter need not.[78]

This illustrates the equivocation of which Durkheim is capable when he handles an issue 'directly'.

In the tradition of pragmatism and social behaviorism, Durkheim also posits a 'relative indetermination' of human behavior which is due to the interposition of thought between stimulus and response.

> The agent endowed with reason does not behave like a thing of which the activity can be reduced to a system of reflexes ... External stimulation, instead of resulting immediately in movements, is halted in its progress and is subjected to a *sui generis* elaboration; a more or less long period of time elapses before the expression in movement appears. This relative indetermination does not occur where there is no thinking mind, and with thought it increases.[79]

This relative indetermination is, on closer inspection, really a very determined determination. Stimulation results, albeit after a delay, automatically in 'movement'. It is recognized by the individual, which because of its humanness can also reflect on and comprehend the nature of the world and its laws. But in the former case as in the latter, this 'recognition' recalls the recognition of a pedestrian in relation to an oncoming truck. Is the human traffic fatality really more free than a 'road kill', because it makes cognitive sense of the inevitable process in which it is inextricably involved?

Durkheim in fact regards the failure to 'recognize' social determinism itself as an illusion, the grand human illusion. This failure is the manifestation of the 'anthropocentric bias' which obstructs the growth of science. 'Man' tends to deny the existence of collective forces:

> this omnipotence, the illusion of which he complacently entertains, has always been a cause of weakness in him . . . his own power over things really began only when he *recognized* that they have a nature of their own, and resigned himself to learning this nature from them. Rejected by all other sciences, this deplorable prejudice stubbornly maintains itself in sociology. Nothing is more urgent than to liberate our science from it and this is the principal purpose of our efforts.[80]

Social forces may be unfelt, but they are real and effective none-theless. Individuals may be 'unconscious' of social determination, but they must not deny it, under penalty of becoming 'victims of the illusion of having ourselves created that which actually forced itself from without . . . the air is no less heavy because we do not detect its weight'.[81]

Durkheim claims that the question 'of knowing whether man is free or not' is a question for 'metaphysics'. Nevertheless, he continues to pose the following necessary (and loaded) question, the choice between two mutually exclusive and unequally reasonable alternatives:

> it is necessary to choose between these two terms, either to *recognize* that social phenomena are accessible to scientific investigation or else to *admit without reason*, and contrary to every induction of science that there are two worlds in the world: one where the law of causality reigns, another where arbitrariness and contingency reign.[82]

(iii) Finally, third, is the figure of internalization. This is intermediate between the mode of determinism now being considered, that of control, and the mode of determinism to be taken up next, that of constitution. In this guise, the social becomes part of the individual, and then controls it from within.[83] This image is predominantly one of the penetration, permeation and pervasion of the individual by society. The social rule, assimilated by the individual, becomes second nature, becomes natural, becomes instinct. In this way, internalization also operates intermediately between the determinism of sovereignty, and the determinism of science.

Social facts have two defining characteristics: they exercise a power of constraint over individuals and they are external to individuals. The attribution of externality to social facts emphasizes that they originate externally to, independently of individuals. They are determined, caused, created by, agencies outside of, meaning agencies other than, the individual. However the quality of externality, which in some places receives so much stress, is elsewhere qualified. Externality is the initial and partial condition of social facts. Social constraints are 'at first external to the individual'.[84] But the collective force is 'not entirely outside of us; it does not act upon us wholly from without'.[85] In fact, the power of constraint which social facts enjoy is to some extent dependent on their ability to insinuate themselves into the individual. Social facts 'pervade' the individual, and they cannot do so 'except by a process that moves from the outside to the inside'.[86]

The process by which external social facts enter the individual is generally constructed through the symbol and image: 'penetration'. The collective force 'must' 'penetrate' the individual.[87] Collective sentiment is conceptualized as 'penetrating' individuals, 'from outside' and 'with a force that its origin gives it'.[88] The ideas of the group are seen to 'penetrate the individual consciousness'.[89] The entire psychic life of the group 'penetrates' the individual psyche, as collective life in general 'penetrates' the individual life.[90] Society in its entirety, Durkheim says, can only exist if it 'penetrates the consciousness of individuals'.[91] Durkheim believes that the idea of the soul, in which the totemic principle (or, in later religions, the divine spirit) is understood as 'penetrating' into individuals, and thereby becoming 'incarnate', 'immanent', 'individualized' in them, is a mystified but essentially accurate reflection of this process.[92]

Social facts and forces, originally external to the individual, become, through a process of penetration, internal to the individual. Social thought and behavior get inside the individual. They thereby become individual thought and behavior, become the individual's own thought and behavior. They become part of the individual, part of the self. The image of the soul includes the act of penetration by an external entity. But once inside individual consciousnesses, the totemic principle 'becomes an integral part of them'. In the same way, social ideas are 'organized in a lasting fashion' within the individual consciousness and become 'elements of our personalities'.[93] The collective force must not only penetrate individuals but must 'organize itself within us'. It thereby 'becomes an integral part of our being'. Social forces form 'a part of our internal life'. Society 'is also represented inside of us'.[94]

Once inside the individual, society and its forces 'transform' the individual, as the divine essence transfigures the individual in whom it becomes manifest. Society can only exist if it penetrates the consciousness of individuals *and* 'fashions it in "its image and resemblance"'.[95] Through internalization society can fashion (*façonner*: to make, work, shape, mold, form, train, fashion) the individual. It can control the individual from within. Social constraint originates externally, but becomes part of the individual, becomes the individual's self-constraint. Social constraint is 'centripetal'. It moves inward to become 'inhibition', defined as the 'means by which social constraint produces its psychological effects'. Social control becomes 'self-control'.[96] The collective sentiment penetrates the individual in order to 'impose itself'. Psychic life penetrates the individual nature and thereby elevates, 'feeds and enriches', it but also tends inevitably 'to subject (*assujettir*) that nature to itself'. The judgements of social morality are 'imprinted' and found 'ready-made within' individuals, 'in most cases without our being aware of having actually formed them'. From this internal position, a moral judgement is able to produce a 'reaction' which is 'spontaneous, even unconscious'; which is 'a type of instinct'.[97]

The process of internalization presents the dual aspects of penetration/assimilation and constraint/control. Society invades the individual and dominates it from the most strategic site, from within. It becomes part of the individual, and dominates it by means of the most effective weapon, by means of itself. Durkheim calls this process 'education' or 'socialization'. It is the sector where education and socialization intersect. Education *qua* socialization, socialization *qua* education, 'teaches us to control and resist ourselves':[98]

> all education is a continuous effort to impose on the child ways of seeing, feeling, and acting which he could not have arrived at spontaneously. From the very first hours of his life, we compel him to eat, drink, and sleep at regular hours; we constrain him to cleanliness, calmness, and obedience; later we exert pressure upon him in order that he may learn proper consideration for others, respect for customs and conventions, the need for work, etc. If, in time this constraint ceases to be felt, it is because *it gradually gives rise to habits and to internal tendencies that render constraint unnecessary* . . . the aim of education is, precisely, the socialization of the human being; the process of education, therefore, gives us in a nutshell the historical fashion in which the social being is constituted. The unremitting pressure to which the child is subjected is the very pressure of the social milieu which tends to fashion him in its own image, and of which parents and teachers are merely the representatives and intermediaries.[99]

Positive determination: constitution

Internalization is a process of control. It is a form of control effected by infiltration: society penetrates the individual to govern and determine it from within. In a sense it causes the individual to control or govern itself, to be self-determining. It is thus less conspicuous, less palpable, less conflictual than social control understood as external power or force. It does not seem like social coercion. Internalization is at one and the same time a less objectionable and a more insidious form of social determination. But it belongs to the same landscape as power and force, the landscape of domination. Through internalization, individuals are induced to think and act in socially determined ways. Internalization is a variant of force as force, with the metaphorical aspect of penetration. It is a specific variant, but it shares a common ground with determination as domination: as power (political metaphor of government) and force (scientific metaphor of physical force).

It has a certain proximity, however, to another modality of social determinism. Force as coercive force is a negative view of the society/individual nexus. Social determination of the individual as force means the social *destruction* of the individual. Durkheim holds this view, but it is the negative moment in a dual conception of society. He always also holds a positive view of society and its relation to individuals. The concept of 'constitution' represents the positive moment of social determinism. In this conception, society is a source rather than a force, or a creative force rather than a coercive force. Social determination of the individual as constitution means the social *construction* of the individual.

This construction is adjacent to the movement of internalization. Education/socialization is not only a process of internalization, but also the process through which 'the social being is constituted'. In each process, society *fashions* the individual, which means that it makes, works, shapes, molds, and forms the individual. However, internalization is a means of directing an extant entity, by inserting elements into it. Constitution is a means of determining all of the elements in an entity, by producing them, by producing the entity itself, 'from scratch', 'from whole cloth'. It is at once more far-reaching control, total control, of the individual by society, and yet it is totally painless

control. There is nothing in the individual to control, because
the individual is always already controlled, controlled from its
inception. The individual is merely an incarnation of society,
simultaneously its creation and its progeny, its product and its
flesh and blood, its servant and itself. The individual is society's
Eve.[100]

Durkheim says that the individual's personality 'can be nothing
but a product of its environment'.

> For where does it come from? One must either say that it is born
> of nothing, that it exists one and indivisible through all eternity,
> a veritable psychic atom implanted in some incomprehensible
> manner in the body; or, if it does have some source, it must
> necessarily be a composite result of various forces derived
> from biological or social sources. Now, we have shown how it
> could not have developed out of any other source.[101]

The individual's personality, its supra-organic, non-physical self,
is constituted, constructed, created by society. Human beings
naturally develop a conception of God, their creator, as a
mystified sense of their real relation to society.[102]

In a general sense, society creates 'human nature'. In the
abstract, human nature is equivalent to, reducible to, civilization,
which is a social creation.

> We speak a language that we did not make; we use instru-
> ments that we did not invent; we invoke rights that we did
> not found; a treasury of knowledge is transmitted to each
> generation that it did not gather itself, etc. It is to society that
> we owe these varied benefits of civilization, and . . . a man is
> a man only because he is civilized.[103]

More specifically, 'human nature' is neither general nor abstract.
It is the particular derivative of a particular society. It is
constituted differently according to the nature of each society.
The social being is 'constituted' in a 'historical fashion'.

> Human nature has varied in time. . . . And it varies geo-
> graphically. . . . And this diversity has sprung out of the
> diversity in human societies, of which the human type is a
> function. . . . man is the product of history.[104]

Human nature is variable, as it derives from the nature of the
creatrix society, which is variable. The 'constitution of man' is

historical, which means that it is social. Society has the ability to produce 'changes' in 'human nature', 'to put a new man in the place of the old', because it has the ability to produce the human being. The physical, mental and moral 'natures' of human beings, including both needs and capacities, shift in relation to social change. 'With societies, individuals are transformed.' In human beings, 'social causes substitute themselves for organic causes' in 'the constitution of human nature'. Therefore, it cannot be said that societies, their diverse structures, or their modifications over time are due to human nature. Social life is not the 'resultant of individual natures, since, on the contrary, it is rather the latter which come from the former'.[105]

Society *creates* individuals. Individuals represent society's 'means' but they are also its 'end', in the sense that 'the aim and fundamental purpose of society is to create the individual'. Social education serves to 'graft' onto the physical individual 'an entirely new man'. It 'creates within him a being . . . the social being'. Education 'creates within us all that lies outside the realm of pure sensations'. It 'fashions' both the mind and the will.[106] Alternatively, humans are the *product* of society. The statement that 'man is the product of history' means that 'man is . . . a product of society'.[107] Man is 'a product of history', read 'society', meaning that 'there is nothing in him that is either given or defined in advance'.[108] Individuals 'are much more a product of common life than they are determinants of it'. The individual is 'much more a product of society than he is its maker', because social phenomena 'form' the individual consciousness. The 'states' of the individual consciousness 'would not have been produced among isolated beings and would have been produced quite otherwise among beings grouped in some other manner'. They are '[p]roducts of group life' and 'it is the nature of the group which alone can explain them'. Society 'rests on' bases in the individual consciousness. But it does not find them 'fully laid out'. Instead, 'it puts them there itself'. 'Everything', in fact, in the individual consciousness, 'comes from society'.[109]

The human individual is created by society as it were out of 'dust from the ground'.[110] Society begins with the individual as a lump of clay, which it shapes: as the malleable raw material which it uses in its production process. Prior to society's intervention as education, the social being exists only as a possibility, in a 'vague, embryonic form'. Childhood, the period before socialization, is the period 'in which the individual, in both the physical and moral sense, does not yet exist'. The educator confronts not 'a person wholly formed – not a complete work or a finished product – but . . . a becoming, an incipient being, a person in the process of formation'.[111] Individual natures 'are merely the indeterminate material' of society's machinery. 'Their contribution consists exclusively in very general attitudes, in vague and consequently plastic predispositions'.[112]

Society then forms/transforms this pliant material into the human, social being. The 'social factor' 'molds and transforms' its human clay.[113] The social factor is a factory, a M/maker. Society is that which has 'made' the individual.[114] In childhood, through education/socialization, the individual 'is made, develops, and is formed'.[115] This creation is not capricious. There is a design behind these machinations of society; a method to the made-ness of the individual. The individual is the 'end' of society's creation process. But it is also society's 'means'. Therefore socialization makes individuals, and makes them social instruments.

The social necessity and utility which underlies, which stands behind the production of individuals is expressed through analogy to the creation of humans by God. Social forces 'fashion' the individual consciousness 'in their image'.[116] Society 'can exist only' on the condition that, Godlike, it 'fashions' the individual consciousness 'in "its image and resemblance"':[117]

> just as society largely forms the individual, it forms him to the same extent in its own image. Society, therefore, cannot lack the material for its needs, for it has, so to speak, kneaded it with its own hands.[118]

Durkheim presents the individual as clay, raw material, a potentiality, in the hands of an interested social constructor, which molds, forms, transforms, creates, animates, the real, social individual. For emphasis, he imagines the unimaginable: the individual deprived of the divine intervention of society. The 'residue' of human nature, eliminating the differences among human beings resulting from their constitution in and by distinct and disparate societies, is 'that which alone can be considered of psychological origin' and which is 'reduced to something vague and rudimentary'.[119] Similarly, the 'residue' obtained by removing from individuals 'everything due to social action' is 'picayune' as well as being uniform.[120] In another vein, without the mediation of society, the individual would be reduced to its physical/animal essence. The personality is 'a social entity' which 'receives everything from without'. Alone, 'left to his own devices', the individual 'could not raise himself beyond his own level . . . the level of animal nature'.

> Take away from man all that has a social origin and nothing is left but an animal on a par with other animals. It is society that has raised him to this level above physical nature.

'Nothing yields nothing.'[121] This is another of Durkheim's images. Without social constitution, the individual is 'nothing'. The ego, alone, 'entirely and exclusively itself', would be 'emptied of all content'.[122] If social elements were withdrawn from the human mind, 'a huge void would be created'.[123] Without the pervasive influence of the physical and, especially, the social world,

> our consciousness would be empty of all content. Each of us is the *point of convergence* for a certain number of external forces, and our personalities result from the *intersection* of these influences. Should the forces no longer converge here, there would remain nothing more than *a mathematical point, an empty place* where conscience and personality could not be built up . . . we are the product of things.[124]

BODY AND SOUL

Durkheim asserts the determinism of the individual by society: by modern as well as by traditional society. In traditional society the individual does not even exist. It is completely absorbed and enveloped in the collectivity; in which it is submerged, with which it is merged, with which it is one. In modernity the individual emerges, but only to be perfectly and totally determined by society. This determinism takes four figurative forms. The individual is absolutely determined by society as an absolute power: the political figure. The individual is mechanically determined by society as a system of mechanical forces: the physical figure. The individual is determined/self-determined by penetrating, assimilated social forces: the figure of internalization.

The individual is determined because produced and constructed by society: the figure of constitution.

Society *makes* the individual, in all senses of the word. It coerces and compels the individual. It causes the individual, the individual's thought and behavior are its effects. It creates the individual, manufactures the individual. Society is Nature, Author, and Authority with respect to its effect, its work, its subject. Through this conceptualization, Durkheim solves a problem, the social problem, the individual. In this formulation the individual appears unproblematic for society because determined by society. However, in solving the social problem, Durkheim creates another problem, a theoretical problem.

The perfectly social, perfectly determined individual; the individual/social harmony of the relation of determination, contradicts Durkheim's assertion of the inevitable, eternal conflict between the individual and society. In eliminating the individual source of social problems, he contradicts his own assertion of the existence of social problems. In denying the individual as an opposing force, a thorn in society's side, Durkheim denies his own conceptual structure. However, ultimately, in another tendency more consistent with his problematic of the individual/society relation as problematic, Durkheim resolves his internal, logical contradiction. He effects this resolution by maintaining another contradiction, the individual/society contradiction.

The classic body/soul or body/mind duality and antagonism is invoked by Durkheim as a means of understanding the individual/society relation as a relation of difference and conflict.[125] In this conception, there are two beings, not one; they are divided, not unified; opposed and not solidary. Society, the social or collective entity, is a spiritual, mental and moral being, essentially immaterial. The individual entity is a material, physical being, essentially a body, an organism. Society and the individual are irreducible and irreconcilable with one another. They are distinct, unlike and hostile. The social being is of course predominant. But the individual being is not simply acquiescent. The individual body is the site of resistance and struggle. It is ultimately determined by society, but it does not give up without a fight. The individual organism is a reality to be conquered. It is a determined thing, but it is a thing. Determination is not, primordially, absolute, total and perfect.

Understood this way, as problematic, social determinism is

seen, in a reversal, as actually more effective in modern than in traditional society. The individual, as a corporeal entity, exists in both modern and traditional society, as the limit of society's power. Even in the collective type, the body cannot be absorbed into the group. Here, 'religion comprises all' and 'religious consciences are identical', in an identity which is 'absolute'. Yet there is still something which exists outside of society; foreign, a stranger and therefore a menace, an enemy. Individual consciousnesses are composed of 'practically the same elements', with one exception: 'save for the sensations pertaining to the organism and to the states of the organism'. In traditional society, 'the individual personality does not exist'. But 'individuals always have a distinct organic life'. No matter how developed the collective type may be, regardless of the extent to which the individual is wrapped in the collective consciousness, there is a sphere which 'varies from one man to another and remains peculiar with each'. This is the individual *qua* individual. This is the part of the individual relating to 'the organism and to the state of the organism'. This sphere represents the 'first foundation of all individuality' which is 'inalienable and does not depend on any social state'.[126]

Through social evolution, the role of the organism is progressively diminished. The individual is slowly liberated from the 'yoke' of the organism and the dominion of the physical world, only to be subjected to social forces, social domination. Psychic life gradually supplants instinctual life, but psychic life is social life. In this sense, the individual could be said to be more autonomous in mechanical society, because it is more physical and therefore more truly individual. Organic society determines the individual more completely, as the physical declines as a factor in human existence, while the ideational becomes preponderant. But of course, the human organism remains, and it remains the point of disruption, of asocial and anti-social tendencies, the locus of social problems and problematic socialization. The sleep of social life is troubled by the life of the body.

This is the external form of the conflict. Society, the mental and moral agent, confronts the body of the individual. But of course Durkheim projects the struggle into the individual, as society projects itself into the individual. The sleep of the body is troubled by the life of the mind, which society awakens within it. Durkheim divides the individual into body and mind or, alternatively, body and soul. The body represents its true, its natural, its primal self. The spirit (*esprit*), including mind and soul, mentality and morality, represents its social self.

Durkheim's classic statement of the internal division of the individual is 'The Dualism of Human Nature'. Humans are 'double', made up of 'two parts', 'two beings'. These are 'composed of very different elements and orient us in opposite directions'. One is 'purely individual and rooted in our organisms'. This is the creature of 'sensations and sensory appetites'. The other is 'social and nothing but an extension of society'. This is the being wherein resides 'the intellectual and moral life'. The two co-exist in antagonism and conflict.[127] Human beings are characterized by an 'inner contradiction':

> man is both 'angel' and 'beast' . . . it is this division that distinguishes us from all other beings. Thus the traditional antithesis of the body and soul is not a vain mythological concept that is without foundation in reality. It is true that we are double, that we are the realization of an antinomy.[128]

The unique division of the human individual into an ideational as well as a material being, creates its unique condition of determination. With respect to its psychic life, the human being is totally determined and constituted by society. Its physical life, its body, represents the incorrigible core of individuality, the intransigent locus of contradiction, of indomitability, poised against society's internal, but strictly mental, hegemony. The individual is both entirely socialized, and partially unsocialized. But socialization and its limit occur in two radically separate spheres. There is no unsocialized aspect of the mental life. There is no socialized aspect of the organism. The war between society and the individual is waged internally between the individual's totally individual body and the individual's totally social soul.

Society is the source of 'all the essentials of our mental life'.[129] Durkheim says that 'everything' in individual consciousness 'comes from society'.[130] Society is the 'nourishing mother' from which humans derive 'the whole of our moral and intellectual substance'.[131] Education, which must 'graft' the social being onto the natural man, 'creates within us all that lies outside the realm of pure sensations'.[132] Devoid of social content, consciousness would be a 'void'. The entirely social psychic life is 'superimposed' onto the physical individual.

This effectively socializes the individual, in two ways. First, the mind of the individual is totally attached to the group, totally merged with the group, is one with the group. There is only one mind, the social mind. The collective consciousness is not a specific delimited instance, located in a particular type of society, or located in a particular region of each society. Consciousness is collective. The individual's mind is not its own. In its psychic life, the individual remains in a relation of complete absorption by society. Psychically, there are no individuals. The individual mind is co-extensive with society, which is co-extensive with the collectivity of individual minds. Thus, the consciousness of the individual is totally socialized as it is totally integrated, as it doesn't exist.

Second, through the superimposition of its consciousness, the individual is socialized because regulated. Society is in a position of determination with respect to the mind. The mind, in turn, is ideally in a position of dominance with respect to the body. One of the two internal beings 'exercises a real pre-eminence over the other'. One being should have more power, 'should tend to exclude the other'.[133] Individuals are social to the extent that their social being, their non-material aspect, can control and direct their individual being, their material aspect. The mind must rule the body, the spirit must rule the flesh. This is the essence of morality, of the dimension of socialization which Durkheim calls discipline.

Both integration and regulation fall short, however, in the presence of the body. The body is the origination of both individualism, or egocentrism; and infinite, insatiable, anomic, anarchic desire. The body is a source of difference, differentiation, dispersion, disintegration, disruption. It is a centrifugal force, it is an unruly force. The person is composed of two sorts of factors. One is 'the spiritual principle', the 'soul of the group', which 'constitutes the very substance of individual souls'. But this substance is disturbed in its unity, separated. 'Another factor intervenes to break up and differentiate this principle: in other words, an individualizing factor is necessary. It is the body that fulfills this function.'[134] The body is that which 'individualizes', destroys the oneness of the group. The mind unifies, the body fragments society.

In addition, while the mind serves as the foundation for integration, the body is the polar opposite foundation of its polar opposite, egoism. The social, mental and moral elements of the human constitution 'connect us with something that surpasses us . . . they turn us toward ends that we hold in common with other men'. The individual, organismic elements 'connect us only with ourselves'. In the conflict between 'the sensations and sensory appetites' and 'the intellectual and moral life', '*it is evident that passions and egoistic tendencies derive from our individual constitutions*'. Sensations and sensory tendencies are opposed to conceptual thought and moral activity as the immoral or amoral to the moral, as the anti-social or asocial to the social. Durkheim equates morality with socialization, integration/attachment, regulation/discipline – with sacrifice, of the individual body on the altar of Alter, of the god that is society, of the collective consciousness.[135]

The dualism of human nature means that the individual consciousness contains itself, the individual consciousness, and its alienation, the collective consciousness. Collective consciousness is itself, is pure consciousness, and is alienated, in the individual mind/matter duality, where it is forced to coexist with matter, as well as with purely individual consciousness, with the consciousness of that materiality, with the individual's self-consciousness. There are thus three levels or realms of alienation and antagonism. Society is alienated in the individual, and the two entities – society, which is essentially psychic, and the individual, which is essentially physical – are divided against each other. The individual contains society within itself, and is self-alienated, both individual and social, physical and mental, divided against itself. Even the individual consciousness is split, fundamentally schizoid, divided between representations which are social, collective, universal and impersonal: the conceptual and moral order, and those which are somatic, individual, idiosyncratic, and personal: the perceptual order.[136]

The religious inspiration of this schema is clear. Society = God. Society/God is the unique universal unity, the one Spirit. It is alienated, it becomes incarnate, in the individual human body, source of all challenge, all sin. Society/God the Perfect, the Good, the omniscient, is poured into corporeal vessels, which contain but also corrupt it. Christ's condition is symbolic of the human condition. On the other hand, as the Social/Spirit is debased, the body is uplifted through this incarnation. The 'superior forms of human activity', broadly defined as all forms of intellectual and moral activity, have a collective origin: 'they are society itself incarnated and individualized in each one of us'.[137] The Social/Spirit acquires a non-spiritual shell, while the individual/body acquires a soul: 'like the notions of religious force and of divinity, the notion of the soul is not without a foundation in reality'.[138] Like the idea of god, the idea of the soul has an 'objective foundation'. As god is a representation of society, the soul is a representation of the social within the individual. The individual/body is 'host' to the Social/Spirit; the psyche/soul of the individual is 'a passing guest which comes from the outside'. Because society 'establishes itself within us', in a sense 'there is divinity in us'. The duality of human nature is due to the fact that 'there really is a particle of divinity in us because there is within us a particle of those great ideas which are the soul of the group'. The soul of the group 'constitutes the very substance of individual souls'.[139]

The Platonic/Hegelian philosophical, secularized version of the Idealist Christian ontology is also visible behind Durkheim's 'scientific' variation.[140] Society, collectivity, represents the singular, unified Essence or Idea. It becomes existence, material reality, becomes manifest, as it is embodied in its individual members. It is thereby realized but at the same time reduced, disfigured, threatened, not-itself, less than itself. The social, the ideal and ideational, must be individualized. But it is imperfectly realized as it is materialized, given form in an alien, material and particular, asocial being. As the material is the denial of the ideal, the existential the denial of the essential, the individual is the denial of the social. It gives it life and destroys it in the same, necessary movement, the movement of alienation. This onto-logical view carries with it a corresponding epistemology, which reiterates the opposition between the individual and society, the material and the ideal, the existential and the essential, the perceptual and the conceptual. The epistemological question will be taken up in Part II.

Chapter 3

The 'individualism' of Durkheim

One tendency in Durkheim's thought is the assertion of the total social determinism of individuals. The individual is reduced to a body, and all supra-organic phenomena are understood as social in origin. Society rules, causes, and constitutes individual hearts and minds, to produce social thought. At the level of thought, society entirely dominates the individual. Society and the individual are merged in thought: social thought is embodied, manifest, incarnate, individualized in individuals, and is co-extensive with individual thought. This social/individual thought in turn dominates individual bodies, to produce social behavior. Individuals are thus completely and mechanically determined, not only in traditional, mechanical society, but also and especially in modern society, where the social, psychic, human dimension assumes decisive preponderance over the individual, physical, nonhuman dimension.

Within the complexity of his work, however, another, opposing, tendency emerges with comparable force. That is the tendency to assert a substantial and progressive individualism as characteristic of society, of modern society in particular. He asserts that individual differentiation and autonomy are not confined to the individual organism but extend to the individual mind. He posits the existence of specifically individual thought and specifically individual behavior: thought and behavior with an individual origin, an individual source. He allows for genuine individual difference and genuine individual freedom. Individualism exists in mental and moral, as well as in physical life. There is an *individual* consciousness. There is an individual *personality*.[1]

THE EXPLICIT INDIVIDUAL: THE INDIVIDUAL AS A SOCIAL FACT

The threshold which opens onto the possibility of individualism is Durkheim's concept of individualization. In 'incarnating' themselves in individuals, collective tendencies simultaneously 'individualize' themselves. Conversely, individuals 'individualize' all social facts. Individualization is basically a physical phenomenon; the concept is closely tied to the mind/body dualism favored by Durkheim. What individualizes social facts is their materialization in individual bodies. Manifestations of social phenomena are individualized in the sense that they depend in part on the particular circumstances as well as the 'organo-psychological constitution' of the individual.[2] The 'individualizing factor' of the collective, spiritual principle or essence, the individual part of the person, is the body.

> As bodies are distinct from each other, and as they occupy different points of space and time, each of them forms a special centre about which the collective representations reflect and colour themselves differently. The result is that even if all the consciousnesses in these bodies are directed towards the same world, to wit, the world of ideas and sentiments which brings about the moral unity of the group, they do not all see it from the same angle; each one expresses it in its own fashion.[3]

Individualization is universal, it necessarily characterizes all societies. However, individuality is a phenomenon unique to modern, complex, organic societies. Modern society is not monolithic; evolution produces an organism which is differentiated into distinct specialized occupations. Similarly, it is differentiated into distinct, specialized individuals. The division of labor produces relations of difference rather than relations of resemblance among institutions and individuals in modern society. The question is: what are the relations between individuals, occupational groups, and organic society? Durkheim tends to mix his metaphors: at times he refers to newly specialized, modern, individuals as 'organs', to emphasize their complementary difference, their interrelated functioning, and their solidifying interdependence.

According to Durkheim's prevailing conceptualization, however, the organized social organism is subdivided into occupational organs, which are themselves composed of individual cells. Durkheim must then answer the question: are the individual human cells of society as thoroughly determined by the organism, and by their respective organs, as are the physical cells in a biological organism? Specifically, do occupational groups, with their internal relations of resemblance, replicate the total socialization of mechanical solidarity and collective consciousness? Does organic solidarity mean the complex interrelations among different occupational organs, which themselves contain determinate identical individual cells?

> One can . . . ask oneself if, in organized societies, the organ does not play the same role as the segment; if it is not probable that the corporative and occupational mind replaces the mind of the native village, and exercises the same influence as it did.[4]

At times, Durkheim seems to answer yes. For example, he refers to 'occupational moralities and laws', 'common corporate opinion', and 'occupational types'. 'Even in the exercise of our occupation, we conform to usages, to practices which are common to our whole professional brotherhood.'[5] Yet Durkheim concludes that professional groups do not exactly resemble traditional societies. They do not completely contain and constrain individuals. Occupational society still constitutes a 'yoke' to which the individual submits, but this yoke 'is much less heavy than when society completely controls us, and it leaves much more place open for the free play of our initiative'.[6]

As society is progressively diversified by occupational specialization, simultaneously:

> in the interior of each occupation the differences are growing. Each individual is more and more acquiring his own way of thinking and acting, and submits less completely to the common corporate opinion.[7]

Occupational regulation, 'because of its very nature', not only tends to 'hinder less than any other the play of individual variation', but in addition, over time, 'it also tends to do so less and less'.[8] Occupational regulation, the rules of law and morality which 'predetermine' functions, necessarily and forcefully exists. But such regulation, however crucial and powerful, still 'does not contract the sphere of action of the individual'.

This is true for three reasons. First, 'the occupational mind can only have influence on occupational life. Beyond this sphere, the individual enjoys a greater liberty'. Second, since occupational rules are the purview of relatively small collectivities, 'they have less authority' than rules emanating from the entire, social collective; they 'have their roots only in a small number of consciences'. Third, 'the same causes which, in a general manner, lift the collective yoke, produce their liberating effect in the interior of the corporation as well as externally'.[9] The occupational group, therefore, leaves a vast 'place open for the free play of our initiative'.[10] Conceived of as a cell in specialized society, the individual has more 'liberty' than its biological counterpart.[11]

Durkheim thus advances the notion that there are three distinct, relatively autonomous, entities in modern society: the social organism, society; the social organs, occupations; and social cells, individuals. In this view, the individual is more than a body, the corporeal component of 'a certain dualism of human nature'. In this view, the individual has a mind. Here, the dualism of human nature is not a mind/body dualism, in which the individual provides the body and society provides the mind, but a dualism of human consciousness. Durkheim asserts that *the individual* has two consciousnesses:

> one contains states which are personal to each of us and which characterize us, while the states which comprehend the other are common to all society. The first represent only our individual personality and constitute it; the second represent the collective type and, consequently, society, without which it would not exist.[12]

The individual consciousness is not depicted here as mere organic consciousness. Some aspects of consciousness are genuinely *individual* without being purely physical. And there is a genuine individual *consciousness*, which is not simply somatic. The body is no longer the sole 'individualizing factor'. The individual consciousness is individual by virtue of the fact that it is 'personal and distinct', rather than by the fact that it is embedded in, and represents, the individual organism.[13]

> We resemble one another a great deal more in the lower and fundamental parts of our being than in these higher parts. It is by these latter, on the contrary, that we are distinguished from one another.[14]

Therefore, 'the differences between men have become more pronounced – in so far as they are more cultivated'.

Individual consciousness does not always exist. Or rather, it initially exists as an animal-like consciousness: totally sensate, totally instinctive. But at some point in time, the individual psyche *qua* psyche is born; henceforth it develops continuously, and inversely with the collective psyche. Specifically, the division of labor, which requires individual differences, requires that the collective consciousness 'leave open a part' of the individual consciousness, 'in order that special functions may be established there, functions which it cannot regulate'. Conversely, collective consciousness, the 'totality of beliefs and sentiments common to average citizens of the same society', contracts as the division of labor advances.[15]

The volume of the common consciousness declines; while the volume of the individual consciousness increases. Collective consciousness regresses over time, in its 'representative element' as in its 'affective element'. The collective consciousness no longer 'completely envelops' the individual consciousness, which itself grows so that, in each particular consciousness, 'the personal sphere is much greater than the other'. The 'personal consciousness' not only grows 'in absolute value' but also grows 'more than the common' consciousness. It is 'emancipated from the yoke of the latter, and, consequently, the latter must have fallen from its throne and lost the determinate power that it originally used to exercise'.[16] The common consciousness, conversely, 'progresses less than individual' consciousness. It becomes 'weak', 'feebler and vaguer', 'more abstract and more indecisive'. It lapses into 'decadence'. Collective consciousness 'has pursued this course in an uninterrupted manner since the most distant times'. Meanwhile,

> Individualism, free thought ... is a phenomenon which begins in no certain part, but which develops without cessation all through history ... This is an inevitable law against which it would be absurd to inveigh.[17]

The collective consciousness does not totally disappear. But it is gradually reduced to 'very general and very indeterminate ways of thinking and feeling which leave an open place for a growing multitude of individual differences'. It cannot grow in extent and strength parallel to the rise of the individual consciousness: 'the two terms vary in a sense inverse to each other'.[18]

Durkheim clearly conceives of an individual consciousness. He makes frequent explicit references to it, as well as references to individual thought and feeling. Thought becomes 'free' and freedom engenders, is 'the first source' of, 'differences'. Individual reflection awakens, and 'as it varies from one man to another in quality and quantity, everything it produces has the same character'. There are individual, as well as collective 'representations'. Consciousness is in some measure 'personal', as are its 'materials', including certain representations and sentiments. The individual consciousness and its 'volume' grow, as individuals have their own 'ideas and sentiments'. Egotism appears in the 'higher representations'. Individuals have their own 'opinions, beliefs and aspirations'. Durkheim says that all consciousnesses 'are not the same, even in the midst of one society'.[19] There is a 'psychic life in the individual', which co-exists with the psychic life of society. *'The contents of men's minds differ from one subject to another.'*[20]

There are several other dimensions of individualism, how-ever, besides the ideational and emotional. Durkheim sees the individual as a locus of originality, initiative and innovation. The individual is thus understood as creative, and as a point of origination, an original source of behavior and ideas, an origin. There is private, personal initiative, which can indulge in 'free play'. The individual is capable of innovations, if left free to do so. The individual is less 'acted upon' and is instead a 'source', of 'spontaneous activity', of action. There is a certain 'individual originality', which must be allowed to 'express itself' if social progress is to occur.

Durkheim also views the individual as, in some real sense, free and autonomous. The individual thus may be influenced by social forces, but is ultimately self-determining. First, society liberates the individual from nature, but without placing the individual in total dependence on itself. For example, heredity is more intractable than common beliefs and practices. 'For the latter are imposed upon the individual only from without and by moral action.' Tradition 'is a considerably less rigid bond than heredity'; one which 'predetermines thought and conduct in a much less rigorous and precise manner'. Society, as opposed to heredity, leaves open a 'larger field' for 'individual variations'.[21]

Second, the effacement of the segmental type, and the emergence of specialization, 'partially lifts the individual conscience from the organic environment which supports it, as from the social environment which envelops it'. The field of individual variations 'enlarges as work is more divided'. The personal consciousness is 'emancipated' from the 'yoke' of the collective consciousness.[22] There is thus a 'double emancipation' of the individual, which 'becomes more of an independent factor in his own conduct'. Individuals are simultaneously 'freed' from 'collective action' and hereditary influences.[23]

Durkheim believes in the existence of individual freedom, which he extends to behavior as well as thought. There is a certain 'sphere of free action of each individual'. The individual is not totally absorbed in the collectivity but 'has a sphere of action which is peculiar to him'.[24] Only certain acts are imposed by public opinion. Others are 'abandoned to private initiative'. There is, first, the possibility of asocial or anti-social egocentric conduct, purely *individualistic* behavior, 'determined by sentiments and representations which are exclusively personal'. But in a broader and more positive sense, Durkheim sees the individual as the center of purely *individual* behavior. Each individual is thus 'a source of spontaneous activity'. The individual becomes 'an autonomous source of action . . . an independent factor in his own conduct'.[25]

Finally, Durkheim insists on individual difference. As society is extended and concentrated, enveloping the individual less and less, it can no longer effectively restrain 'divergent tendencies', and 'individual variability grows'.[26] On one hand, individual difference is universal, because in the same environment 'each individual adapts himself to it according to his own disposition and in his own way, which he prefers to all other ways'. On the other hand, individuals become 'increasingly differentiated from one another', as the result of 'the progressive disintegration of the common consciousness and of hereditary influences'. This 'development of individual differences' is 'necessarily accompanied by a greater diversity of tastes and aptitudes'.[27] In large societies, 'collective tyranny declines' and 'individual diversities can . . . more easily have play'.[28] This is 'in accordance with a general law' that 'differences among individuals increase with the expansion of the environment'. As the field of social relations widens, and social control and uniformity decline concomitantly, differences which are 'unique to each individual' 'inevitably develop', becoming 'more numerous and more significant', 'sharpened and systematized'.[29]

Durkheim's summary concept for all these aspects of individualism, of the individual – individual consciousness, individual originality, individual freedom, individual behavior, individual difference – is 'personality'. Modern society is distinguished from traditional society because modern society contains not one entity, not one personality, but two: the collective personality co-exists with the individual personality. In simple, mechanically integrated, collective society, 'individuality is nil'. More precisely: 'Individuality is something which the society possesses'. The 'individual personality' is absorbed into the 'collective personality'. Conversely, 'the collective personality is the only one existent'. In this form of social organization, individual personality *'did not exist'*.[30]

However, the individual personality, originally 'lost in the depths of the social mass' later 'breaks away'. Personal consciousness becomes 'emancipated' from the collective consciousness until, in each particular consciousness, 'the personal sphere is much greater than the other'. This 'growth of psychic life in the individual' is the development of personality as the development of personal ideas, of personal consciousness; as the development of a 'personal manner of feeling and thinking'.[31] But personal 'tendencies' develop also. There is, increasingly, an individual personality, defined as a 'sphere of action' peculiar to each individual. To be a 'person' is to be 'an autonomous source of action'; the individual personality 'develops itself' as it becomes such a source.[32] The individual becomes 'an autonomous centre of activity, an impressive system of personal forces'.[33]

Finally, personality means – in addition to individual consciousness, action, and autonomy – individual distinction. 'But what makes our personality is how much of our own individual qualities we have, what distinguishes us from others.' Personality is 'that in us which is personal and distinct, that which makes us an individual'. The individual acquires the quality of being a 'person' to the extent that 'there is something in him which is his alone and which individualizes him'. The individual personality rises up out of the collective personality as 'the individual, disengaging himself from the mass', becomes 'a being personal and distinct, *not only as an organism, but also as a factor in social life*'.[34]

THE IMPLICIT INDIVIDUAL: THE POSSIBILITY OF ESCAPE

Durkheim makes a strong, if implicit argument against the total social determinism of the individual. This stance suggests at least partial individual self-determination. It is effected through Durkheim's emphasis on individual deviance; and through his understanding of deviance as the asocial, the anti-social.[35] If socially induced thought and behavior is conceived of simply and restrictively as legal, moral, collective and collectively acceptable thought and behavior, then the illegal, the immoral, the localized and the unacceptable stand as proof of the possibility of escape from society and social forces. Society is not ubiquitous if it does not control all individuals, and all individuals totally. Individuals are not entirely social, socialized, socially controlled and constituted, if some of their activity lies outside of, in fact opposed to, social influence. All societies may be despotic, but none is totalitarian, omnipotent, as long as deviance is conceived of, and as long as it is conceived of as a non-social, an individual phenomenon.

Durkheim of course believes that deviance, as excessive individualism/insufficient socialization is characteristic of modern, and especially transitional society. But it nonetheless features in traditional, apparently monolithic, society. The repressive law which preponderates in traditional society demands total conformity, total uniformity, the absence of individuality/deviance. But it fails to produce this condition. In fact, it exists to attempt to prevent potential violations and to punish manifest violations. Where social forces do not 'have their way' with individuals, individuals violate the collective consciousness. This individual violation or violence against the social order belies the facticity of social facts, even in the heartland of sociality, the total society, the inviolable society.

The formulations which Durkheim invokes to understand the determination of individual thought and behavior by the collectivity, necessarily imply their own opposites. They necessarily involve a tension, between society and the individual, between social tendencies and individual tendencies. This theoretical framework undercuts the social determinist position itself. Social determinism in the form of norms is actually a dichotomy, a pair of opposites: normal/abnormal or normative/deviant. Social determinism as conformity automatically contains nonconformity; obedience, disobedience; resemblance, dissemblance. Integration and regulation are social, centripedal movements countering and countered by the individual, centrifugal movements, egoism and anomie. Social constraint, authority, coercion, obligation, control and force are confronted, in a dialectical unity, by their failure, by individual resistance and rebellion.

The transition from traditional to modern society, the twilight of one form of society, the dawn of another, is a period characterized by the escape of individuals from social forces. It is a time when 'society, weak and disturbed, lets too many persons escape too completely from its influence'. It is a period without social solidarity, without unified public opinion, without a collective belief system. It is a time of pronounced alienation, or egoism, when society is decomposed into atomistic, self-centered individuals, who are 'detached' from social life. At this moment, 'society is not sufficiently integrated'. It is 'not sufficiently integrated . . . to keep all its members under its control'. There is a 'weakening', a dangerous relaxation of the 'social fabric'. The breakdown or inordinate absence of society means, conversely, the ascendance or inordinate presence of the individual. Society disintegrates into disintegrated individuals. The bond attaching the individual to society becomes 'slack'. The ties uniting the individual with others are 'slackened or broken'. The metamorphosis of society therefore entails excessive or exaggerated individualism, overindividuation. The individual ego is enabled to assert itself 'to excess, in the face of the social ego and at its expense'. The individual somehow 'frees himself from the social environment'. It becomes possible for the individual to be *unsocialized*.[36]

As the members of society lose their social center of gravity, and thus disperse as free-floating, asocial beings, they simultaneously lose their locus of control. Anomie, or anarchy, emerges in the absence of a social entity able to impose limits, restraints on individuals.[37] Anomie is the condition of individual consciousnesses suffering from a 'lack of rule', wherein human activity is 'lacking regulation'.[38] It arises in the moral vacuum created as one social organization is transformed into another, as the 'old morality and law' are displaced, with no 'new judicial and moral order' to replace them. Anomie means that individual passions, appetites, and desires know no bounds. It is a 'state of disarrangement, excitement, frenzied agitation, which do not spring from social activity and which even make it suffer'.[39] It means that the nascent social relations of the division of labor have no rules, have no pattern. It means that it is possible for individuals, their drives, activities and relations to be *unregulated*.

Anomie results from 'the lack of collective forces at certain points in society'. As such, it shares an 'identical cause' with egoism. They both result from the 'disaggregation' of society. Anomie and egoism have 'an affinity for one another' and are 'two different aspects of the same social state'. Produced by the same cause, they occur together. The egoist has a tendency to non-regulation; 'since he is detached from society, it has not sufficient hold upon him to regulate him'. Conversely, the unregulated individual is egoistic; 'if one were highly socialized one would not rebel at every social restraint'. Egoism and anomie represent two forms of 'the disease of the infinite'. Anomie is a centrifugal infinity; unregulated individuals aspire to infinite heights. Egoism is centrifugal with respect to society but centripetal with respect to the individual; the self-absorbed individual faces an introspective infinity, the infinite vortex of the self. Both anomie and egoism occur in the infinite void into which the individual is cast in the absence of society. In the absence of society, individuals can neither 'become attached to higher aims' nor 'submit to a rule'. In the absence of society, the individual is 'free . . . from all social pressure', abandoned 'to himself'. Individuals 'tumble over one another like so many liquid molecules, encountering no central energy to retain, fix and organize them'. Egoism is the lack of society as collective activity, as external, altruistic object for individual thought and behavior. Anomie is the lack of society as a check-rein on individual passions.[40] Both indicate *'society's insufficient presence in individuals'*, society's *'absence'*.[41]

Of course, the transition from traditional to modern society is an anomaly, an abnormal situation by definition. It is the exceptional case, the aberrant case. However, Durkheim's conception of the status of society and individuals during the transition contains a fundamental element of his problematic. It is the very *possibility* of the non-socialization, the non-regulation of the individual by society, and not their normality or prevalence, which is crucial, which represents an intransigent obstacle to any radical theory of social determinism. To conceive of any individual, ever, to any extent, escaping society, is to reject the notion that all individuals are always, already and completely socially determined and constituted. To understand any part of any individual as at any time unsocial, asocial, anti-social, non-social, extra-social is to contradict Durkheim's own tendency to assert the primacy and absolute determinancy of society vis-à-vis the individual, the whole vis-à-vis the part, the structure vis-à-vis the element. To admit the possibility of individual indeterminacy is to deny the necessity of social determinism.

The transitional moment, the moment of social upheaval, chaos, anarchy, is in some sense bracketed by Durkheim, as atypical, as counter to the nature of society because characterized by the absence of society. Yet in another sense it is understood by him not as an exceptional social condition but as an extreme social condition. Durkheim sees the escape of the individual from society as prevalent during the transformation from one social state to another; but he sees it as possible in any social state; in modern society, and even in traditional society. In all societies, in society in general, social facts are coercive. They are defined by their capacities of obligation and constraint. They impose, compel, resist, prevent, hinder, dominate, restrain, command, individuals and their thought and behavior. They have the power of exerting pressure on individuals. They weigh on the individual. They have authority, and they govern the individual. They control the individual by force, by their superior force.[42] In fact, collective tendencies are 'forces as real as cosmic forces'. And their equivalent reality is demonstrated as physical force is demonstrated: 'by the uniformity of effects'.[43] But yet, social facts are not determinant of individuals in the strict sense. Their power is limited; their effects contained. They are more like influences than absolute, exhaustive constituent causes. There is an important distinction between physical and social constraint, between the pressure 'exerted by one or several bodies' and 'that which the consciousness of a group exercises on the consciousness of its members'. Social constraint operates not through 'the rigidity of certain molecular arrangements', but through the relatively ethereal property of 'prestige'.[44] Unlike the mandates of the internal or external physical universe, collective beliefs and practices are imposed 'only from without and by moral action'.[45] Social pressure exercises itself 'in spiritual ways', as a fact which is 'wholly ideal', as *'moral authority'*.[46]

Unlike physical forces, social forces leave open the possibility of disobedience, of refusal, of deviance. Social forces can be ineffective. Individuals in any society can escape from them, or rebel against them. It is not *normal* for them to do so, but it is *possible* for them to do so. The extensity and intensity of unsocialized, unregulated, thought, behavior and individuals, vary according to the social context. But the unsocialized and the unregulated may occur in *any* social context. In fine, the unsocialized and the unregulated may occur. The reality of collective tendencies, the proof that they are 'forces as real as cosmic forces' supposedly lies in the 'uniformity' of their effects. But these effects are remarkable precisely for their non-uniformity. The effects of social forces leave their mark as uniformity. But they have a counterpart in their own ineffectuality, and its sign, deviance. Deviance, disobedience of social laws, is at once the complement and limiting condition of conformity, of the individual effects of social determination. In any society there is uniformity, and there is a limit to uniformity. A uniformity so 'universal and absolute' as to prevent crime, is 'utterly impossible'. In any society there is standardization, and there is a limit to standardization. 'A society without criminality would necessitate a standardization of the moral conceptions of all individuals which is neither possible nor desirable.' In short, 'there cannot be a society in which the individuals do not differ more or less from the collective type'. And since such individual 'divergences' include 'the originality of the idealist' as well as 'the originality of the criminal', creative as well as destructive tendencies, 'individual originality' is not only inevitable but also desirable.[47] All consciousnesses, and therefore all conduct, 'are not the same, even in the midst of one society'. There are 'normal' consciousnesses, which are 'the most general in society'. But of course normalcy is only part of a duality, of the pair normal/abnormal. The general is necessarily paired with the exceptional. There are 'healthy' consciousnesses in every society, consciousnesses which contain the sentiments that 'crime shocks'. But the concept of health contains the concept of sickness. And there are, universally, 'adults who do not know these fundamental rules or do not recognize their authority'. This 'ignorance or insubmissiveness' constitutes 'an undeniable sign of pathological perversion'. The collective consciousness of a society includes the 'totality of beliefs and sentiments common to average citizens of the same society'. But some individuals fall outside of the collective consciousness, outside of the collective, outside of society. The common bears the un-common; the average bears the un-usual, the extra-ordinary. In any society there is a certain 'minimum of resemblances without which the individual would be a menace to the unity of the social body'. But such individuals exist. Society contains its own menace. Resemblance is reflected in dissemblance, in the 'dissemblance' between the agent of a crime and the 'collective type'.[48]

Social laws, social facts and forces, are both effective and ineffective, both determinative and non-determinative, because they do not constitute the only impulsion to which the individual is subject. The individual is partially indeterminate in relation to society because the individual is partially self-determining. There are two impulses, or a 'double impulse', operating on any individual. Individuals are to some extent 'solidary with the group', participating in collective tendencies, 'exposed to their influence'. To this extent, individuals are 'drawn in a social direction'. On the other hand, the other side of this 'double existence' is that individuals, to the extent that they have a 'distinct personality', try to 'rebel against' and try to 'escape' collective tendencies. To this extent they tend to 'follow the inclinations' of their 'own natures'.

Social forces are not omnipotent, individuals are not totally social because social forces are not the only forces in society. There are actually two 'antagonistic forces' which confront each other. 'One, the collective force, tries to take possession of the individual; the other, the individual force, repulses it.'[49] The social force acts as a 'restraint' with respect to the individual force, which represents 'centrifugal tendencies'. The social environment is a force which opposes and resists the force of individual differences and divergences.[50] The group 'strives' (but only strives) to 'model' individuals, 'to impose on them its ways of thinking and acting and to prevent any dissent'.[51] Society invokes its authority to impose logical and moral conformity; to forestall 'dissidences' in thought and behavior, against 'revolutionary fancies'.[52] Social authority is necessary, 'to halt, to contain rebellious forces'.[53] Under normal circumstances, the common sentiments of the collective consciousness have a certain force; the social organization, a certain force of resistance, against 'subversive tendencies'.[54] Society offers 'lively resistance' to individual attempts 'to pass beyond it or rebel against it'; against individual efforts 'directed against social facts with the intent to destroy or change them'. Social forces are challenged by individuals. They react with a superior energy, an energy which is 'usually' irresistible. One of the outward signs of social facts is, in fact, 'the resistance with which the social group opposes individual deviations from certain ways of doing or thinking'.[55] What is interesting in these formulations is not society's 'superior force' vis-à-vis the individual. What stands out is the assertion of an individual force, capable of attempts to rebel against or escape society, capable of efforts to destroy or change social facts. The tendency of social forces to predominate over the individual and prevent divergence and dissidence is not remarkable. What is exceptional is that Durkheim constructs an individual capable of even the tendency to deviation.

SOCIALIZATION AS PROBLEMATIC

The possibility of escape from society indicates the incomplete nature of social determinism as social control, of social laws as rules and norms, of society as a dominating force. But for Durkheim, society is also a creative force which determines individuals by constituting them. And, within the individualist tendency of his thought, this aspect of the society/individual relation is also only partial. Society does not entirely create the individual. The individual is not entirely constituted by society. There is a real individual, psychic as well as somatic, an extra-social mental and moral being, an individual consciousness, a 'personality', which confronts society, which pre-exists and survives society's constitutive effect. The socialization of the individual is neither automatic nor total. Instead it is a challenge, a conflict, a contest. It is a process rather than an absolute fact. It is subject to limitation and failure. From the standpoint of society, it is problematic.[56]

Of course, socialization is more problematic in modern, individuated society. And it is most problematic in transitional society, the moment of society's insufficiency or absence. In fact, in the post-mechanical world, it is necessary for society to undertake socialization as a conscious, deliberate, urgent project. The outcome of socialization is never necessarily certain, never guaranteed, but in metamorphosis and modernity, even the occurrence of socialization is uncertain. It becomes artificial, a contrivance, rather than a spontaneous, natural function of the social structure. Socialization must be introduced into society. In fact, Durkheim himself serves as an architect of this social programme, as he devotes himself to the development of 'moral education' and the resuscitation of the corporation.

When society is disintegrating, when it is 'weak and disturbed', 'breaking down', it has an 'insufficient presence in individuals', its influence is 'deficient', 'lacking'. The individual is freed 'from all social pressure' and abandoned 'to himself'. This allows the individual to escape or disobey social mandates. But it also means that the individual has escaped society primordially, from the beginning; that, in nature and development, individuals are unsocialized. The individual who escapes, the renegade who reneges on the social contract, the social outlaw, violates social rules, deviates from social norms, because it has not been formed by society, 'fashioned in its image', to begin with. Suicide, the social fact which reveals the ineffectiveness of social facts, is endemic to modern and especially transitional society not only because lawlessness prevails there, but also because 'too many' individuals 'escape too completely' from society in the first place. Individuals are predisposed to break social laws because, in the absence of social constitution, individuals are not social beings but are self-constituting. Individuals are anti-social because they are non-social. In transitional society deviance is the norm partly because there is a lack of rules. But it is also rife because of a dearth of social forces in the form of institutions which concentrate social tendencies and instill them in individuals, which envelop and pervade individuals. That is why Durkheim suggests as remedial measures not only the development of a new morality, a new system of juridico-moral rules and regulations suited to specialized society, but also the development of the means of inculcating social beliefs and behaviors: a secular system of moral education, and intermediate, occupational, groups to serve as proximate and effective agents of socialization. He is advocating the deliberate social production of the individual in its spontaneous absence.

It is even necessary, in transition and modernity, to both increase society's power and to convince the individual of that power. Education empowers society, as its socializing agent. It creates attachment and discipline between the individual and society. It inculcates society's norms, beliefs and values into individuals. It transmits social laws, as well as rational arguments demonstrating the need to submit to them. It is itself a social force, it represents society directly, in the sense that it acts on individuals. At the same time it represents society to individuals indirectly, in the sense that it depicts society, in such a way as to inspire individuals with awe, respect, and an obedient spirit. The corporation is also seen as the means to both ends. Secondary groups, specifically the corporation, are necessary because in a vast society they alone are 'near enough to the individuals to attract them strongly in their sphere of action and drag them, in this way, into the general torrent of social life'. Modern, specialized and extensive society, in its entirety (through the aegis of the state), proves to be too remote, external and intermittent 'to penetrate deeply into individual consciences and socialize them within'.[57] The corporation can fill this social void. It is the solution for the fact that society 'is not sufficiently integrated at all points to keep all its members under its control'; for the fact that society is 'weak and disturbed' and 'lets too many persons escape too completely from its influence'. The 'remedy' for this 'ill' is, first, 'to restore enough consistency to social groups for them to obtain a firmer grip on the individual'. This can be done by resurrecting corporate societies. Secondly, it is necessary that the individual 'feel himself bound to them . . . He must feel himself more solidary with a collective existence which precedes him in time, which survives him, and which encompasses him at all points'. The corporation is also charged with this function, 'to reimpress on man this salutary sentiment of solidarity' by persuading individuals of society's transcendence.[58] Finally, it is the task of sociology to dispel the popular conception of the impotence of society, and enlighten individuals by revealing its strength: of course, through its socializing effect on individuals, the revelation itself serves to strengthen society. Sociology must prove that religion, jettisoned by modernity, is a mystified but fundamentally correct stance by individuals in relation to society, and reestablish the stance – of devotion, worship, obedience and sacrifice – if not religion itself. It must counter the tendency of individuals to sense their own omnipotence. This sense, presumably developed in the relative social vacuum of non-traditional society, is nonetheless false. Durkheim insists simultaneously that society must be built up, fortified; and also that it exists, powerfully, only individuals fail to recognize this truth.

> Each of us has such an exorbitant sense of our own self that we no longer perceive the limits which surround us on all sides. Creating an illusion of our own personal power, we aspire to self-sufficiency. . . . It is necessary to react with all our forces against this dispersive tendency. It is necessary for society to regain consciousness of its organic unity; for the individual to feel the social mass which envelops and penetrates him, for him to always feel it as present and active, and for this feeling to constantly rule his conduct. . . . sociology is capable of restoring these ideas. It is sociology which will make the individual understand what society is, how it completes him and to what extent he is insignificant, reduced to his own forces. It will teach him that he is not an empire within another empire, but the organ of an organism . . . [59]

Durkheim's mission is the dual and contradictory one of restoring society's dominance, and at the same time restoring people's belief in its persistent dominance. Nonetheless, he shows that it is possible, tendential, in the stage of transition or modernity, for society to fail to even attempt socialization, the incorporation of individuals into itself through the incorporation of itself within individuals, the colonization and control of individuals through the construction of individuals. Further, even in the stage where society evinces a total and totalizing socialization effort, even in mechanical, collective society, where society is everything and individuals are nothing, socialization encounters resistance, encounters a limit, encounters the individual. Durkheim most commonly describes social determinism in the form of social control as 'coercion', 'constraint', 'restraint', terms which imply that there is *something*, some individual force or tendency, for society to oppose, to coerce, constrain and restrain. He most commonly describes social determinism in the form of socialization as 'penetration', 'invasion'. These terms imply that there is *something*, some individual existence or substance, to penetrate and invade. Rather than the individual's finding society already formed, society finds the individual, if not already completely formed, at least already *there*, prior to and independent of, if susceptible to, social influence. Social thought and behavior are 'engraven' or inscribed *on* something; on individual consciousnesses. Social facts are characterized by their externality. They are external *to* something, to the individual. Social facts are individualized, actualized, generalized, through an internalization process, through socialization or education. Since they derive from society, 'they cannot pervade individuals except by a process that moves from the outside to the inside'. Social facts must pervade *some thing*, the individual. Social facts must move from the outside to the inside, to the inside of something, to the inside *of* the individual. Society with its force penetrates and organizes itself within the individual, and thus 'becomes an integral part' of the individual, of 'our being'.[60]

In this, individualistic, aspect of his thought, Durkheim clearly believes that the individual is not totally socialized, but is, apart from society and social influence, something. It is something more than a body, something more than an empty vessel which society fills. The individual consciousness has individual content. The individual is a mental and moral entity, an entity with its own mental and moral essence. It is an autonomous being, which to some extent originates, produces and determines itself, its own thought and behavior. The individual is not merely 'the point of convergence for a certain number of external forces'. The personality is not merely the 'intersection of these influences'. Isolated from these forces the individual would not be reduced to 'a mathematical point, an empty place'. Individuals are not simply 'the product of things'. Durkheim actually sees an individual core, a center of substance, originality, volition and freedom, a real and really individual nucleus. The individual is, here, an agent. And Durkheim adds to his conception of the collective social subject, a second, an individual *subject*. But he is then forced to answer his own question, the question posed by his determinist alter ego. Deterministically, he states that 'personality can be nothing but a product of its environment'.

One must either say that it is born of nothing, that it exists one and indivisible through all eternity, a veritable psychic atom implanted in some incomprehensible manner in the body; or, if it does have some source, it must necessarily be a composite result of various forces derived from biological or social sources.[61]

Durkheim the individualist must respond to Durkheim's social deterministic challenge concerning the existence of an extra-social individual reality, an individual subject. 'For where does it come from?'

WHENCE THE INDIVIDUAL?

Given Durkheim's determinist tendencies, and given his tendency to posit mechanically integrated, segmental society in particular as totally and absolutely determinative of individuals, the emergence of the individual as an authentic entity is theoretically problematic. If individuals are originally totally determined, how do they elude this determination initially; how do they become self-determining, even in part, from a position of absolute dependency; how do they move from being effects to being, at least partially, autonomous? If it is possible to conceive of total social determinism, how is it possible to conceive of less than total, less than absolute, social determinism? How can individual freedom and originality be understood? How can an individual, pre-social, non-social core be understood? If the individual is not exclusively and exhaustively the 'result' of a combination of biological and social sources, can it be anything other than 'born of nothing . . . one and indivisible through all eternity, a veritable psychic atom implanted in some incomprehensible manner in the body'? The question remains: 'For where does it come from?'

Durkheim occasionally provides some unsatisfying, tautological explanations, such as the following. 'In the early stage, the individual personality is lost in the depths of the social mass and then later, by its own effort, breaks away.'[62] But for the most part his explanation centers on five distinct but interrelated factors. First is, ironically, the social factor itself. In some ways, Durkheim sees society as liberating rather than determining individuals. While at times he compares social forces to physical forces as literal equivalents, at other times he stresses the difference between them. Society is less deterministic than nature, and thus, because humans are social as opposed to natural beings, they are extricated from a consummate causality. In addition to being less despotic than physical nature, society actively liberates the individual from it. In conquering nature, society delivers the individual from its power as internal instinct and external environment. Liberty is 'the subordination of external forces to social forces'. It is realized only as 'man raises himself above things and makes law for them . . . in so far as he becomes a social being'. The human being can 'escape nature only by creating another world where he dominates nature'. That world is, of course, society.[63]

> Left to himself the individual would become dependent upon physical forces. If he has been able to escape, to free himself, to develop a personality, it is because he has been able to shelter under a *sui generis* force . . . capable . . . of neutralizing the blind and amoral forces of nature. This is the collective force . . . liberty can become a reality only in and through society.[64]

To the extent that humans are socially determined, a proportion which advances progressively over time with the advance of civilization, as the social world establishes hegemony over the physical world, they are relatively indeterminate.

The most important social developments behind the emergence and emancipation of the individual, however, are these dual historical realities: the expansion of society, and the differentiation of society. The inevitable increase in society's population and geographical purview cause the division of labor to occur, inevitably. Together they cause the birth and development of the individual.

> As societies become greater in volume and density, they increase in complexity, work is divided, individual differences multiply, and the moment approaches when the only remaining bond among the members of a single human group will be that they are all men.[65]

Individualism expresses the fact of individual differentiation and the formation of unique individual personalities. These are inextricable parts of the inexorable social tendencies to extension and centralization, as well as to specialization.

A large society is 'less restrictive'; it offers less 'resistance' to individuals. First, as society becomes more extensive, it no longer consists of a single, uniform environment. Instead, it increasingly contains a diversity of 'conditions of existence'. Therefore, the homogeneity of individuals gives way to a heterogeneity which is both possible and necessary. Second, as society grows, it becomes increasingly centralized, and therefore more distant from individuals. With its decreased proximity, it loses its capacity for 'surveillance', 'supervision', and 'restraint' of individuals. Large societies are characterized by moral density, by the increased frequency and intensity of interaction among individuals. But they are simultaneously characterized by discontinuity and diffusion, by the reduced frequency and intensity of interaction between individuals and society. 'In short, for social control to be rigorous and for the common conscience to be maintained, society must be divided into rather small compartments completely enclosing the individual.'[66]

Second, the division of labor is necessarily associated with individuality as opposed to uniformity. The division of labor is synonymous with differentiation, as different occupations distinguish specialized individuals vis-à-vis other, specialized individuals and specialized groups vis-à-vis other, specialized groups. In addition, it necessitates individuation, in two senses. As an antecedent, individuation must be at least a potentiality, if not a reality, in order for diverse occupations to appear in the first place: '. . . for the division of labor to be born and grow, it is very necessary that individual variations be possible'.[67] Then, once established, the division of labor is productive of extraoccupational as well as occupational diversification: heterogeneous economic activity is the base from which heterogeneous individual personalities and subcultures arise, as identical labor had determined identical individuals and a singular collective culture. Individual independence, along with individual variations and individual personality, 'progresses regularly with the division of labor'.[68]

Individualization also occurs as an indirect consequence of societal growth and the division of labor. It develops in a whole constellation of interrelated conditions which describe the evolution of the social organism into its complex, advanced, modern state.

As we advance in the evolutionary scale, the ties which bind the individual to his family, to his native soil, to traditions which the past has given to him, to collective group usages, become loose. More mobile, he changes his environment more easily, leaves his people to go elsewhere to live a more autonomous existence, to a greater extent forms his own ideas and sentiments.[69]

As the expansion of society and the division of labor advance, segmental society and mechanical solidarity are gradually 'effaced'. The collective consciousness, too, is 'effaced', fragmented into specificity, into group and individual consciousnesses. What remains of it becomes abstract and general; indefinite and indeterminate; flexible and plastic; and subject to rational legitimation requirements, rather than simply and absolutely imperative. The transformation of the social structure, and the decline of the collective consciousness, are accompanied by a transformation of social solidarity; social integration and regulation. They simultaneously presume and preserve difference rather than identity. Finally, tradition and traditionalism are eroded. Tradition, already seen to be a weaker force than natural law, becomes even more dissipated, more dilute, under conditions of social diversity and change. And traditionalism itself is outmoded, as too rigid, too arbitrary, too forceful, too irrational, a system of rule for a complex, variegated, and shifting social landscape.

Finally, Durkheim's vision of modernity constitutes *the* social configuration productive of individual freedom. Durkheim insists that the emancipation of the individual can only occur in the very specific conjuncture of: a large society, centralized in a large state, and subdivided into relatively autonomous secondary groups. And these are precisely the conditions encompassed by social evolution as Durkheim sees it. Social evolution is nothing other than the expansion and centralization of society, as well as its organic disaggregation into occupational groups. The state frees the individual from domination by secondary groups: the family, the community, the corporation; from 'collective particularism'. It acts as a countervailing force, preventing the secondary group from becoming a repressive mechanical society. In turn, secondary groups, specifically occupational groups, act as a countervailing force, preventing the state from becoming despotic. 'It is not a good thing for groups to stand alone, nevertheless they have to exist. And it is out of this conflict of social forces that individual liberties are born.'[70] Thus social groups not only 'regulate and govern' individuals, but also 'form one of the conditions essential to the emancipation of the individual'.

Modernity engenders individualism. It is a form of society which opens up and liberates the individual. But there is a more radical social openness than that of modernity, and a more radical individualism. It is the openness of a void, of the disintegration of society. It produces the overindividualization of extreme, unmediated atomization and anarchy. The transition from mechanical to organic solidarity, from traditional to modern society, occurs through the destruction of solidarity, the demise of society. The individual emerges out of the fragments of a shattered society, out of society's ruins, in its absence. Specifically, free individual thought is born in the lacuna of collective consciousness. Free inquiry first appears as a need, a need caused by 'the overthrow of traditional beliefs'. Conscious reflection 'intervenes to fill the gap that has appeared, but which it has not created'. The autonomy of individual consciousness asserts itself to the extent that public opinion is unformed, that a social belief system is non-existent; and a new opinion, a new system of beliefs, has not yet arisen. The transformation in social structure renders the old superstructure of traditions and customs asynchronous, obsolete. It is only in this relative darkness that 'light is sought' in the form of a quest for knowledge. It is after religion 'has lost its sway' that philosophy, followed by the sciences, are given a *raison d'être*, and are born. Knowledge is sought in the wake of the destruction of accepted opinions, the downfall of faith and 'irrational beliefs and practices'. In fact, knowledge is 'the only remedy' for this evil. The quest for knowledge, like suicide, is the product of the death of society prior to its rebirth; of the moment when the chrysalis is newly lifeless but the imago has yet to awaken. 'Man seeks to learn and man kills himself because of the loss of cohesion in his religious society.' Science, as well as the precepts it uncovers, will ultimately replace religion as a means of integrating and regulating individuals. Social science in particular is to discover the awesomeness of society, and to persuade individuals to attach themselves to it, as they had to the divinity in which they had previously mis/recognized society. It is also to determine the social laws necessitated by the new social order, and to explicate their necessity, with the end of exhorting individuals to obedience. But as reflection, like suicide, is transitional, it is similarly temporary.

> If a new system of beliefs were constituted which seemed as indisputable to everyone as the old, no one would think of discussing it any longer. Its discussion would no longer even be permitted; for ideas shared by an entire society draw from this consensus an authority that makes them sacrosanct and raises them above dispute.[71]

The obsolescence first of tradition, and then of critical inquiry, is part of a general, dialectical movement described by Durkheim. Traditional, collective society exists as thesis. Transitional, chaotic, alienated, anomic society: non-society, exists as anti-thesis. Modern society is to emerge as a synthesis, containing both collective and individual tendencies, both socialization and individualization. After the 'rudimentary' or insufficient individuation of mechanical solidarity, and the 'excessive individuation' of transition, an intermediate, healthy, necessary level of individualism will be sustained. After the excess repression of traditional society, and the excess permissiveness of transitional society, a balance will be forged, an equilibrium between society and the individual, between collectivism and individualism. Integration will reemerge to dispel absolute egoism. However, it will not be total; the individual will not disappear into the social mass. Integration will be tempered by the very egoism it displaces. Regulation will reemerge to dispel absolute anomie. However, it will not be total; the individual will not be over-regulated, fatalistic. Rather, regulation will be tempered by the very individual liberty it displaces. A golden mean will prevail, between over- and underintegration, between over- and under-regulation. Two relatively autonomous entities will confront and limit each other: the authentic, relatively autonomous individual entity, which had not even existed in collective society; and the transcendent, but no longer unique, social entity, which had been eclipsed in the disruption of transition. Durkheim allows the individual to become a reality, but anticipates the reestablishment of social reality, as social evolution ends in modern society.

RECUPERATION

There is clearly a tension in Durkheim's work between determinism and individualism. In some passages this tension is resolved in favor of determinism. Elsewhere, it is resolved in favor of individualism. At times, Durkheim boldly assaults the individualist sensibilities of his milieu with an uncompromising social determinism. At other times, he makes concessions to these same sensibilities, and even shares them. The two tendencies co-exist separately, parallel to one another, without confrontation. The contradiction between them remains latent. For example, deviance is sometimes posed as an individual, sometimes as a social phenomenon. Modern society sometimes seems to contain relatively autonomous individuals; elsewhere modern individuals seem totally determined, by a combination of the occupational organ and the societal organism; mechanical and organic solidarity; natural and social forces.

However, there are instances where Durkheim explicitly addresses this ambiguity. And in these instances, he resolves the tension, he recovers from the contradiction, by performing the following mediation between the two antagonistic systems of thought. He declares himself an individualist, asserting the existence of individual liberty, individual identity. But he re-defines these terms in a deterministic sense, relocates them within the field of determinism. Individual liberty is understood as obedience and conformity to social laws. Individual personality is understood as a social product. While Durkheim elsewhere maintains many genuinely individualist positions, in this case he assumes individualism as an acceptable cover over a more controversial, social determinist, content. He defines away the specificity of individualism, retaining only the name. He resolves his own internal theoretical conflict by dissolving individualism into determinism.[72]

Durkheim makes such complex and arbitrary manoeuvres sporadically throughout his text. For example, he declares the autonomy of the individual in modern society, comparing it to the autonomy of an organ in an evolved organism. But he insists equally on the strictly regulated nature of a specialized organ, its functional determination. He posits individual difference, specifically attributable to the division of labor. But he stresses the conformity of the individual to specialized, localized, occupational conventions. He links his theory of social statistics with the existence of free will by pointing out that social forces, while comparable to physical, chemical, biological and psychological forces, merely determine rates of behavior, without determining the behavior of specific individuals. Further, he claims that since non-social forces are compatible with human freedom, social forces should not be understood to preclude it.

But in addition to such incidental statements, Durkheim's work contains several explicit and systematic statements reconciling individualism and determinism. First, liberty is equated with regulation. Liberty is described as the 'product' of regulation, the 'fruit' of regulation. Regulation is seen as natural, as a necessary aspect of all natural life. Everything that is natural exists as a part of the universe, and is therefore necessarily influenced and limited by the rest. Human nature specifically requires regulation, particularly to the extent that humans are freed from the physical constraints of environment and instinct.[73] Externally, society conquers the environment on behalf of the individual, but on the condition that individuals participate in, submit to, society itself: 'liberty can become a reality only in and through society'.[74]

> liberty itself is the product of regulation . . . it results from social action . . . it is a conquest of society over nature . . . liberty is the subordination of external forces to social forces . . . this subordination is rather the reverse of the natural order. It can, then, realize itself progressively only in so far as man raises himself above things and makes law for them, thus depriving them of their fortuitous, absurd, amoral character; that is, in so far as he becomes a social being. For he can escape nature only by creating another world where he dominates nature. That world is society.[75]

> The individual submits to society and this submission is the condition of his liberation. For man freedom consists in deliverance from blind, unthinking physical forces; this he achieves by opposing against them the great and intelligent force which is society, under whose protection he shelters. By putting himself under the wing of society, he makes himself, also, to a certain extent, dependent upon it. But this is a liberating dependence. There is no paradox here . . . It is to

society that we owe the power over matter which is our glory. It is society that has freed us from nature.[76]

Internally, society conquers the instincts of the individual. This second emancipation is effected through the self-regulation of the individual. 'Through the practice of moral rules we develop the capacity to govern and regulate ourselves, which is the whole reality of liberty'. Self-limitation is 'the necessary condition of happiness and health'.[77] Self-control, 'the power to contain, regulate and overcome oneself', is 'one of the essential characteristics of the individual'.[78]

External, environmental control is supplanted by external, social control. Internal, instinctual control is replaced by internal self-control. And this, according to Durkheim, is the fulfillment of human nature as well as human freedom. Duty and sacrifice are not violations of this nature. Rather, it is through 'submitting to rules and devoting himself to the group' that the individual 'becomes truly a man'. Moral regulation stimulates the individual 'to realize his own nature as a man'.[79]

In addition, since society itself is part of nature, since the individual exists in a social milieu, the individual is necessarily and naturally limited and regulated in its relations with the other social elements. It is only part of the social universe, and cannot ignore that fact, except through the individually and socially pathological conditions of alienation and anomie:

> man is a limited being. Physically, he is part of the universe; morally, he is part of society. Hence, he cannot, without violating his nature, try to supersede the limits imposed on every hand . . . Man's nature cannot be itself except as it is disciplined.[80]

The health and welfare of the individual organism, as of the social organism, require that individuals are social, which is to say, subject to social law. Humans become human, and become free, through society and its mandates:

> liberty is the fruit of regulation . . . 'Rules' and 'liberty' are far from being exclusive or antithetical terms. The latter is only possible by virtue of the former. The idea of regulation . . . deserves to be cherished.[81]

The individual is natural through submission to natural law. It is social, human, and free through submission to social law. And this is the only freedom to which the individual can aspire. Individual freedom, autonomy, and power constitute an illusion, a self-delusion, which sociology intends to dispel; from which sociology intends to deliver – or, liberate – humanity.

There is, however, another dimension of freedom which is potentially open to human beings, beyond the freedom of regulation. And that is *enlightened* obedience or *informed consent* to social regulation. For Durkheim, social laws, like natural laws, are immutable and inescapable. But he maintains that conscious, deliberate behavior, even if necessary and determined, is somehow different from involuntary, reflexive behavior. If reflection intervenes between cause and effect, stimulus and response; if reasoned adherence is granted to social imperatives, then, in addition to being necessary and determined, they are freely chosen. An 'intellectual operation intrudes' between a rule and its execution, which makes social conformity 'reasonable, deliberate behavior' as opposed to 'automatic reflex'.[82] External stimulation does not result immediately in behavioral response but 'is halted in its progress and is subjected to a *sui generis* elaboration; a more or less long period of time elapses before the expression in movement appears'. This interpolation of thought and understanding into the determinative process constitutes, for Durkheim, 'relative indetermination'.[83] The individual must 'submit' to social rules, but the submission is, ideally, 'of his entire free will'.[84] The individual should understand, in a general way, 'the intelligible reasons for the subordination demanded of him'; i.e. the individual should understand the power and superiority, the omnipotence and transcendence, of society. Further, the individual should understand the reasons for specific regulations; these should be rational in the first place, and their rationality should be demonstrated to the individual. 'The rule must be related to conditions of time and place.'[85] The individual should evince a 'desire' to conform, as well as a desire for the rule itself, based on an understanding of 'the reasons that justify the rule' along with a judgement that they are well-founded. It is this understanding of its constraints and their necessity which constitutes the individual's autonomy. The faculty of understanding distinguishes human individuals from physical life, characterized by automatism. 'The agent endowed with reason does not behave like a thing of which the activity can be reduced to a system of reflexes.'[86] The individual is only a 'thing' to the extent that it submits 'passively, unconsciously, without knowing why' to social laws. If, on the other hand,

> he is aware of what they are, of his reasons for submitting and being receptive to them; in that case he is not passive, he acts consciously and of his own accord, knowing well what he is about. The action is in this sense only a passive state, whose *raison d'être* we know and understand. The autonomy an individual can enjoy does not, then, consist in rebelling against nature – such a revolt being futile and fruitless, whether attempted against the forces of the material world or those of the social world. To be autonomous means, for the human being, to understand the necessities he has to bow to and accept them with full knowledge of the facts. Nothing that we do can make the laws of things other than they are, but we free ourselves of them in thinking them, that is, in making them ours by thought.[87]

The 'first degree of autonomy' for the human being is the fact that it can represent the world to itself internally, it can know the world. Then, in so far as humans 'understand the laws of everything', they can 'understand the reasons for everything ... for the universal order'. On this basis, they can 'conform, not simply because we are physically restrained and unable to do otherwise without danger, but because we deem it good and have no better alternative'. This conformity is not 'passive resignation' but 'enlightened allegiance'.

> Conforming to the order of things because one is sure that it is everything it ought to be is not submitting to a constraint. It is freely desiring this order, assenting through an understanding of the cause. Wishing freely is not desiring the absurd. On the contrary, it implies wishing what is rational ... the desire to act in agreement with the nature of things ... To the extent that science builds itself, we, in our relationship with the physical universe, tend increasingly to rely only on ourselves. We liberate ourselves through understanding; there is no other means of liberation. Science is the wellspring of our autonomy. In the moral order there is room for the same autonomy; and there is place for no other. Since morality expresses the nature of society ... individual reason

can no more be the lawmaker for the moral world than that of the physical world ... However, it is possible through science to get hold of this order, which the individual, *qua* individual, has not created and for which he has not deliberately wished. We can investigate the nature of these moral rules ... We can investigate the reasons for their being, their immediate and more remote conditions. In a word, we can create a scientific study of the moral order ... Our ascendancy has gained its goal. We are masters of the moral order ... we can freely conform to it. For to wish that it be other than is implied by the natural make-up of the reality that it expresses would be to talk nonsense under the pretext of free will. Thus, on condition of having adequate knowledge of moral precepts, of their causes and of their functions, we are in a position to conform to them, but consciously and knowing why. Such conformity has nothing of constraint about it.[88]

However, while the science of morality is 'the means of liberating ourselves', the means to 'moral autonomy',

a thing does not stop being itself because we know the why of it ... because the science of morality teaches us the reason for the imperative quality inherent in moral rules, these latter do not on that account lose their imperative character. Because we know that there is something useful in that which is commanded, it follows not that we fail to obey but that we obey voluntarily. We can understand very well that it is in our nature to be limited by forces outside us; accordingly, we accept this limitation freely, because it is natural and good without being any the less real. Only through the fact of our informed consent it is no longer a humiliation and a bondage ... in a sense, we are still passive with respect to the rule that commands us. However, this passivity becomes at the same time activity, through the active part we take in deliberately desiring it. We desire it because we know the reason for its existence. It is not passive conformity that, taken by itself, constitutes a reduction of our personality. It is passive conformity to which we consent without full knowledge of the cause for it. When, on the contrary, we blindly carry out an order of whose meaning and import we are ignorant, but nonetheless understanding why we should lend ourselves to the role of a blind instrument, we are as free as when we alone have all the initiative in our behavior. This is the only kind of autonomy to which we have any claim ... we fashion it ourselves to the extent that we achieve a more complete knowledge of things. It does not imply that the human being, in any of his aspects, escapes the world and its laws ... We can only conquer the moral world in the same fashion that we conquer the physical world; by building a science of moral matters.[89]

Social regulation is thus 'a remarkable mixture of subordination and power, of submission and autonomy'.

When we try to rebel against it, we are harshly recalled to the necessity of the rule. When we conform to it, it liberates us from this subservience by allowing reason to govern the same rule that constrains us.[90]

This unique type of freedom, enlightened and consensual obedience, is specific to human beings, the highest form of life. Further, it is increasingly characteristic of humanity over time, a specific feature of modernity, the highest form of society. Modern society gives birth to a third moral imperative, besides attachment (integration) and discipline (regulation).[91] This is 'the understanding' of morality:

we must have knowledge, as clear and complete an awareness as possible of the reasons for our conduct. This consciousness confers on our behavior the autonomy that the public cons-cience from now on requires of every genuinely and completely moral being ... Morality no longer consists merely in behaving, even intentionally behaving, in certain required ways. Beyond this, the rule prescribing such behavior must be freely desired, that is to say, freely accepted; and this willing acceptance is nothing less than an enlightened assent.[92]

But the modern ideal of individualism, as autonomy of reason and freedom of thought, is never equivalent to 'intellectual and moral anarchy'. It does not involve escape from social authority. Rather, it involves knowledge of the reasons for such authority. This is the meaning of 'enlightened consent'.[93] Democracy, in particular, illustrates this concept. Democracy is a system 'based on reflection'. Therefore, 'it allows the citizens to accept the laws of the country with more intelligence and thus less passively'.[94]

Besides his reduction of individual liberty to social determinism, Durkheim reduces individual personality to social constitution. Human personality is a social product first in the sense that it can only develop in society; in so far as the individual is released from physical bondage, from nature. And, if the individual has been able 'to escape, to free himself, to develop a personality', this is because 'he has been able to shelter under a *sui generis* force . . . capable . . . of neutralizing the blind and amoral forces of nature'.[95] The personality represents a 'relative autonomy' in relation to its environment, which only society can create.[96] Personality is also social to the degree that it suggests the individual's conquest of its own nature, which is accomplished through the intervention of society and its exigencies. The affirmation of social rules and the denial of purely individual inclinations mutually imply each other. Thus, the individual is more an individual, more a personality, to the extent that it is less of an individual; to the extent that it acquires autonomy over itself, in deference to society. Self-control, or 'the power to contain, regulate and overcome oneself' is 'one of the essential characteristics of the individual'.[97] Personality 'presupposes, as its central element, a self-mastery that we can achieve only in the school of moral discipline'.[98] The personality is enhanced in the measure that its social obedience is informed, reduced in the measure that it is ignorant. 'It is not passive conformity that, taken by itself, constitutes a reduction of our personality. It is passive obedience to which we consent without full knowledge of the cause for it.' The important point is that personality involves social rather than individual thought and behavior. It is understood as 'conformity', in the same way that 'passivity' is understood as 'activity', and 'the role of blind instrument' is understood as freedom.[99]

But 'a person' is more than 'a being who disciplines himself'. It is also 'a system of ideas, of feelings, of habits and tendencies, a consciousness that has a content'. Crucially, Durkheim thinks of this content of the personality as social, as the product of socialization. Thus, the 'civilized man' is 'a person in greater measure than the primitive; the adult than the child'.[100]

The substance or essence of personality is the supra-somatic aspect of the individual consciousness; the higher, mental and moral, forms of psychic life. And these Durkheim attributes, with increasing decisiveness and exclusivity, to society. As he moves from *The Division of Labor* to *The Elementary Forms of Religious Life*, Durkheim's initial individualist impulse is gradually eclipsed by an idealist form of social determinism. Society is a collective mind immanent in the bodies of its members. It is a great spirit substantiated in individuals. *Elementary Forms* contains his most elaborate statement of the dichotomy between the individual and society posed as a dichotomy between body and soul. The individual is merely a mortal receptacle for the divine, the social. Society alone creates and imparts this *esprit*, human mind and spirit, the mental and moral essence individualized as a soul or 'personality'. As the divinity is the mystified symbol of society, the soul is 'the symbolic representation of the personality', that 'fragment of the divine'/society that each individual carries within itself.

The personality consists of that which is specifically human in the individual. And the specifically human is of course the specifically social. That part of the individual which is not in 'immediate dependence upon the organic factor', all of the 'superior forms of psychical activity', is social in nature and origin. Notably, both reason and morality, which are unique to human beings, derive from society. The individual is subject to 'logical conformity' as well as 'moral conformity' in order to be truly human.

> Does a mind ostensibly free itself from these forms of thought? It is no longer considered a human mind in the full sense of the word . . . we cannot abandon them if our whole thought is not to cease being really human.[101]

> . . . man is man only because he lives in society. Take away from man all that has a social origin and nothing is left but an animal on a par with other animals. It is society that has raised him to this level above physical nature.[102]

> . . . a man is only a man to the degree that he is civilized. That which makes us real human beings is the amount that we manage to assimilate of this assembly of ideas, beliefs and precepts for conduct that we call civilization . . . deprive man of all that society has given him and he is reduced to his sensations. He becomes a being more or less indistinct from an animal.[103]

'Man' is 'a product of society'.[104]

But Durkheim carefully points out that it is not just the individual's humanity, human-ness in general, which is social. The personality itself is not an individual but a social, an impersonal, phenomenon. The personality is 'a social entity' which 'receives everything from without'. The 'mental life' which it comprises is wholly sustained by the social milieu just as physical life is sustained by the 'cosmic milieu'.[105] The personality:

> can be nothing but a product of its environment ... a composite result of various forces derived from biological or social sources ... we have shown how it could not have developed out of any other source.

> Each of us is the point of convergence for a certain number of external forces, and our personalities result from the intersection of these influences. Should the forces no longer converge here, there would remain nothing more than a mathematical point, an empty place where conscience and personality could not be built up ... we are the product of things.[106]

'For' – otherwise, apart from these sources – 'where does it come from?' The alternative explanation is that: 'it is born of nothing, that it exists one and indivisible through all eternity, a veritable psychic atom implanted in some incomprehensible manner in the body'. And, in fact, this is not the case. In the beginning, before socialization, the personality *is not*. In childhood,

> the individual, in both the physical and moral sense, does not yet exist ... he is made, develops and is formed ... The educationalist is presented not with a person wholly formed – not a complete work or a finished product – but with a becoming, an incipient being, a person in the process of formation.[107]

In a sense, the individual enters into the constitution of the personality. But it does so only as a body. Body and soul, individual and social aspects, are conjoined in the individual personality:

> the notion of the person is the product of two sorts of factors. One of these is essentially impersonal: it is the spiritual

principle serving as the soul of the group. In fact, it is this which constitutes the very substance of individual souls. Now this is not the possession of anyone in particular: it is a part of the collective patrimony; in it and through it, all consciousnesses communicate. But on the other hand, in order to have separate personalities, it is necessary that another factor intervenes to break up and differentiate this principle: in other words, an individualizing factor is necessary. It is the body that fulfills this function.[108]

However, not only is the individual contribution strictly confined to the corporeal, the phenomenal. In addition, this is an insignificant aspect of personality. The social soul 'may well take from the body the outward form in which it individualizes itself, but it owes nothing essential to it'. Individuation 'is not the essential characteristic of the personality'.

Besides its dominance relative to the body as the real essence of personality, the individualized, incarnate soul literally 'dominates' the body from within. But this represents a reprise of the familiar mind/body duality. Durkheim follows Kant in declaring the body not only secondary to the soul, but actually the enemy of the soul it houses. To do so, he must entirely renounce the individual aspect of personality, and again construct personality as exclusively and conterminously soul, exclusively and conterminously social. 'The senses, the body and, in a word, all that individualizes' is, ultimately for Durkheim as for Kant, actually 'the *antagonist* of the personality'.

> So it is not at all true that we are more personal as we are more individualized. The two terms are in no way synonymous: in one sense, they oppose more than they imply one another. Passion individualizes, yet it also enslaves. Our sensations are essentially individual; yet we are more personal the more we are freed from our senses and able to think and act with concepts. So those who insist upon all the social elements of the individual do not mean by that to deny or debase the personality. They merely refuse to confuse it with the fact of individuation.[109]

A final way in which Durkheim effects a mediation between a social, determinist philosophy and individualism, is through his concept: *the cult of the individual*. In the first place, he reconciles the collective consciousness with individualism. The two are not incompatible, he says, because individualism becomes the active content of the collective consciousness. Thus individuals are merged, identical, and unified, on the very basis of individual distinction, difference, and autonomy. Individualism becomes the collectivizing religion of the modern, individualized collectivity. In fact, Durkheim says that the 'antagonism between the individual and society' is resolved in 'moral individualism', itself a social creation.[110]

> *This is how it is possible, without contradiction, to be an individualist while asserting that the individual is a product of society rather than its cause.* The reason is that individualism itself is a social product, like all moralities and all religions. The individual receives from society even the moral beliefs which deify him.[111]

Durkheim is careful to qualify this new social religion, this individualism which supplants collectivism even while recreating the collective consciousness on a different foundation. The 'cult of the individual' is, in Durkheim's conception, not equivalent to egoism or anarchism. It is not the worship of the concrete individual, but a 'sympathy for all that is human'. It is a religion not of the individual as *self*, but of the individual as *other*, and of the individual as *all*. First, it is a belief in the absolute, inviolable sanctity of the other individuals in society, as opposed to a belief in the sanctity of their collective form, the group or society alone. It is a religion of the 'rights of man', 'rights of the person', a *cult of individual rights*. This represents not individual self-aggrandizement but self-circumscription, deference by *ego* to *alter*. The sphere of *ego* is not infinite, but ends where the sphere of *alter* begins. Second, it is a belief in the sanctity of that which is common to individuals, their humanity or human nature, 'mankind in general', as opposed to a belief in the sanctity of their individuality itself. The cult of the individual, redefined as the cult of humanity, becomes a new form of the cult of the collectivity. The 'religion of humanity' or the 'cult of man' is:

> very different from egoistic individualism ... Far from detaching individuals from society and from every aim beyond themselves, it unites them in one thought, makes them servants of one work. For man, as thus suggested to collective affection

and respect, is not the sensual, experiential individual that each one of us represents, but man in general, ideal humanity as conceived by each people at each moment of its history. None of us wholly incarnates this ideal, though none is wholly a stranger to it. So we have, not to concentrate each separate person upon himself and his own interests, but to subordinate him to the general interests of humankind. Such an aim draws him beyond himself; impersonal and disinterested, it is above all individual personalities.[112]

The individualism of Durkheim is 'the individualism of Kant and Rousseau'. It is not a religion of utilitarianism nor egoism but of 'man in abstracto', 'man in general', the human being. It is 'individualistic' only in the sense that it has 'man', not society, as its object; 'individualism thus understood is the glorification not of the self but of the individual in general'.[113]

The common humanity of individuals, composed of the characteristics which constitute human nature, the 'human person in general', 'man himself', is of course that aspect of the individual which derives from society, the 'personality'. For Durkheim, the human is the social. The reality underlying Durkheim's cult of the individual/cult of humanity is, therefore, the 'exaltation of human personality', the cult of personality. And the cult of personality is a cult of society, not a cult of the individual. It is true that this cult is not directed to the collectivity itself. But it is directed to the collectivity, to society, as it appears in socialized individuals. The individual becomes sacred only to the extent that it becomes social, only to the extent that it is imbued with a social nature, or personality; only to the extent that it contains and personifies the only genuinely sacred entity, society itself. And this is why the cult of the individual arises in modern society. In modern society the individual is actually less of an individual, less profane; because more socialized, more civilized. Durkheim describes two conditions in which the individual personality does not exist. First, it does not exist in traditional, collective society. And second, it does not exist in childhood. In both instances, it is the intervention of society which institutes the personality of the individual. In the first instance, it is the progressive growth of civilization itself. In the second, it is the progressive inculcation of that civilization into the individual.

Personality is the social aspect of the individual. The cult of personality is addressed to society, in its manifest existence within the individual. When Durkheim explains individualism in terms of the fact that each individual 'embodies something of humanity ... the divine ... sacred and inviolable', he is no longer discussing individualism. Individuals become sacred because they each embody something of 'society ... the divine ... sacred and inviolable'. Theological religion worships God and the particle of God's spirit animating the unholy human creature: the divine/individual soul. Durkheim's secular religion worships society, which it perceives as the reality behind the theological/ideological veil. And, increasingly, it worships the individual personality, which is society incarnate: the social/individual soul. Durkheim's paradoxical form of individualism is really a religion of society, as it animates the individual body. It is the cult of '*the individualized forms of collective forces*'.[114]

Part II

Durkheim's (social) epistemology

Chapter 4

Ideology and truth
Individual and collective knowledge

DURKHEIM'S THEORY OF KNOWLEDGE

Durkheim's theory of knowledge can best be described as sociological rationalism. Durkheim's epistemology is systematically constructed in alignment with his ontological theory. His epistemology is also systematically constructed in opposition to alternative epistemologies: biological reductionism, individualism, idealism, materialism, a priori rationalism, and empiricism. Durkheim's position in the onto-epistemological debate is based on his specific conception of the subject and object of human knowledge.

With respect to the object of knowledge, Durkheim is a rationalist.[1] He conceives of reality as relational, relations as real, and relational reality as intelligible.[2] He rejects empiricism, because of its tendencies to atomism and mysticism as opposed to relational, objectivist realism. He rejects materialism, because of its tendencies to reductionism and nominalism, as opposed to social emergentism, and social and psychological realism. With respect to the subject of knowledge, Durkheim is a sociocentrist.[3] He conceives of the subject of true knowledge as collective, and the knowledge of individual subjects as ideological. He rejects a priori rationalism because of its tendencies to individualist idealism or mysticism, as opposed to collectivist, objectivist constructionism. He rejects biological reductionism because of its tendencies to individualism and perceptualism, as opposed to sociologism and conceptualism.

Ultimately, Durkheim posits the collective consciousness or social mind as the supreme subject and object of rationality and therefore of true knowledge. Conversely, the individual human being is the subject and object of empirical knowledge, and therefore an inferior subject and object of truth. According to sociological rationalism, true knowledge is possible; it is simultaneously socially constructed and objectively grounded. True sociological knowledge is rationally constructed *by* and objectively grounded *in* the collective mind.[4]

Durkheim rejects biological reductionism, and maintains that even in individuals, thought is ultimately transcendent with respect to its material substratum. A system of ideas or 'representations', once formed, attains a state of 'relative autonomy' in relation to its physical foundation. However, Durkheim does not believe that thought originates with individual minds, even understood as operating in partial independence of their underlying organisms.

In Durkheim's view, individuals themselves in effect form the material substratum of a social mind. Individual minds are comparable to cerebral cells. Individuals, or social cells, like physiological brain cells, enter into combination and thereby release a psychic power, which presupposes but also surpasses its material matrix. It is thus society, the collectivity of individual bodies and minds comprising the collective mind, which actually produces thought. Individuals are merely constituent parts of the collective mind, and passive recipients of its mental activities.

Durkheim refuses to explain psychic life organically, as originating exclusively in the brain of the individual body. But he also refuses to see it as inexplicable; either as the product of strictly spontaneous individual activity, or as without origin, as eternally present and never produced.

> If reason is only a form of individual experience, it no longer exists. On the other hand, if the powers which it has are recognized but not accounted for, it seems to be set outside the confines of nature and science. In the face of these two opposed objections the mind remains uncertain. But if the social origin of the categories is admitted, a new attitude becomes possible, which we believe will enable us to escape both of the opposed difficulties.[5]

Thought is produced, and it is produced systematically. It is produced in and by society. Thought has a 'cause', and that cause is social.

Because it [psychic life] is partly independent of the organism, however, it does not follow that it depends on no natural cause, and that it must be put outside nature. But all these facts whose explanation we cannot find in the constitution of tissues derive from properties of the social milieu ... the social realm is not less natural than the organic realm. Consequently, because there is a vast region of consciousness whose genesis is unintelligible through psycho-physiology alone, we must not conclude that it has been formed of itself and that it is, accordingly, refractory to scientific investigation, but only that it derives from some other positive science, which can be called socio-psychology. The phenomena which would constitute its matter ... arise from social causes.[6]

Durkheim advocates psychological 'naturalism', which neither places mental phenomena beyond the realm of nature, nor reduces them to either 'the individual mind' or 'organic matter'. It explains thought, yet without reducing it to matter. It is neither idealist nor materialist, but 'sociological'.[7] Thought has *specificity*. It constitutes a specific level of existence, which is different from matter, but nonetheless real. And it is specific to the concrete, particular society in which it exists, and on which it depends. Thought is neither ethereal, insubstantial and epiphenomenal (materialism) nor eternal, universal and primary (idealism), because it is social.

Durkheim's 'sociological theory of knowledge' is a sociological theory of rational knowledge. He describes this theory as situated in the interstices between empiricism and a priori rationalism. It opposes them both, and at the same time it incorporates elements of each of them.

The rationalism which is imminent in the sociological theory of knowledge is thus midway between the classical empiricism and a priorism. For the first, the categories are purely artificial constructions; for the second, on the contrary, they are given by nature; for us, they are in a sense a work of art.[8]

Durkheim rejects idealist or a priori, Kantian rationalism; the theory that rational thought and its categories pre-exist concrete human beings and their experience:

it is no explanation to say that it is inherent in the nature of the human intellect. It is necessary to show whence we hold this surprising prerogative and how it comes that we can see certain relations in things which the examination of these things cannot reveal to us.[9]

Durkheim's theory of knowledge represents a form of rationalism, but at the same time, it opposes the notion that the categories of thought are 'given by nature'. Classification is neither 'innate' nor 'individual' nor 'given in things'. Without inculcating 'ways of thinking which are the result of an entire historical development', the adult mind would produce no more than 'a continuous flow of representations which are lost one in another', or at most 'fragmentary' 'distinctions'.[10]

We have no justification for supposing that our mind bears within it at birth, completely formed, the prototype of this elementary framework of all classification ... neither the tangible world nor our mind gives us the model.[11]

Thus Durkheim distances himself from a priori rationalism, in the direction of empiricism. The categories of rational thought are in fact 'artificial constructions' in the sense that they are *constructed*. They are not spontaneously and eternally immanent in human minds. Further, while they may be eternally immanent in reality, they are not spontaneously and unproblematically projected from that reality into human minds.

On the other hand, the sociological theory of knowledge is itself 'rationalism'.[12] It shares the rationalist principle that 'the world has a logical aspect which the reason expresses excellently'. It stands opposed to the empiricist notion that the categories are 'artificial constructions' in the sense that they are *false*. There is more to reality than the sensory phenomena of empirical experience. 'Reality' is not the same as, cannot be reduced to, empirical reality. Although the mind is neither transcendent nor prior with respect to experience, experience 'is not sufficient unto itself'; it does not constitute knowledge. Empirical knowledge is 'that which is brought into our minds by the direct action of objects'. But knowledge of reality cannot be direct and unmediated. It cannot be experiential. It is characterized by an *intervention*. To be truly understood or known, reality requires 'conditions' which are 'exterior and prior' to experience: it requires the categories of thought.[13] While rationality is in fact constructed rather than immanent, it is nonetheless realist, rather than nominalist in nature. It corresponds to the rationality inherent in reality. The sociological theory of knowledge is, then, a theory of rationality which represents it as both artificial and apodictic; as neither automatic nor false.

INDIVIDUAL EMPIRICISM, COLLECTIVE RATIONALITY

Empirical knowledge as individual knowledge

Despite his conception of thought as essentially social, and his contention that individual thought is not an independent but a derivative process, Durkheim nevertheless has occasion to acknowledge individual thought, as such. He discusses individual thought: individual consciousness and individual representations; as distinct from, and in contradistinction to, social thought: collective consciousness, collective representations. Individual thought is largely presented as base; as selfish and somatic in nature. It arises from and reflects the body and its states. Social thought is higher; more properly mental, as well as moral, in nature. It is both ideational and idealistic. This fundamental contrast, between individual and social representations, underlies a more general distinction, between the two central, divergent tendencies in thought per se: empiricism and rationalism. The empirical tendency is seen as the specifically individual in thought; while the rational tendency is seen as specifically social.

According to Durkheim, there are 'two sorts of knowledge'. Intelligence does not present the aspect of a unity but that of a duality. It is split into 'two opposite poles': the poles of experience and reason, the empirical and the rational.[14] The realm of empirical experience is the realm of the senses. The empirical dimension of intelligence is the dimension of sense perception. The *subject* of sense perception is the physical organism. It is material and particular. The *object* of sense perception is the immediate concrete world. Parallel to its subject, this object is both material and particular. This means that the character of empirical knowledge is both specific, to its particular object and subject, and also ephemeral in nature. It reflects the state of a certain, unique object and a certain, unique subject; at a certain, unique moment in time. It is imbued with the singular nature of a peculiar subject, the singular nature of a peculiar object, and the singular nature of a peculiar point in time.

The *subject* of empirical perception is the body. It is a particular and material point in space. This partially accounts for the specificity of its sensations. The sensation 'holds closely to my organism' and 'cannot be detached' from it.[15] Sensations are 'closely dependent on my individual organism'. Therefore, perceptions 'belong' to distinct individuals, and cannot be communicated or shared among them.[16] The perceiving body is also a point in a particular time. Thus, empirical data, a sensation, 'expresses the momentary condition of a particular consciousness'.[17] Finally, the perception is specific to the idiosyncratic nature of the perceiver. Empirical knowledge is 'composed of individual states which are completely explained by the psychical nature of the individual'.[18] The sensation 'holds closely' to the 'organism and personality' of the individual sentient/sensate entity, and 'cannot be detached from them'. It is 'dependent' on the individual organism; 'proper' to the individual. It is a phenomenon of a 'particular mind'.[19]

The duality of knowledge, as composed of the opposites, empirical and rational knowledge, mirrors the central duality which Durkheim establishes between individual and society. The individual, already identified with the physical and with the organism, is of course readily identified with the empirical mode of knowing. The dichotomy between reason and experience is actually a dichotomy between reason and *individual* experience.[20] Experience, particularly sensory experience, is an individual phenomenon. Sensations and images result from sensuous, individual, experiences.[21] Empirical data, in the form of sensation or image, 'is *essentially* individual and subjective'.[22] The world of perception, of the senses, is variable, unstable, concrete, particular, personal: it is the 'individual' world. The 'world of matter and sense' is one of 'two antagonistic worlds'. It is the world of individuality, of the 'peculiar point of view' of each separate individual.[23]

The conflict between individual and society is a conflict in which sensations are arrayed, along with sensory appetites, passions and egoistic tendencies, on the side of the individual. These are seen to derive from 'individual constitutions'.[24] The two opposed forms of psychic life are associated with the two antagonistic beings which comprise each individual. Empirical thought is the work of the being 'that represents everything in relation to itself and from its own point of view', the being that 'has no other object but itself'. This is the being which knows only 'the body and its states', the 'sensory being'. This is the individual being, 'individuality'.[25] Experience and sensations, like instincts, sensitivity and individual impulse, are opposed to reason as one side of the epistemological duality, as: 'the mentality which results from individual experiences'.[26]

The object of empirical perception is concrete, substantial matter. It is specific and present. It is a *thing*. The sensation relates to a particular or 'determined' object. 'A sensation or an image always relies upon a determined object.'[27] Sensations necessarily represent the concrete, that which speaks to the 'sensory being': they represent 'life' itself.[28] The relationship between the empirical, present, object and its subject is therefore direct and immediate. The senses apprehend immediate, distinct objects in their immediate and apparent states. Empirical knowledge is 'that which is brought into our minds by the direct action of objects'.[29] Perception is definitionally the simple, mechanical internalization of sensuous appearances, of external material reality. These determined objects are also both spatially and temporally singular. Therefore, empirical perception is not only confined to phenomena in isolation, in immediacy or presence, and in manifest apparentness. It is also confined to objects in spatial and temporal succession: the concrete is an infinity of specific instances, in infinite transformation.

The essential component of empirical knowledge is the perception. Perceptions are inherently different from, antithetical to, radically heterogeneous with respect to, the essential components of rational thought, conceptions. The two, conceptions and perceptions, stand in relation to each other as diametrical opposites. The immutable and universal concept: 'is opposed to sensual representations of every order – sensations, perceptions or images'.[30] The intellectual and the corporal, conceptual thought and sensations, are 'opposed to one another', in a relation of 'conflicts' and 'antagonism'.[31] Durkheim identifies 'two worlds' – two 'antagonistic' worlds – the world of 'matter and sense' and the world of 'pure and impersonal reason'.

Concepts also stand in a certain, more specific relation to perceptions. Most frequently this relation is understood as the relation of a frame or framework and its contents. The categories form a 'solid frame which encloses all thought', beginning with sensual perceptions. For example, the category of time functions as 'an abstract and impersonal frame' which 'surrounds . . . existence'.[32] The category of class functions as 'the external framework of which objects perceived to be similar form, in part, the contents'.[33] The category of causality serves as a 'framework in which our empirical ascertainments arrange themselves', and thereby 'enables us to think of them'.[34] The category of space or spatial representation consists in 'a primary co-ordination of the data of sensuous experience'.[35] The conceptual 'framework' is thus seen to organize and classify as it 'contains' its perceptual 'contents', 'matter', 'substance'. It connects and separates, unites and divides, empirical phenomena. Conceiving things is understanding their relations to each other; learning their 'place' as well as their 'essence'.

There are other ways of describing this relation between the conceptual and the perceptual. Concepts are said to 'add to' sensory information. Social representations, including the categories, 'add to' individual representations. Collective thought, associated with the abstractions of religion, science and philosophy; with the concepts of god and country and currency, occurs when 'the mind adds to the immediate data given by the senses'.[36] Animals can only 'perceive by experience' but humans have 'the faculty of conceiving', the faculty of ideation, which consists in 'adding something to the real'.[37] There are 'two worlds', and ideation represents the supplementation of the world of experience through the superimposition over and above it of another, a new, a conceptual world.

This superimposition can alternatively be understood as the replacement of one world by another, as a substitution of the ideational world for the empirical world. It is possible to 'substitute' 'a new way of representing reality' for the 'impressions of the senses'.[38] In this way, a 'conceptual' idea of the world is 'substituted' for a 'sensuous' idea of the world.[39] 'In a word, society substitutes for the world revealed to us by our senses a different world that is the projection of the ideas created by society itself.'[40]

Superimposition – as supplementation or substitution – is not a relation of parity. It does not represent a compromise between two equal parties, but rather a victory for the realm of reason over and above the realm of the senses. The conceptual world and the perceptual world stand in a relation of conquest to each other, an imperial relation, a relation of colonizer and colonized. For another way to describe their relation is to invoke the notion of 'domination'. The lesson of conceptual thought, the secret of its ability to produce knowledge and its triumph over nature, lies in its propensity 'not to leave the mind enslaved to visible appearances, but to teach it to dominate them'.

Philosophy and science are the fruits of conceptual thought, which, beginning with religion, is able to 'make a law' for the impressions of the senses.[41] The conceptual framework which enables us to think of its empirical contents not only 'contains' but also 'surpasses and dominates' this substance.[42] For example, in relation to experiential reality, the principle of causality is 'superior'. It 'dominates and rules imperatively' over the 'flow' of individual, sensory, representations.[43]

Rationality stands in a relation of opposition, and ultimately of domination, vis-à-vis empirical knowledge.[44] The conceptual stands in the same relation to the perceptual as that maintained by society with respect to the individual. And for good reason. Because, just as the empirical is essentially individual, the rational is essentially social. Conceptual thought is social thought; social thought is conceptual thought.

> In order to make a law for the impressions of the senses and to substitute a new way of representing reality for them, thought of a new sort had to be founded: this is collective thought ... to create a world of ideals through which the world of experienced realities would appear transfigured, a super-excitation of the intellectual forces was necessary, which is possible only in and through society.[45]

Rational knowledge as collective knowledge

The social nature of rational or conceptual thought, which Durkheim insists on, is conceived by him in several distinct ways. According to Durkheim, thought reflects the particular social milieu in which it exists: there is a correspondence between thought and its social structural basis. Rational thought can be said to 'translate social states' or 'express social conditions' for at least two separate reasons.[46] First, society is the *subject* of thought in the sense that it is the thinker of thought. Society is the subject of the verb 'think'. Society, the collective mind, produces thought, meaning that it creates and constructs thought. Second, Durkheim sees social life as an *object* of thought. Thought reflects society because it initially takes society as its model, and then understands other realms of experience through constructs developed in this consciousness of society. In other words, society first becomes conscious of itself, and it is this self-consciousness which then enables it to think the rest of reality.[47]

Rational or conceptual thought is equated with social thought through an understanding of society as the *subject*, author, agent . . . as the thinker of such thought. If conceptual thought is a collective product, it is because society is a collective subject. Collective subjectivity has two aspects. In the first place, the social body acts collectively: there is social, normative, collective behavior. In the second place, the social mind thinks collectively: there is social, communal, collective thought. Specifically, the collective mind thinks or produces collective representations.

Society, as established above, is seen by Durkheim as an entity or 'being'. This is the meaning of the pervasively reiterated statement that society constitutes a reality *sui generis*. Society is actually, literally, a 'special being'. It is an 'observable being'. It is an 'individuality', with its own nature, its own 'personal physiognomy' and idiosyncrasies. Society is a 'particular subject'. It is collective as well as particular, as it is 'a subject which contains all the individual subjects within it'. And it has a mental aspect. Social life embraces 'at once both representations and practices . . . ideas as well as acts'. Society is, in a very important sense, 'a synthesis of human consciousnesses'. Collective representations are produced cooperatively, by a collective mind or collective consciousness, which consists of a 'multitude of minds'. The social mind is 'a unique intelligence, where all others meet each other'. The collective consciousness is 'the highest form of psychic life'. It is a 'consciousness of consciousnesses'.[48] This means that society as such *thinks*. The existence of collective thought signals the existence of collective thinking.

Logical and rational thought are specifically described by Durkheim as 'impersonal', as 'collective thought'.[49] Logical understanding is 'a function of society, for it takes the forms and attitudes that this latter presses upon it'.[50] Social life is the 'origin' of logical life.[51] Society is the 'source' or 'cause' of logical thought. Reason is 'possible only through a group of individuals;

it supposes them'.[52] Reason is 'social'.[53] Between empirical representations and rational representations 'there is all the difference which exists between the individual and the social'. In the schism between sensations and intellect, the former 'derive from our individual constitutions', while 'our rational activity – whether theoretical or practical – is dependent on social causes'.[54]

Logic and reason are both composed of concepts and categories.[55] Concepts 'belong to the whole social group'. Concepts 'express the manner in which society represents things'.[56] The concept 'is an essentially impersonal representation'. It 'bears the mark of no particular mind'.[57] Concepts are *independent of every particular subject*.[58] Categories, in turn, are simply more 'general concepts'.

Concepts and categories alike are thought or *produced* by society. They are 'products' – or fabrications – of the social mind or collective consciousness. They are 'forged', 'constructed', 'elaborated', 'founded' by society. Society 'makes' and 'furnishes' them. They are the 'work' of society, the 'result' of society's collective mental labor. Concepts are 'the product of an anonymous and impersonal action'.[59] The concept is 'the work of the community'. It is 'elaborated' by a unique, collective, intelligence. Categories are 'the work of the group'. They have been 'elaborated by society', society has 'founded' them.[60] Categories are – like their original source, religious thought – 'social affairs and the product of collective thought'. Categories are social objects 'which the human groups have laboriously forged through the centuries'. The idea of class, for example, 'has obviously been constructed by men'.[61] The law of causality, like the magical thought from which it developed, is 'a product of social causes . . . elaborated by groups'. The category of causality is 'the work of the group, and is given to us ready-made'.[62]

Concepts and categories, which constitute rational and logical thought, are, essentially, collective representations.[63] Collective representations, in general, are:

> the result of an immense co-operation, which stretches out not only into space but into time as well; to make them, a multitude of minds have associated, united and combined their ideas and sentiments; for them, long generations have accumulated their experience and their knowledge. A special

intellectual activity is therefore concentrated in them which is infinitely richer and complexer than that of the individual.[64]

Concepts are the fundamental elements of categories and thus of logical and rational thought. Concepts are intimately, primally related to words. Thus conceptual thought is inherently, inextricably interwoven – or co-extensive – with language. Durkheim says that 'ideas ... correspond to the diverse elements of language'.[65] 'Concepts ... are constituted by means of words'.[66] They are 'formed in and through language'.[67] The nature of this primary relationship, this constitution, is ambiguously presented by Durkheim. At one moment of the text, language 'translates' and 'expresses' concepts. While 'every word translates a concept', the whole of language 'expresses' the whole 'conceptual system'.[68] At another moment, concepts are derived from language. It is said of the majority of concepts that: 'we get them from language'.[69]

Durkheim's ambivalence centers on the question of relative primacy – the question of which comes first, the word or the concept. However, the following point emerges unscathed from this ultimately unresolved confusion. 'Language is not merely the external covering of a thought; it also is its internal framework'.[70] To put it another way, 'the concepts with which we ordinarily think are those of our vocabulary'.[71] In some crucial sense, the word and the concept are one, and together they are one with thought. Words make concepts possible, and concepts make thought possible. Their 'inseparability' is in fact due to their unity, their identity.

Concepts, categories and classes are the 'tools' or 'instruments' of thought.[72] In fact, the categories are *inseparable* from the normal working of the intellect'. Reflecting 'the most universal properties of things', they form the 'solid frame which encloses all thought'. The individual *cannot think* of objects which are not in time and space, which have no number, etc.'. Thought 'does not seem to be able to liberate itself' from categories 'without destroying itself'. In the form of the concepts and categories of logical thought, society furnishes 'moulds which are applicable to the totality of things and which *make it possible to think of them*'.[73] Ultimately, logically, thought occurs in/through concepts; thought = concepts, as concepts = words. Thinking is essentially classifying, and classifying is essentially naming.

Concepts and categories are intimately related to language, and just as language is a social product, they too are constructed by society. Concepts are 'constituted by means of words', and

> neither the vocabulary nor the grammar of a language is the work or product of one particular person. They are rather the result of a collective elaboration, and they express the anonymous collectivity that employs them.[74]

Concepts are 'collective' ideas, since they are 'formed in and through language, which is a collective thing'.[75] 'Now it is unquestionable that language, and consequently the system of concepts which it translates, is the product of a collective elaboration.'[76, 77, 78]

The world of ideas and concepts, which includes the world of logical categories, is primarily the world which society perceives or experiences, the world *as* society perceives or experiences it. In other words, there is one world of reality, which individuals can only perceive sensuously, and which society or the collective mind is able to conceive, to conceptualize, to 'ideationalize'. The individual subject responds to the real world physically. It is *acted upon* by the physical world in the form of sensations which the physical world stimulates. The collective subject responds to the real world mentally. It *acts upon* the physical world, by creating ideas or concepts which represent it; and by categorizing and rationally comprehending it. This is only possible because of the special nature of the mentality of the collective subject, which is infinitely rich and complex. It is the total, all-inclusive subject of subjects, consciousness of consciousnesses.

In addition, conceptual knowledge is possible because of the special nature of the *object* of social thought. It is the total, all-inclusive object. The object of collective thought, of the collective subject, is the universe. The universe exists only as it is thought of, and '*it is not completely thought of except by society*'.[79] Society is a collective, psychic subject. Reality in its entirety is the object of its thought. It thinks, it sees, it regards, it embraces, it represents, it *knows* reality. When this total subject and its total object are combined, they form the absolute totality, 'the totality outside of which nothing exists'.

Concepts are collective representations in the sense that they are collectively thought or produced. They are representations of the collective environment. Concepts 'correspond to the way in which this very special being, society, considers the things of its own proper experience'. Concepts are thus the collective equivalents of individual (empirical) representations: 'they are as concrete representations as an individual could form of his own personal environment'. The interwoven structure/s of language/'the system of concepts which it translates' together express 'the manner in which society as a whole represents the facts of experience'.[80] In this sense, society constructs concepts as it thinks and knows things, reality, the world, the universe. Concepts are representations of objects external to, but thought and known and therefore internalized by, society as a subject.

Again, 'concepts express the manner in which society represents things'. Or, cumulatively, 'the world expressed by the entire system of concepts is the one that society regards'. In this manner, the exterior universe 'becomes a part of society's interior life'.[81] The collective consciousness contains collective 'impressions' of its 'collective environment'.[82] The schism between the empirical and rational is only, ultimately: 'the duality that exists between the mentality which results from individual experiences and that which results from collective experiences'.[83]

The object of rational thought is characteristically *non-particular*. Rational knowledge is not the knowledge of any specific object any more than it is the knowledge of any specific subject. The rational is not related to the concrete objects of concrete experience. Rather, it is general, universal, abstract, and absolute in nature. Conceptual and categorical knowledge, as opposed to empirical knowledge, is distinguished by its generality and 'universality'. Concepts pertain to 'the totality of things'.[84] Categories, 'the most general concepts', are applicable not to particular and concrete objects, but 'to all that is real'.[85]

The categories of time and space, for example, represent time and space 'in general', as opposed to the time and space which are concrete, perceived, felt, known by the senses. Time 'in general' corresponds to 'the rhythm of a life which is not that of any individual in particular, but in which all participate'. Causality does not reflect a 'personal state of expectation' but 'the conception of a universal order of succession' which 'imposes itself upon . . . all events', and which is therefore only accessible to a universal, omniscient subject which is able to perceive 'all events'.[86]

Concepts capture not only the general aspects of things, but also their 'permanent' aspects. Concepts are characterized by their 'stability' and 'immutability'.

> Sensual representations are in a perpetual flux ... On the contrary, the concept is, as it were, outside of time and change; it is in the depths below all this agitation ... it resists change. It is a manner of thinking that, at every moment of time, is fixed and crystallized.[87]

In general, conceptual thought is 'a definite form with fixed outlines'.[88] Thinking conceptually is 'relating the variable to the permanent'. The concepts and categories which constitute logical thought reflect 'stability and impersonality' to the extent that they are 'universal and immutable'.[89] Conceptual thought and knowledge are *outside of and above individual and local contingencies*.[90] Rational or logical thought, as exemplified by the concept of causal relationship, is thought which rises *above all particular minds and events*.[91]

Conceptual thought extends beyond the general and permanent to the abstract. Not only is it independent of specific objects, but it transcends the realm of real, perceived, existing objects. A 'class' of objects includes 'the whole group of all *possible* objects which satisfy the same condition'. Concepts can be applied to 'an undetermined number of things, *perceived or not, actual or possible*'.[92] This independence from concrete, material, experienced reality derives from the fact that concepts express 'the most universal properties of things'.[93] Concepts are not only 'independent of every particular subject'. They are *not attached to any particular object*.[94]

It seems obvious that what concepts, or collective representations, actually represent are the objects of the collective consciousness, which together form the collective environment. The collective subject perceives the outside world conceptually. Concepts are to the collective mind what percepts are to the individual mind: reflections of the universe, relations with the universe. However, this is not the only way in which Durkheim understands the thought of the social subject. Sometimes he understands it this way, as consciousness of the objective world. But other times, he understands it instead as society's consciousness of itself.

This conception is related to the idea that society serves as a model for understanding the universe. For Durkheim, society is the most complex object of knowledge in the universe, the ultimate combination of penultimately complex elements, human individuals. Society is the ultimate and all-inclusive reality. At the same time, it is the most complex subject of knowledge, the combination of all individual knowing subjects. Thus, when society regards itself, it produces the highest form of knowledge, as well as categories which are universally applicable to the rest of nature in its relative simplicity. As a subject of knowledge, society constructs a 'new world of ideas', or representations, which are completely different from individual representations, and which 'add something' to the latter.[95]

These representations are not only constructed by society, they are representations of society, which serves as their object. They 'express' society and the nature of social reality. 'For society has constructed this new world in constructing itself, since it is society which it expresses.'[96] More explicitly, Durkheim says that concepts 'are the work of the group', 'they have been elaborated by society'. But, in addition,

they are social in another sense. They not only come from society but the things which they express are of a social nature. Not only is it society which has founded them, but their contents are the different aspects of the social being.[97]

INDIVIDUAL, EMPIRICAL KNOWLEDGE AS IDEOLOGY/COLLECTIVE, RATIONAL KNOWLEDGE AS TRUTH

The object of truth: reality

Durkheim's most important formulations about the nature of reality are interrelated, and lead directly to his epistemology. He views reality as essential and relational, rather than as existential and substantial.[98] There are two levels of reality, and the deeper, more internal, less visible level is the most important, the determinative level. Because he poses this surface/depth, external/internal, appearance/essence, effect/cause, phenomenon/structure dichotomy, he believes that it is impossible to know reality empirically. The abstract is more real and true than the concrete. Concepts, categories, logic and reason must be invoked, to mirror or model the essences and relations which underlie, interconnect, and give meaning and order to, the manifest objects of the universe.

Concepts express reality because they express the *essence* of things. Conceiving something is, first, 'learning its essential elements', its 'general and permanent qualities'.[99] The 'function' of concepts is 'to express the reality to which they adhere'. The conceptual idea is 'a symbol of a thing and makes it an object of understanding'. It gives a 'faithful analysis and representation of reality' because it reflects the factual, the real object: it reflects 'the inherent properties of the object . . . its nature'.[100] Thus, at the level of individual objects, concepts create 'harmony' between human minds and 'the nature of things'. The *raison d'être* of the concept is 'being true', rendering 'things, thought of as adequately as possible'.[101] Therefore, 'the world expressed by the entire system of concepts' is the universe; the real, true, essential universe.

More important than concepts, the categories of logic and reason serve to express universal reality, natural as well as social reality, because they express not individual things in essence, but the more essential *relations* among things. Conceiving something is, second, 'locating it in its place'.[102] The categories 'represent the most general relations which exist between things'. 'The fundamental relations that exist between things – just that which it is the function of the categories to express – cannot be essentially dissimilar in the different realms'. Thus, while the categories are a 'work of art', that is to say, socially constructed, it is 'an art which imitates nature'.[103] Irrationalism is false: the categorical thinking of logic and reason has 'objective reality', which is to say that it is based in reality, it accurately reflects reality, it derives from the nature of reality. The rational is the real, the real is rational. The 'true laws of nature', which comprise the 'natural law' of the social and physical worlds alike, are 'the regulations according to which facts are really interconnected'.[104] There is, in fact, and not merely in thought, a *natural order of things*. This means that 'the phenomena of the universe are bound together by necessary relations, called laws'. These necessary relations indicate 'the manner in which things are logically related', and signify a 'universal determinism'. Therefore, Durkheim asserts that: *what is natural in this sense of the word, is also rational*.[105] Nature or reality, or the nature of reality, is rational, which is to say relational. Because such a logical, rational order actually exists in reality, in nature, this order must be represented in thought for thought to be accurate. Not only is rationality not an artifice, it is the only way to understand the universe. Relations and not just things must find expression before truth is at hand:

> For to explain is to attach things to each other and to establish relations between them which make them appear to us as functions of each other and as vibrating sympathetically according to an internal law founded in their nature.[106]

The essential and relational nature of reality makes it difficult to know reality. Specifically, the nature of reality invalidates the easy, ready knowledge of the senses, of the immediate, of appearance. Reality is only accessible through the more arduous, mental, processes of conceptual thought and reason. Knowing reality is problematic. It requires concerted, cerebral, effort and labor. The process of knowledge is a process of intellectual production. On the one hand, 'logical understanding' prevents humans 'from seeing reality as their senses show it to them'. On the other hand, since to explain is 'to attach things to each other and to establish relations between them', reality as revealed by the senses 'has the grave inconvenience of allowing of no explanation'. 'But sensations, which see nothing except from the outside, could never make them disclose these relations and internal bonds; the intellect alone can create the notion of them'.[107] The senses *see*, and only from the *outside*. The intellect *makes* things disclose their *internal* bonds and *relations*, it *creates* notions of them.

> The essential thing was not to leave the mind enslaved to visible appearances but to teach it to dominate them and to connect what the senses separated; for from the moment when men have an idea that there are internal connections between things, science and philosophy become possible.[108]

The senses operate on the level of *visible appearances*, and thereby *enslave* the mind. The senses *separate* things. The mind *dominates* the senses. It *connects* things. The mind works. It digs deep to discover and uncover the *internal connections* among things. While the senses passively receive appearances of reality, the mind actively seeks knowledge of reality. It thereby paves the way, the only way, for science and philosophy, the only paths to true knowledge. 'Our senses . . . can touch only realized and known conditions, each separate from the others; the internal process uniting these conditions escapes them.'[109] Realized and known conditions; obvious, apparent, manifest, superficial and separate conditions, are the purview of 'external experience'. On the other hand, the internal process uniting conditions, causality for example, is the purview of 'psychic life'.

Reality is essential and relational; therefore it is resistant, resistant to knowledge. This is true of all the domains of nature: the physical world, the social world, and even the psychic world, where knowledge resides. While only the mind can know reality, it does not follow that the mind can know reality directly, immediately, individually. And it does not follow that the mind can know itself. Like the rest of nature, the mind is not knowable through experience alone.

> The facts of individual psychology . . . are by definition purely mental, yet the consciousness we have of them reveals to us neither their nature nor their genesis . . . it gives us confused, fleeting, subjective impressions of them but no clear scientific notions or explanatory concepts.[110]

Psychic life provides the best example of the stubborn, elusive nature of 'facts', because it appears to be the easiest, closest, most comprehensible reality. Because the psyche is not easily and simply known, even by itself, the difficulty of knowing the rest of the world is demonstrated:

> psychical life, far from being directly cognizable, has on the contrary profound depths inaccessible to ordinary perception, to which we attain only gradually by devious and complicated paths like those employed by the sciences of the external world.[111]

Things are not *directly cognizable*. They have *profound depths* which are *inaccessible to ordinary perception*. The depths of psychical as well as physical reality are attained *gradually*, by the *devious* and *complicated* paths of science.

If psychic life is not directly cognizable, social life is even more inaccessible, despite appearances to the contrary. Like psychic life, social life appears immediately knowable. 'The sociologist seems to move in a sphere perfectly transparent to his view.' However, in fact, 'consciousness is even more helpless' in knowing social reality than in knowing its own reality.[112]

> If we had really only to open our eyes and take a good look to perceive at once the laws of the social world, sociology would be useless or, at least very simple . . . Never would consciousness have dreamt, of its own accord, of the necessity which annually reproduces demographic phenomena in equal numbers . . . Still less can it discover their causes, if left to its own devices.[113]

Social reality, like psychic reality, cannot be known by means of *opening the eyes* and *taking a good look*. This is especially true of its *laws*, its *necessity*, and the *causes* which operate within it. Consciousness cannot be merely *left to its own devices* if the objective is to *discover* the reality underlying the appearance.

Knowledge of society is particularly difficult; society is a particularly resistant object of knowledge. At the same time, society is the ultimate object and quintessential model of true knowledge. Scientific knowledge originates as a reflection of society, because it is the relations which constitute society that are most immediately apparent to humans. The basic elements of the categories are 'taken from social life' because 'the relations which they express could not have been learned except in and through society'. Social time, space, classes and causality are 'the basis of the corresponding categories, since it is under their social forms that these different relations were first grasped with a certain clarity by the human intellect'. The collective consciousness 'does not create these moulds artificially; it finds them within itself'. These social relations themselves are only one instance of the relations which extend throughout the universe, holding it together and determining its constituent things and events.

The molds of conceptual thought, rationality and science are first based on human relations, yet they are 'applicable to the totality of things' because they 'translate the ways of being which are found in all the stages of reality but which appear in their full clarity only at the summit'.[114] The categories 'originally only translate social states'. The categories are modelled on society, but they 'are not made to be applied only to the social realm; they reach out to all reality'.[115] But society is 'part of nature', the social realm is 'a natural realm'. And 'fundamental relations' are both universal and universally similar in all of nature.[116]

Psychic life and social life are only specific aspects of general, natural reality. In general, 'reality' is such that:

> In order to discover it, external signs are first used which most clearly reveal it. Then, as the investigation proceeds, these outward tangible signs are replaced by others. Only when one has gone beyond the level of tangible appearances does it become possible to discover the innermost characteristics of the thing, which pertain to its very essence.[117]

To know reality is to *discover* it. Knowledge of reality proceeds from the *outward* to the *innermost*, from *signs* to *characteristics*. It moves from *external* and *tangible appearance* to internal *essence*. Essence is another *level* of reality, which lies *beyond* the level of appearance. This conceptualization enables Durkheim to conclude that rationality is real. Rationality is: 'an *objective* rationality which is *immanent in reality*, a rationality which is *given in things themselves*, and in which the scientist *discovers* and *deduces* but does not *create*'.[118] Reality can be 'translated into an intelligible system of notions and relationships' because reality is essentially intelligible. Reality is rational. Because it is rational, comprised essentially of relations, reality can only be known rationally. Through rationality, 'we can see certain *relations* in things which the examination of these things cannot reveal to us'. Durkheim believes, with rationalism, that: '*the world has a logical aspect which the reason expresses excellently*'.[119]

The method of truth: rationality

With respect to the relation of truth and untruth or truth and error, truth and falsehood, truth and ideology, Durkheim draws less of a distinction than a continuum. There is knowledge which is more true and knowledge which is less true, but there is no knowledge which is not knowledge: there is no pure ideology, no pure illusion. However, two crucial and interrelated qualifications must be made.

First, Durkheim *does* invoke the concept of ideology. He normally uses it to differentiate what he terms 'introspection' from science. He believes that philosophical speculation is misguided because its method consists in the examination and articulation of the ideas – preconceptions and prejudices – as they already exist in the mind of an individual thinker. Thus, introspection is the study of ideas; hence the term 'ideology'. Science, by contrast, is the study of facts. It is only possible when preconceptions and prejudices, or ideas, are cleared away so that objective reality can appear.

However, there is another sense in which Durkheim invokes the concept of ideology. And that is to differentiate between individual, subjective, perceptual sensation and experience: ideology, on the one hand; and social, objective, conceptual knowledge: truth, on the other. This second form of ideology delineated by Durkheim is actually related to the first. Individual, subjective, perceptual and experiential 'knowledge' is in fact the basis for the false preconceptions and prejudices which obstruct true, conceptual, rational, scientific knowledge. Thus the first rule of the sociological method, *'Consider social facts as things'*, and its first corollary, *'All preconceptions must be eradicated'*,[120] are ultimately related to the distinction between individual, empirical knowledge and social, rational knowledge.

The 'ideas' and 'preconceptions' which interfere with the objective knowledge of facts, and which constitute ideology, are formed by individuals, subjectively, experientially, empirically.

> At the moment when a new order of phenomena becomes the subject matter of a science, these phenomena are already represented in the mind not only by rather definite perceptions but also by some kind of crudely formed concepts . . . These ideas or concepts, whatever name one gives them, are *not legitimate substitutes for things. Products of everyday experience,* their primary function is to put our actions in harmony with our environment; *they are created by experience and for it.* Now, a representation may successfully fulfil this function while *theoretically false.* Several centuries have elapsed since Copernicus dissipated the *illusions of the senses* concerning the movements of heavenly bodies; and yet we still habitually regulate our time according to these *illusions.* In order to evoke the reaction required by the nature of a certain stimulus, *an idea need not express that nature faithfully* . . . In fact, many times they are as dangerously *incorrect* as they are *inadequate.* By elaborating such ideas in some fashion, one will therefore never arrive at a discovery of the laws of reality. On the contrary, *they are like a veil drawn between the thing and ourselves, concealing them [sic] from us the more successfully as we think them more transparent.*[121]

To study these preconceptions is to produce 'an *ideological analysis*'.[122] Pre-conceptions, which is another way of describing *perceptions*, are for Durkheim (following Bacon): *notiones vulgares* or *praenotiones . . . idola*. They 'take the place of facts'. They are 'illusions that distort the real aspect of things' and are 'nevertheless mistaken for the things themselves'. And of course these preconceptions/perceptions which constitute idola/ideology, are 'especially . . . likely to exercise undue ascendancy over the mind and to be substituted for the study of facts' in the social realm, as opposed to the physical realm of nature.[123] The method that the scientist must follow, which is particularly difficult in sociology, is to:

> emancipate himself from the fallacious ideas that dominate the mind of the layman; he must throw off, once and for all, the yoke of these *empirical* categories, which from long continued habit have become tyrannical.[124]

The scientist must methodically be divested of the 'mystical doctrine' which examines sentiments pertaining to things rather than things themselves, sentiments which:

> have been formed in the course of history; they are a product of human experience, which is, however, confused and unorganized. They are not due to some transcendental insight into reality but result from all sorts of impressions and emotions accumulated according to circumstances, without order and without methodical interpretation.[125]

To remain in the sphere of experience is to favor 'the inferior faculties of intelligence over the superior', to 'prefer the immediate and confused syntheses of first impression to the patient and luminous analyses of reason'.[126] This approach or method (nonmethod, anti-method), this mystical doctrine: *'like all mysticism, is essentially a disguised empiricism, the negation of all science'*.[127]

Durkheim employs nouns such as illusion, veil, mysticism, negation of all science . . . ideology. These entities perform actions of concealment and distortion. And they are described as ideas, representations, substitutes for things, expressions of reality, which are illegitimate, incorrect, inadequate, mistaken, unfaithful, false, fallacious . . . ideological. Thus, the second qualification to the continuum theory is that, although truth lies on a continuum and is not radically, heterogeneously distinguished from ideology, Durkheim does impose a distinction *within* this continuum. A radical demarcation occurs between knowledge which is sensate and individual, and knowledge which is conceptual and social because this is where Durkheim would place the ideology/truth relation.

Durkheim's described method, the scientific method, is the means of attaining truth rather than ideology, illusion and falsehood. This method eschews 'mysticism', which is not only 'closely related' to empiricism, but is actually, always, essentially, 'a disguised empiricism'. Therefore, Durkheim's apodictic method, his epistemology, is first and foremost a renunciation of empiricism. True knowledge is to be sought by employing the instruments of conceptual thought associated with rationalism: concepts, categories, logic and reason. These instruments and modes of thought, on the truth end as well as on the truth side of the truth continuum, the truth/ideology dichotomy, are all social, and they are all superior to the instruments and modes of thought (non-thought) characteristic of the individual. The crucial moment in this continuum/dichotomy is the immediate juxtaposition, perception/concept.

The concept is superior to its opposite, the perception, in that it is true. Conceptions relate to the essential aspects of things. The concept, as opposed to the perception, is characterized by objectivity or impersonality, and permanence or stability; and: 'Impersonality and stability are the two characteristics of truth.' The concept provides human minds a 'harmony with the nature of things . . . it had a reason for existence only on condition of being true'. Through concepts minds communicate as they should, which is 'in regard to things, thought of as adequately as possible'.[128] The 'moulds' of thought 'are applicable to the totality of things'. They 'translate the ways of being which are found in all the stages of reality'.[129] The 'function' of concepts is 'to express the reality to which they adhere'. It is 'a symbol of a thing and makes it an object of understanding'. It provides a 'faithful analysis and representation of reality'.[130]

Concepts are 'explanatory', unlike the 'confused, fleeting subjective impressions' of perceptions.[131] In fact: 'We understand only when we think in concepts.'[132] Concepts express and translate reality; faithfully, adequately. Therefore, 'the world expressed by the entire system of concepts' is nothing more or less than 'the universe' itself.[133] This dual condition – the opposition of concepts to perceptions, along with the essential truth of concepts – makes it tautologically the case that perceptions are essentially untrue, ideological. And when looking at their relationship as a relationship of difference, distinction, and division, this is the conclusion latent if not manifest in Durkheim's thought.

However, as noted, this opposition is not the only shape that their relationship takes. Because, in a very real sense, Durkheim views all knowledge as lying on a continuum, in a relation of continuity and progressive perfection. In this light, the perception becomes the crude form, the primitive matter which is only relatively untrue, and then only until it is processed and refined by higher, relatively true forms of knowledge. And the adjacent, immediately superior form of knowledge is of course the concept. In this relation, the concept is only more true than the perception: better, but not qualitatively heterogeneous. Thus while on the one hand the conceptual idea of the world is 'substituted' for the sensuous idea of the world, on the other hand the former results from 'an examination and elaboration' of the latter.[134] The sensate is 'transformed' and 'transfigured' as it *becomes* conceptual. In this guise, 'Thinking by concepts . . . is projecting a light upon the sensation which illuminates it, penetrates it and transforms it'.[135]

Examination, elaboration, illumination and transformation are markedly different, pacifistic and cooperative relations, in comparison with antagonism, conflict, and opposition. The superiority/inferiority relation remains, but in an attenuated form. Concepts and perceptions thus have a dual relationship. They both negate and complement each other. They are both radically different, and substantially the same. Concepts are of another world than perceptions, and begin by renouncing them. At the same time, they are *of* perceptions, and begin *as* perceptions. This dual relationship of transformation, of production, of an operation which effects a qualitative change, is expressed in the following passage.

> But sensory reality is not made to enter the framework of our concepts spontaneously and by itself. It resists, and, in order to make it conform, we have to do some violence to it, we have to submit it to all sorts of laborious operations that alter it so that the mind can assimilate it. However, we never

completely succeed in triumphing over its resistance. Our concepts never succeed in mastering our sensations and in translating them completely into intelligible terms. They take on a conceptual form only by losing that which is most concrete in them, that which causes them to speak to our sensory being and to involve it in action; and in so doing, they become something fixed and dead.[136]

Violence is present in this transformation. Perceptions are killed as perceptions before they can be reborn as concepts. But a difference which can be nullified by transformation, however violent, is not as radical a difference as an absolute opposition. Concepts are the framework and perceptions are their contents. Concepts are the finished product and perceptions are their raw material. Rather than being absolutely separated by their absolute difference, they are intricately and inextricably linked to each other. They are linked in substance, as perceptions are the substance of concepts. They are not two different, irreconcilable things. They are *the same thing*, in different forms.

The relation of continuity within hierarchy between concepts and perceptions is the beginning of the hierarchical continuum of knowledge. As concepts are a higher form of perceptions, categories are a higher form of concepts. Categories *are* concepts. Categories 'are themselves concepts'. And yet they are superior to concepts. Concepts express the essence of things, the general and abstract nature of things, which must be extracted from their particular and concrete existence as isolated, empirical things. Categories move even further from specific, individual things. They don't express things at all, even in their abstract essence, but only the more abstract relations which obtain among things. Categories 'represent the most general relations which exist between things'. The 'function' of categories is to 'express ... the fundamental relations that exist between things'.[137] Concepts are simple, mere elements of categories, which are complex and comprehensive. As concepts are the framework of perceptions, categories are the framework of concepts. Categories are 'pre-eminent concepts', whose 'function' or 'role' it is 'to dominate and envelop all the other concepts'.[138]

As concepts comprise perceptions, and as categories comprise concepts, logic and reason comprise both concepts and categories.

'Logical thought is made up of concepts.' Logical thought 'commences with the concept'.[139] Concepts are 'the material of all logical thought'.[140] Reason is 'all the fundamental categories taken together'.[141] And of course, logic and reason operate in the domain of truth. They comprehend all the concepts/essences and all the categories/relations which together exhaustively and accurately constitute the truth of the universe.

> In fact, logical thinking is always impersonal thinking, and it is also thought *sub species aeternitatis* – as though for all time. Impersonality and stability are the two characteristics of truth. Now logical life evidently presupposes that men know, at least confusedly, that there is such a thing as truth, distinct from sensuous appearances.[142]

Ultimately, 'reason' is allied with 'truth', and opposed to 'experience', 'perceptions', 'sensations', 'instincts', 'sensitivity and individual impulse'. The triumvirate of 'truth . . . reason and morality' together constitute the 'higher' plane of human existence.[143]

Durkheim upholds the realism of rationalism against the nominalism of empiricism. He 'keeps . . . intact' the a priorist principle that 'knowledge is made up of two sorts of elements, which cannot be reduced into one another', the empirical and the rational. Logic and reason are real and true; they refer to an 'objective reality':

> forcing reason back upon experience causes it to disappear, for it is equivalent to reducing the universality and necessity which characterize it to pure appearance, to an illusion which may be useful practically, but which corresponds to nothing in reality; consequently it is denying all objective reality to the logical life, whose regulation and organization is the function of the categories. Classical empiricism results in irrationalism.[144]

Logic and reason are only penultimate methods of divining truth, themselves the ingredients of the highest, truest form of knowledge: science. Science represents the end of the truth continuum, united with concepts, categories, logic and rationality in that it is similar to them, and composed of them. Yet it is different from these instruments and methods by virtue of the fact that it is an even more perfect method, productive of an even more perfect truth. At the same time it is both different from perceptions and empirical knowledge, as the apex of rationality and the negation of the negation of empiricism; and yet it is linked to them by virtue of the fact that it represents their ultimate refinement, their most perfect moment, their truest form. The continuum of knowledge symbolizes the progressive development knowledge must undergo as it becomes truer, as it becomes truth. And science is the most developed form of knowledge, the best and most methodical method for ascertaining or producing truth.

Science is opposed to all empirical knowledge, as the most true is opposed to the least true. It is further from empirical knowledge than conceptual knowledge *per se*, as it lies at the polar opposite end of the knowledge continuum. Thus, the contrast between the scientific and the sensual is less *immediate* than the face to face confrontation and stark contrast between the radically heterogeneous realms of concepts and perceptions. But at the same time, science is more distant, more different from empirical knowledge than the merely conceptual, as it represents an elaborative transformation of the latter. Science is in one sense simply reason. 'Reason thus understood is simply science'.

With reason, as reason, science is generally, definitionally opposed to the empirical. That 'collective impersonal reason called science', or the pair: reason/science, is opposed and opposite in relation to the pair: empiricism/mysticism.[145] Just as the rational is opposed to 'the particular and the concrete', which 'baffles the understanding', so the concrete is 'refractory to science'.[146] Like the rational, and unlike the empirical, which is subjective and personal, science is 'objective' and 'impersonal'.[147] Science is opposed to 'sentimental subjectivism', which is 'a form either of empiricism or mysticism, two closely related ways of thinking'. To move from the 'unscientific' to the scientific, it is necessary 'to eliminate . . . what is necessarily individual, subjective, contingent', spontaneous and instinctive knowledge, in favor of what is 'general 'impersonal' and 'objective'.[148]

Rationality/science, like morality, is universal in nature. It transcends individual subjects and objects, and operates according to the categorical imperative. 'Rational thinking' is parallel to moral acting, in that it is 'thinking according to the laws which are imposed upon all reasonable beings . . . In other words, science and morals imply that the individual is capable of raising himself above his own peculiar point of view and of living an impersonal life'. Thus in relation to the 'two antagonistic worlds . . . the world of matter and sense on the one hand, and the world of pure and impersonal reason on the other', science, like morality, is part of the latter world, foreign and hostile to the former.[149] The world of perceptions is the world of 'confused, fleeting, subjective impressions', while the world of rationality is the world of 'explanatory concepts' and 'clear and scientific notions'.[150] There are two ideas of the world, 'the sensuous idea' and another, which is 'conceptual' and 'scientific'. The latter must be 'substituted' for the former.[151] The empirical is an inferior, obscuring, ideological mode of understanding. The conceptual, rational and scientific mode of understanding is superior, enlightening, and adequate to its object. Of course, 'a science that would adequately express all of reality . . . is an ideal that we can only approach ceaselessly'. Nonetheless, the *raison d'être* of a science 'is to express, objectively and adequately . . . reality'.[152]

Science is a part of the conceptual, rational mode of thought and knowledge, with which it has a relation of conjunction. It is *other than* empirical, sensual knowledge, with which it is related by contradiction; by disjunction, disunity, dissimilarity, difference, diametric opposition. However, it also exhibits relations of similarity with the empirical, as the culmination of the progressive development of knowledge. Science is *not merely* conceptual or rational knowledge, and thus in a sense it is *not* equal to them. There is a relation of difference separating science from the conceptual and the rational, a difference which consists in the relation of elaboration. There are only 'differences of degree' between scientific and other concepts; all concepts, including the scientific, are 'approximative', and no concept, including the non-scientific, is ever 'wholly inadequate for its subject'. Yet even a difference of degree is a difference. There are 'scientifically elaborated and criticized concepts', which are, moreover, only a 'very slight minority'.[153] This difference of elaboration and criticism, which distinguishes science from conceptual thought and rationality in general, which specifies it, at one and the same time connects it to empirical knowledge. For if scientific knowledge is an elaboration of conceptual/rational knowledge, which is itself an elaboration of empirical knowledge, scientific knowledge finally, ultimately elaborates, refines and perfects empirical knowledge. The empirical must first be subjected to a revolution, to a radical break, as it becomes conceptual. Then it is subjected to an evolution, to a development, as the latter becomes scientific. The process through which a scientific idea of the world is 'substituted' for the sensuous idea of the world is not only a process of contradiction, opposition, conquest and destruction, but also a process of 'examination and elaboration'.[154] Perceptions are not only the negation but also the raw material of concepts. And since concepts are themselves the raw material of science, the empirical and the sensate are not just untrue or less true forms of knowledge: they are the rawest material of truth.

Durkheim has a recurrent example of the relation of similarity/difference according to which the various forms of knowledge are both united and divided. This is the metaphorical example of the knowledge of heat and light. There is knowledge of heat and light which is more crude, and less true. That is empirical knowledge. Then there is knowledge of heat and light which is less crude, and more true. That is conceptual, rational, scientific knowledge. There are 'unobjective vulgar notions' of 'heat, or light, or electricity', just as there are 'auditory and visual sensations' of 'sound or color'. These are analogous to the moralist's own conception of morality, or the layman's 'confused notions of society'. The common denominator is the *inadequacy* with which these sensations and notions nonetheless 'express' their objects, physical or social.[155] To discover reality, it is necessary to go 'beyond the level of tangible appearances', to 'the innermost characteristics' and 'very essence' of things. This is analogous to the way in which light and electricity are known first *only* by the senses, and then subjected to 'deeper analysis'.[156] Psychological facts, for example, are in a sense known by consciousness.

> It permits us to know them up to a certain point, just as our sensations give us a certain familiarity with heat or light, sound or electricity; it gives us confused, fleeting, subjective impressions of them but no clear and scientific notions or explanatory concepts.[157]

The knowledge/non-knowledge of psychological and social facts by the individual consciousness is both opposed to/replaced by, and also elaborated/completed by, the sciences of psychology and sociology. Perceptions are knowledge, but perceptions are empirical knowledge and therefore they are limited, subjective, particular, contingent. 'Thus the physicist substitutes, for the vague impressions of temperature and electricity . . . the thermometer or the electrometer.'[158] Perceptions *correspond* to an object, and *express* it. However, this correspondence and expression are partial and limited at best; they obscure and distort the object at worst.

> If a scientist states it as an axiom that the sensations of heat and light which we feel correspond to some objective cause, he does not conclude that this is what it appears to the senses to be. Likewise, even if the impressions which the faithful feel are not imaginary, still they are in no way privileged intuitions; there is no reason for believing that they inform us better upon the nature of their object than do ordinary sensations upon the nature of bodies and their properties. In order to discover what this object consists of, we must submit them to an examination and elaboration analogous to that which has substituted for the sensuous idea of the world another which is scientific and conceptual.[159]

There is an ideology of society, which is religion. It is not false, because it really corresponds to a real object. However, there is also a science of society, which is more true, which discovers the truth of reality by discarding the ideology of religion. Yet it does not throw out the infant truth with the ideological bath water. It recognizes the truth of religion, which is the transcendental, omnipotent real entity, society. But it recognizes that religion, as an empirical, mystical knowledge, obscures, distorts and veils society even as it reveals its existence. Perceptions always reveal and conceal, disclose and distort, their objects. They always constitute knowledge, but empirical knowledge is always ideological. Science always only reveals and discloses its object, closes the gap between knowledge and reality, becomes one with its object, as truth. The distance between science and ideology, between truth and falsehood, between knowing/knowing more and not knowing/knowing less, between perfect and imperfect knowledge, is the distance between empirical knowledge and rational knowledge. And that is the distance between the individual: individual/body/perception and society: society/collective consciousness/conception. The common, salient, crucial feature of the methods productive of true knowledge, the feature which distinguishes the nexus of language, concepts, categories, logic, rationality and science, from the non-method of empirical, perceptual sensation, is the fact that they are all non-individual, they are all collective methods of representation, they are all *social*.[160]

The subject of truth: society

The quality of being collective or social is thus the central characteristic of the subject of knowledge, society; and the product of knowledge, truth. The object of knowledge, the universe and all of its immanent relations, is an object which can only be known by society, the collective, objective, rational subject.

> Since the world expressed by the entire system of concepts is the one that society regards, society alone can furnish the most general notions with which it should be represented. Such an object can be embraced only by a subject which contains all the individual subjects within it. Since the universe does not exist except in so far as it is thought of, and since it is not completely thought of except by society, it takes a place in this latter; it becomes a part of society's interior life, while this is the totality, outside of which nothing exists.[161]

The methods of truth are themselves social products – 'collective representations' – from elemental words and language through concepts, systems of concepts, and categories.[162] Collective representations reflect:

> the way in which the group conceives itself in its relation to objects which affect it. The group differs from the individual in its constitution, and the things that affect it are therefore of a different nature. Representations or concepts that reflect neither the same objects nor the same subjects cannot be traced to the same causes. To understand the way in which a society thinks of itself and of its environment one must consider the nature of society and not that of individuals.[163]

Collective or 'social representations' therefore 'reflect a reality different from the individual's reality'.[164] As opposed to the individual representation, the collective representation 'presents guarantees of objectivity by the fact that it is collective'.

The larger processes of knowledge – logic, rationality and science – are equally social and collective in nature. The 'part of society in the genesis of logical thought' is essential.

> This is possible only . . . when, above the fugitive conceptions which they owe to sensuous experience, men have succeeded in conceiving a whole world of stable ideas, the common ground of all intelligences . . . logical thinking is always impersonal thinking.[165]

In the 'duality' which exists between 'the mentality which results from individual experiences and that which results from collective experiences', the collective subject and the collective experience are productive of reason, which is 'social'.[166] Reason is 'able to go beyond the limits of empirical knowledge' because it is a 'special intellectual activity infinitely richer and complexer than that of the individual'. It is the intellectual activity of a 'unique intelligence', a collective intelligence, society. The dual nature of the human being, as 'an individual being which has its foundation in the organism' and 'a social being which represents the highest reality in the intellectual and moral order' has as an intellectual consequence: 'the irreducibility of reason to individual experience'.[167] Of course reason and science are equated, although they can be distinguished. 'Reason, thus understood is simply science.' And 'that collective and impersonal reason called science' is 'a pre-eminently social thing'.[168] Ultimately, 'science, because it is objective, is an essentially impersonal affair and cannot progress except through collective labor'.[169]

The individual subject is an inadequate subject, incapable of conceptual thought, reason, and true knowledge. Individuals *qua* individuals are devoid of all the elements of truth: words, language, concepts, categories, logic, rationality, science. The individual is an empirical and subjective subject, and empiricism and subjectivity are antithetical to truth, which issues solely from rational and objective – thus collective – thought processes. The individual consciousness on its own is empty, without content, without thought, apart from perceptions imposed internally by the body and externally by the physical world. Without the conceptual/rational knowledge produced by the collective subject, individual knowledge would be reduced to the strictly perceptual level of animal 'knowledge'.

Concepts 'contain much that surpasses the knowledge of the average individual'.[170] The individual must 'assimilate' the social 'scheme of ideas'. However,

> the assimilation is always imperfect. Each of us sees them after his own fashion. There are some which escape us completely . . . there are others of which we perceive certain aspects only. There are even a great many which we pervert in holding, for as they are collective by nature, they cannot become individualized without being retouched, modified, and consequently falsified.[171]

The categories of logical thought are particularly antithetical to individual minds. The categories are 'pre-eminent' concepts, as they are comprehensive, enveloping and dominating lesser concepts. A class of objects is a 'mould including the whole group of all possible objects which satisfy the same condition'. Classes and categories refer to and are organized around the idea 'all'. And this idea is inaccessible to individuals. In the objects which the individual has 'perceived directly' there is no indication of 'all': 'there is nothing there which could give me the idea of a class'.

> This idea of all . . . could not have come from the individual himself, who is only a part in relation to the whole and who never attains more than an infinitesimal fraction of reality.[172]

As categories are pre-eminent concepts, embracing 'all' things in a specific class, so the category 'totality' is the pre-eminent category, embracing all things and all classes of things. And this is particularly, infinitely, beyond the scope of the individual:

> as the role of the categories is to envelop all the other concepts, the category *par excellence* would seem to be this very concept of *totality* . . . it really surpasses the contents of each individual consciousness taken alone to an infinite degree.[173]

Reason can be inculcated by the individual. The individual is capable of 'raising himself above his own particular point of view'. But in the process the individual is 'forced to do violence to himself by leaving his individuality'. And reason itself is violated. Reason, like morality, is actually 'dissipated by incarnating itself in individuals'.[174] Reason, like morality, is essentially impersonal; essentially social; and therefore essentially extrinsic to individuals:

> there is something impersonal in us *because there is something social in all of us,* and since social life embraces at once both representations and practices, this impersonality naturally extends to ideas as well as to acts ... Between the world of the senses and appetites on the one hand, and that of reason and morals on the other, the distance is so considerable that the second would seem to have been able to add itself to the first only by a creative act. But *attributing to society this preponderating role in the genesis of our nature* is not denying this creation; for society has a creative power which no other observable being can equal.[175]

The very foundation of conceptual thought – language – is beyond the purview of the individual subject.

> Very frequently a term expresses things which we have never perceived or experiences which we have never had or of which we have never been the witnesses. Thus there is a great deal of knowledge condensed in the word which I never collected, and which is not individual; it even surpasses me to such an extent that I cannot even completely appropriate all its results.[176]

Concepts and categories, reason and conceptual thought, words and language, essentially precede, exceed, and surpass individual consciousness. The individual subject cannot even know itself.[177] 'The facts of individual psychology ... are by definition purely mental, yet the consciousness we have of them reveals neither their nature nor their genesis.'[178] In a Freudian moment, Durkheim discusses not only the inability of consciousness to understand itself, but also the misrecognition that individuals experience of their own motives. Not only do humans 'know very imperfectly the relatively simple motives that guide us'.[179] There is actually a self-deception which occurs in the psychic domain.

> Human deliberations, in fact, so far as reflective consciousness affects them, are often only purely formal, with no object but confirmation of a resolve previously formed for reasons unknown to consciousness.[180]

The 'agent's motive' is beyond 'self-observation'. 'How often we mistake the true reasons for our acts!' Durkheim sounds like Freud as he discusses how 'petty feelings' and 'blind routine' can be represented by the individual subject as 'generous passions' and 'lofty considerations'.[181] There can be 'a positive contradiction between the actual state of a thing as it is and as it appears in the mind'. For example, love can appear as hate. There are even psychic facts which are *unconscious*, and therefore inherently inaccessible to conscious introspection.[182]

However, it is Durkheim the sociologist rather than Durkheim the Freudian who attributes the individual's incapacity for self-knowledge to the individual's inability to understand deterministic causality in general, and social causality in particular. The individual is unable to understand its own behavior because it is unable to recognize the social forces which act upon it; unable to understand itself and its thought and behavior as socially determined. The individual 'left to its own devices' has only its senses, and:

> senses only enable us to perceive phenomena which co-exist or which follow one another, but nothing perceived by them could give us the idea of this determining and compelling action which is characteristic of what we call a power or force. They can touch only realized and known conditions, each separate from the others; the internal processes uniting these conditions escapes them.[183]

> ... by himself, the individual observes the regular succession of phenomena and thus acquires a certain feeling of regularity. But his feeling is not the *category* of causality. The former is individual, subjective, incommunicable ... The second is the work of the group, and is given to us ready-made. It is a framework in which our empirical ascertainments arrange themselves and which enable us to think of them.[184]

The individual is unable to perceive causality, because the individual is unable to perceive *relations*. The 'constituent elements of the categories' are 'taken from social life' because:

> the *relations* which they express could not have been learned except in and through society. *If they are in a sense immanent in the life of an individual, he has neither a reason nor the means*

for learning them, reflecting upon them and forming them into distinct ideas.[185]

The individual is especially at a loss to comprehend causal relations, and then especially blind with respect to social causes. The scientific method of studying phenomena externally, as things, is even more necessary for social than for psychological facts, because *'consciousness is even more helpless in knowing them than in knowing its own life'.*[186] This is the case despite the illusion whereby the sociologist 'seems to move in a sphere perfectly transparent to his view'.[187] Social facts in particular must be studied objectively, because: *'social facts . . . result from syntheses which take place outside us and of which we have not even the confused perception which consciousness can give us of internal phenomena'.*[188] There is an 'incompetence of consciousness' concerning 'the laws of the social world'.

> Never would consciousness have dreamt, of its own accord, of the necessity which annually reproduces demographic phenomena in equal numbers, had it not received a suggestion from without. *Still less can it discover their causes, if left to its own devices.*[189]

This 'incompetence', the congenital ignorance of social laws on the part of the individual, is even more apparent as the individual consciousness regards itself. It specifically fails to see social laws regulating its own life. For example, suicide is a social phenomenon par excellence, as Durkheim demonstrates. Yet: 'The reasons ascribed for suicide . . . or those to which the suicide himself ascribes his act, are usually only apparent causes.'[190] More generally, the discoveries of sociology notwithstanding, there is 'only a very small number of individuals who feel that their duties have a social origin'.[191]

Where the individual subject is incompetent and helpless, however, the social subject is competent and proficient. Where the individual subject is blind, the social subject sees. Where the individual consciousness is sensate and subjective – empirical – the collective consciousness is conceptual and objective – rational. Thus while the individual subject can only produce inferior, empirical knowledge or ideology, the social, collective subject can produce rational, scientific knowledge, or truth. The social subject is only affected by 'general and permanent qualities'. It is 'part of its nature to see things in large and under the aspect which they ordinarily have'.[192]

> The collective consciousness is the highest form of the psychic life, since it is the consciousness of consciousnesses. Being placed outside of and above individual and local contingencies, it sees things only in their permanent and essential aspects, which it crystallizes into communicable ideas. At the same time that it sees from above, it sees farther; at every moment of time, it embraces all known reality; that is why it alone can furnish the mind with the moulds which are applicable to the totality of things and which make it possible to think them . . . Attributing social origins to logical thought . . . is relating it to a cause which implies it naturally.[193]

The subject, ultimate object, and methods of attaining truth are collective and social, and so is truth itself. The impersonality and stability which characterize logic and which require a collective subject, are 'the two characteristics of truth'. Truth is 'distinct from sensuous appearances', as sensuous appearances are founded in individual experience whereas truth is founded in 'collective experience'.[194]

> It is under the form of collective thought that impersonal thought is for the first time revealed to humanity . . . From the mere fact that society exists, there is also, outside of the individual sensations and images, a whole system of representations which enjoy marvellous properties . . . there is a world of absolute ideas . . . a whole intellectual kingdom . . . This is the first intuition of the realm of truth.[195]

Society is at one and the same time the perfect subject and the perfect object of truth. As the perfect object of truth, the 'constituent elements of the categories' are 'taken from social life' because society, as a part of nature, operates according to the universal laws of nature. It does so on an elevated level, which makes the laws not less but more valid for nature in general.

> The social realm is a natural realm which differs from the others only by a greater complexity . . . The fundamental relations that exist between things – just that which it is the function of the categories to express – cannot be essentially

dissimilar in the different realms ... ideas which have been elaborated on the model of social things can aid us in thinking of another department of nature. From the fact that the ideas of time, space, class, cause or personality are constructed out of social elements, it is not necessary to conclude that they are devoid of all objective value. On the contrary, their social origin rather leads to the belief that they are not without foundation in the nature of things.[196]

Society is the perfect subject and object of truth, because the relations which the categories express 'could not have been learned except in and through society'. In contrast to the social subject/object, the individual 'has neither a reason nor the means for learning them, reflecting upon them and forming them into distinct ideas'. However:

It is a different matter with society. This is possible only when the individuals and things which compose it are divided into certain groups, that is to say, classified, and when these groups are classified in relation to each other. Society supposes a *self-conscious* organization which is nothing other than a classification ... it alone can furnish the mind with the moulds which are applicable to the totality of things and which make it possible to think them. It does not create these moulds artificially; it finds them within itself; *it does nothing but become conscious of them.* They translate the ways of being which are found in all the stages of reality but which appear in their full clarity only at the summit, because the extreme complexity of the psychic life which passes there necessitates *a greater development of consciousness.*[197]

Rational knowledge is social knowledge in a double determination. Rational knowledge is social knowledge because society serves as its maker, or subject. Rational knowledge is social knowledge because society serves its model or object. The perfect, absolute and total subject of knowledge, combined with the perfect, absolute and total object of knowledge, constitute truth: perfect, absolute and total knowledge; the perfect, absolute and total merger of thought and reality; the perfect, absolute and true totality.

Since the world expressed by the entire system of concepts is the one that society regards, society alone can furnish the most general notions with which it should be represented. *Such an object can be embraced only by a subject which contains all the individual subjects within it.* Since the universe does not exist except in so far as it is thought of, and since it is not completely thought of except by society, it takes a place in this latter; it becomes a part of society's interior life, while *this is the totality, outside of which nothing exists.*[198]

Truth, like reason, is opposed to experience, perceptions, and instincts. Truth, like reason and morality, is 'social'.[199] In fact, because it is social, truth is variable or *relative.* It is a product of society, and its nature corresponds to the nature of society. The relativity of institutions to the social milieu includes: 'the theoretical order . . . thought itself . . . speculative thought . . . the content of truth'.[200]

Speculative and theoretical thought varies as practice varies . . . speculation and its value are variable . . . consequently, *truth, too, is variable.*[201]

Chapter 5

Collective ideology

THE SOCIOLOGICAL THEORY OF KNOWLEDGE: RELATIVISM OR RATIONALISM?

The epistemological assertion that social knowledge is superior, truer, than individual knowledge derives from the dual equations: (1) rationality = social thought and (2) rationality = truth. This is sociological rationalism, the sociological theory of knowledge.[1] This position is opposed to empiricism, which it denounces as equivalent to irrationalism and mysticism. Therefore, it would seem that the theory, in its rationalism, posits the existence of truth (as essence and relations) and the possibility of knowledge (conceptual and rational approximations of essence and relations). However, the sociological aspect of the theory tends to imply an epistemological relativism, in contradiction to the premises of rationalism. Does Durkheim's unique, sociological, rationalism contain a fundamental contradiction? Does its sociologism contradict its rationalism? Does the fact that the method of knowledge (conceptual thought and rationality) and the product of knowledge (truth) are social, and that the subject of thought, knowledge, and truth (society) is social, supersede the rationalist theory that truth is true? Is the sociological theory of knowledge necessarily a relativistic theory of knowledge?

There are certainly indications of sociological relativism in Durkheim's epistemology. Beginning with religious conceptions, ideas are 'the products of the social environment'. In general, there is a 'mental system' in each society, which 'depends' on, and changes with, its 'anatomical constitution', the 'social structure'.[2] Even abstract ideas such as time, space and causality; as well as entire 'modes of reasoning', are 'closely connected with the corresponding social organization'.[3] 'The principle of causality has been understood differently in different times and places; in a single society it varies with the social environment.'[4] Sociologism necessarily introduces 'relativism'. The 'relativity of institutions' to social milieu or environment means that they co-vary with one another. There are different 'types' of institutions, corresponding to different social types. They include 'the theoretical order . . . thought itself . . . speculative thought', and even 'the content of truth'. Speculative and theoretical thought are variable and 'consequently, truth, too, is variable'. The variations which characterize thought and truth, rendering them socio-historical in nature, 'take place . . . in time . . . between one type of historical society and another'.[5]

'Sociocentrism' is another term for the 'sociological' theory of knowledge. It refers specifically to the following theory. 'The centre of the first schemes of nature is not the individual; it is society.'[6] In fact, for Durkheim, society, as versus the individual, is the *'centre'* of all genuine thought, knowledge and truth. In other words, society, as versus the individual, is the *subject* of thought, knowledge and truth. This *subjectivity* necessarily involves *relativity*.

> If society is something universal in relation to the individual it is none the less an individuality itself, which has its own personal physiognomy and its idiosyncrasies; it is a particular subject and consequently particularizes whatever it thinks of. Therefore collective representations also contain subjective elements, and these must be progressively rooted out, if we are to approach reality more closely.[7]

A subject, whether collective or individual, is characterized by its specificity. And the specificity of a subject automatically entails the specificity of its thought, even its 'true' thought: 'the nature of the subject is a factor in the representation and alters the shape of the thing represented'.[8]

According to the sociological theory of knowledge, then, society rather than the individual is the subject of knowledge. Society, as opposed to the individual, is the *genuine* subject of knowledge, as rationality; including conceptual thought, science, and truth, which are inherently collective, inherently non-individual. And society, as opposed to the individual, is the *superior* subject of knowledge. Social knowledge, or rational knowledge, is superior to individual knowledge, or empirical knowledge. But this does not mean that it is the *infallible* subject of knowledge. It is better than the individual subject, but it is not a perfect, omniscient subject. The collective consciousness of society thinks and knows through its own, collective, representations, which serve as knowledge and truth. But these representations do not merely reflect their objects in reality. They also reflect their subject, society. To the extent that they correspond to reality, they are objective and eternal, or true. To the extent that they correspond to society, they are subjective and variable, or relative. Which is to say that collective representations may appear as true in their own milieu; they may be *socially* or *subjectively* true. But insofar as 'truth' signifies a non-subjective relationship between an idea and a thing, a representation/object relation, they are not *objectively* true, they are not *truly* true.

The sociological theory of knowledge does imply epistemological relativism. But relativism is only a minor, furtive tendency in Durkheim's thought, a tendency of accident and implication. It runs counter to his dominant theoretical tendency, which is rationalism. Durkheim clearly believes that the crucial relations sustained by ideas are with reality rather than with society. Society is the subject of ideas, but this fact is productive of truth. Society is the only subject which can conceive of reality adequately, accurately, comprehensively. It is the only subject which can formulate ideas which correspond to reality. Society is the only subject which can produce truth. Collective subjectivity is qualitatively as well as quantitatively distinct from individual subjectivity. Collective subjectivity is objectivity, and collective representations are true representations, which is to say they truly represent their objects. The sociological theory of knowledge is compatible with both relativism and rationalism. It is a theoretical innovation which produces a theoretical tension. But for Durkheim, for the most part, the tension is resolved in favor of rationalism, sociological rationalism. This means that Durkheim's thought tends, overall, to objectivism and realism; even, in a certain sense, materialism.[9]

The word representation itself is 'loaded' or biased against relativism. Individual sensations and collective ideas are 'representations' (*représentations*), which means that they are representations *of* something; of things, of objective reality. Representation is in fact the recurrent and central metaphor in Durkheim's work for the relationship between ideas and reality, between words and things. This relationship is portrayed variously but consistently as: reflection, expression, translation, symbolization, imitation, approximation. In general, within human thought the 'symbol' 'represents' 'reality'.

For example, categories are 'objective'. They 'express' relations. They are modelled on social relations, and beyond this, they have an even more 'objective value'. They have a 'foundation' in 'the nature of things'. While categories are social constructions, a social 'work of art', nonetheless they are works of a type of art which 'imitates nature with a perfection capable of increasing unlimitedly'.[10] More generally, concepts are *collective* representations. They 'belong to' the group, the 'very special being' which is society. But they are objective representations. They correspond to the way this being 'considers the things of its own proper experience', just like individual representations of the individual environment.[11]

Concepts ensure harmony between individual minds because they ensure 'their harmony with the nature of things'. The concept has 'a reason for existence' which consists in 'being true, that is to say objective'. The concept is impersonal 'only as a consequence of its objectivity'. The concept is the means of communication only because it is 'in regard to things, thought of as adequately as possible, that minds ought to communicate'.[12] Concepts 'express the manner in which society represents things'.[13] Concepts are 'collective' and they are 'constructions'. Society substitutes 'for the world revealed to us by our senses a different world that is the projection of the ideals created by society itself'. But in most cases, the ideal is 'a symbol of a thing', which only serves to make it an 'object of understanding'. The 'function' of the majority of these 'ideals', the function of the concept, is 'to express the reality to which they adhere'. Conceptual ideas provide 'the faithful analysis and representation of reality'. Thus concepts are related to the 'real', 'the inherent properties of the object', 'the given'.[14]

Rationality, composed of concepts and categories, Durkheim's designated vehicle of truth, is 'objective'. Rationality for Durkheim is: 'an objective rationality which is immanent in reality, a rationality which is given in things themselves, and which the scientist discovers and deduces but does not create'.[15]

At the most general level, the collective representation is objective.

> A collective representation presents guarantees of objectivity by the fact that it is collective . . . If it were out of accord with the nature of things, it would never have been able to acquire an extended and prolonged empire over intellects . . . Therefore, it could not be wholly inadequate for its subject [read: object].[16]

Scientific concepts are a 'methodically controlled' subset of collective representations. Collective representations *per se* are not methodically controlled, but are controlled nonetheless. They are 'imperfect symbols', but they are still symbols. Scientific representations are methodical, but are 'approximative' nonetheless. Therefore, 'scientific symbols' are more perfect, but they are still only symbols.[17] Simply put, ideas are determined by material, objective reality.

> Among peoples as among individuals mental representations function above all as an expression of a reality not of their own making; they rather spring from it and, if they subsequently modify it, do so only to a limited extent.[18]

The decisive factor is that ideas always relate to things, objects, reality, the world. They have a social subject, but they have a real object. They are socially constructed, but they are *not* socially relative. Their origin in a social subject enhances rather than reduces their objectivity, their ability to represent objects. Ideas are social products, but they are not arbitrary. They are grounded in material reality. They do not relate primarily to society or to other ideas. They relate primarily to things. Thus Durkheim's sociological rationalism is still rationalism. It posits a different subject and method from classic rationalism, but it does not renounce the existence of truth. Rational ideas are social, and rational ideas are true. Rational ideas simply reconstruct the rational nature of the world.

In social ideas, collective representations,

> the individual at least obscurely takes account of the fact that above his private ideas, there is a world of absolute ideas according to which he must shape his own; he catches a glimpse of a whole intellectual kingdom in which he

participates, but which is greater than he. This is the first intuition of the realm of truth.[19]

Social ideas are not only not relative, they are *absolute*. The realm of the collective consciousness and its representations is the realm of *truth*. Durkheim may propose a sociological rationalism, but he actively opposes any sort of relativism. His rationalism can be seen as an attack on empiricism, not only as an inferior method of knowledge, but also as a form of relativism, as 'mysticism' or 'irrationalism'. He sees in empiricism not only a lesser truth, but a denial of truth itself. If knowledge is only subjective and contingent, particular with respect to subject and object alike; specific to time, place, event and individual – in other words, if knowledge is empirical – then there is no knowledge that Durkheim could call truth. And this is the real threat of empiricism. Empiricism is a menace to the empire of truth not so much as a pretender to the throne, but as a radical challenge to the existence of the empire itself.

Durkheim rewrites rationalism as sociological rationalism, and thereby unintentionally introduces an apostasy, a potential tendency to relativism. Yet he consciously remains fiercely loyal to the anti-relativist principles of rationalism, and militantly battles relativism on all fronts. He seeks out, and seeks to destroy, all forms of relativism, from the non-knowledge and anti-truth of empiricism, to the 'multiple' or 'amorphous' 'truths' of pragmatism.[20] When Durkheim declares collective representations to be relatively or partially 'autonomous',[21] he is not making a relativistic statement.[22] He is declaring the independence of social ideas, but not from the object world. He is freeing them from their social structural matrix, from their social subject, in order that they might in fact be even more bound, more true, to their object, the real world.[23]

Because he is an anti-relativist rationalist, Durkheim's sociologism leads to another theoretical tendency or trap. And this is precisely the tendency to see social knowledge as absolute, as absolutely true. Durkheim often appears to assume that because social thought is rational thought and rational thought is true thought, then social thought is automatically, necessarily, always already true thought.[24] According to Durkheim, individual and empirical knowledge is less true, or false, relative to social and rational knowledge.[25] This tends to be his only criterion of truth. It is one which is shocking because of the quality and quantity of knowledge it disqualifies as truth. But this shock serves as a distraction from the quality and quantity of knowledge it implicitly honors as truth. There is a strong inclination, pervasive in Durkheim's work, to consider all social thought to be knowledge, true knowledge.

The two most important products of the collective consciousness, representation and morality, or ideas and ideals, are accepted by Durkheim, taken at face value, as given. They are both seen as inevitable and right, by virtue of their relations of correspondence: collective ideas correspond to the objects which they represent, as collective representations; collective morality corresponds with the social structure it expresses and sustains. The thought and behavior of a society, its mentality and morality, are *social facts* for Durkheim. Which is to say that they are as unquestionable, as necessary, as beneficial, as natural facts. This is one of the most conservative moments of Durkheim's thought. Whatever a society thinks is true, whatever it does is good.

Durkheim delimits the realm of ideology as the realm of *individual* knowledge, as he delimits the realm of immorality as the realm of *individual* behavior. Society's realm is the realm of the *right*, in the double sense of truth and goodness. So from the question of whether social knowledge is relative, and therefore always untrue, emerges the question of whether social knowledge is absolute, and therefore always absolutely true. Ironically, the answer to both is negative.

There is a concept, within Durkheim's thought, of collective representations which are untrue, or wrong. He acknowledges the existence of social thought and knowledge which is inaccurate, or false. And therefore, he admits the possibility of ideology as a collective and social, rather than a purely individual, phenomenon.[26] The collective consciousness is not simply infallible, in relation to the individual consciousness. In fact, it is itself capable of error. This is a different issue from the issue of relativity. Durkheim does not merely posit the radical separation of ideas and reality, and relegate human consciousness to the world of ideas: a world always apart from the real world; a world always relative only to itself and its subject; a world characterized by an absolute absence of relations with the real world.

The concept of error, the possibility of untruth which

operates in Durkheim's thinking, is actually predicated on the possibility of truth; on the possibility of a meaningful relationship between ideas and reality, a relationship which is somehow betrayed when ideas are untrue. Ideas are not necessarily adequate to their objects, but it is against their objects, relative to their objects, that they must be judged. They do not constitute an autonomous world, a parallel universe. They are related, either truly or falsely, to the world of reality. Ideas *can and should* accurately represent the real world, but they do not *necessarily* do so.

In this conception, public opinion is divested of the sanctity with which it is endowed in other moments of Durkheim's work. The existence of social ideology precludes the absolute truth of social thought. At the same time, because of the objectivist criterion which simultaneously creates social ideology and demarcates it from social truth, the absolute relativity of social thought is denied.

Ideology, as false ideas about reality, exists at the individual level as empirical sensation. At the social level, it exists as pre-scientific or non-scientific collective thought: collective pre-conceptions and prejudices; traditions and myths; common sense and accepted knowledge. Social ideology is conventional wisdom which is unwise. It is public opinion gone awry. The collective consciousness, though predisposed to truth through its social structural determinateness and its rational methodology, can wander, go astray, err. And when it does, it rather predictably resembles the individual consciousness.

False consciousness at the social level is characterized by empiricism, subjectivity, sentiment, and lack of method. It is nonrational and unscientific. If all rationality, science and truth are collective and social, it does not follow that all collective and social thought is rational, scientific, and true. Collective ideology, like individual knowledge/ignorance, tends to resist science and particularly social science; to be blind to determinism, particularly social determinism; to reside at the level of illusion: external, experiential appearance and practical truth, as opposed to the level of reality: internal, rational essence and theoretical truth. Collective knowledge can be right, which is to say, rational and scientific. But it can also be wrong, which is to say it can be like individual, sensate knowledge.

THE SUBJECT/S OF COLLECTIVE IDEOLOGY

In one sense, incorrect collective knowledge is simply an aggregate form of individual knowledge/ideology, a social incarnation of the individual's epistemological mistakes. In another sense, though, social ideology has a social subject. But the collective subject of social fallacy is not the same as the collective subject of social truth. The subject of social untruth is: primitive society as opposed to modern society *en masse*; and, within modern society, it is: the ordinary observer, the common man, the laity, the masses. In other words, the subject of true social knowledge is a collective subject, but it is an élite collective subject, composed of modern, rational men, imbued with the scientific spirit. The subject of true social knowledge is a homogeneous collectivity of men like Durkheim himself.

The social groups falling outside of this enlightened minority think collectively, but instinctively. They produce knowledge collectively, but it differs little from that which they produce individually. This misguided majority conceives such untruths as: empiricism, individualism, religion, socialism, feminism, and racism. The unenlightened many, in other words, think collectively but ideologically. Individual preconceptions/misconceptions are not the only form which intellectual mistakes can take. There are, additionally, '*collective preconceptions*'.[27]

The collectivity in question, in error, can be a part of society, a collectivity within the larger collectivity. Sometimes the less sentient group is a minority within society, and its lack of knowledge is related to its delimited nature. There are many diverse segments in society, and each taken alone 'only expresses one aspect, and not always very faithfully'.[28] Sociology must necessarily oppose the social doctrines of 'interest groups' or 'parties' within society, with their narrow perspectives and interests.[29]

Alternatively, the misinformed constitute the majority within society, and they are misinformed relative to an enlightened élite. The most characteristic example of such a majority is the laity, defined by contrast to a minority, the scientific élite. The laity is the greater community, the community which is external to the scientific community. Durkheim has a fixation with 'the layman' and 'lay' ideas. His frequent allusions to the 'ordinary' or 'vulgar' observer, 'the non-scientist', 'the common man', and the ideas held by them, refer less to specific individuals and individual consciousnesses than to general groups and modes of thought pervasive in society. The 'layman' is simply one member of the collectivity 'laymen', not so much a distinct individual as a generic symbol of the laity. The consciousness which corresponds to this group is collective, but it is an unscientific collective consciousness. The knowledge of the 'common man', 'lay' knowledge, is common, collective, but it is also fundamentally inferior and incorrect. For example, the vulgar observer is 'unable to perceive' real forces at play in society. The representation that the common man has of moral matters 'cannot correspond to the reality'.[30] If science and truth are essentially social and collective, so too are their contraries.

A second example of a relatively unintelligent majority is the citizenry of an enlightened and benevolent democracy. There are two psychic lives in society, 'two kinds' of social thought. They are both collective, but one is 'diffused throughout the entire social body'. 'There is nothing deliberately thought out in all this activity. There is something spontaneous, automatic, something unconsidered, about this whole form of life.'[31] The other is 'localised in a specific organ', the 'organ of social thought', the brain of society, the state. The difference between these two collective consciousnesses is analogous to the difference between 'the subconscious' and 'the ego' of the individual.

In order to reach the correct decisions, based on correct knowledge, in order 'to act with full knowledge of the facts', society must rely on the deliberations occurring within its rational conscious mind, the government, rather than succumb to the tyranny of the majority in the guise of direct democracy and rule by public opinion. Government makes decisions which are 'valid for the whole community', and which 'do not square with the state of social opinion'. It 'thinks and decides for' society.

> The role of the State, in fact, is not to express and sum up the unreflected thought of the mass of the people but to superimpose on this unreflective thought a more considered thought, which therefore cannot be other than different.[32]

True democracy is thus necessarily rule by an élite. The state should not simply 'represent the mass of individuals'. It should not attempt to ascertain 'what the society is thinking' but rather to determine 'what is in its best interests'. It is 'better placed' than 'the mass' or 'the crowd' to do so. The state finds its proper role in 'subordinating' the 'sentiments of the mass of people' to 'clearer and more reasoned ideas', rather than 'in servitude to the citizens . . . reduced to being a mere echo of their will'.[33]

The predominant tendency within Durkheim's thought then, in relation to collective untruth, is to delineate a collective majority, an unenlightened 'mass' and its common sense, lay knowledge, and public opinion; and a collective, enlightened scientific or governing knowledge élite. Thus he can say that concepts are collective and science is collective, but not all concepts are scientific. In fact, scientific concepts are 'in the very slight minority'.[34] At each moment of history, which is to say in each society, as in the mind of each individual, 'there is a determined place for clear ideas, reflected opinions, in short for science, beyond which it cannot normally extend'.[35] Durkheim often appears to accept all collective representations uncritically and unquestioningly, as inherently true because collective, or as simple reflections of social structure. But he answers this criticism, that he idealizes and hypostatizes public opinion as it exists, or effectively 'subjugates the mind to the prevailing moral opinion', by allowing that collective representations can be invalid, incorrect, untrue, wrong.

The problem here, besides the fact that these two conceptualizations are contradictory to one another, is that Durkheim becomes the arbitrary arbiter of social truth and falsehood, right and wrong. Social thought which he agrees with is automatically established as correct, because collective and reflective. Social thought with which he disagrees is automatically established as incorrect, because unscientific or diffuse.[36] Thus, to give just one example, in *Suicide* he can affirm one collective sentiment, the one which proscribes suicide. And he can simultaneously condemn another collective sentiment, the one which endorses unbridled, individualistic and materialistic, economic competition.

Through this epistemological contradiction, he can have his ontological, socio-political cake, and eat it too. Since he believes that 'the nature of the subject is a factor in the representation and alters the shape of the thing',[37] he can focus on the subject to distract attention from the representation and the thing. When he agrees with the collective subject, he contrasts its apodicticity favorably with that of the individual subject, and stands behind it. When he disagrees with it, he divides society against itself, and declares that he stands on the side of truth and reason, science and the state, opposed to the falsehood of the masses, the unreason of the rabble.

He even goes so far, and enters into such deep conflict with his own theme that social knowledge is essentially true, as to suggest that the collective knowledge of entire societies can be incorrect. Primitive societies, for example, operate in 'sensations and movements of sensibility, not in concepts'. The primitive collective consciousness thinks in terms of the particular, which is 'unintelligible'; and the concrete, which 'baffles the understanding' and is 'refractory to science'.[38]

More generally, Durkheim locates tradition, collective social thought *par excellence*, in primitive societies. And in an astonishing, anomalous reversal of his 'sociological theory of knowledge', he asserts that tradition, or collective thought, is not only false, but it also positively inhibits individual thought, which is here inexplicably associated with reason and truth.

> The pressure exerted by the group on each of its members does not permit individuals to judge freely the notions which society itself has elaborated and in which it has placed something of its personality. Thus the history of scientific classification is . . . the history of the stages by which this element of social affectivity has progressively weakened, leaving more and more room for the reflective thought of individuals.[39]

It is possible, then, for social knowledge to be a lie. And this is true even in modern society. In general, in modern as well as primitive society, it is possible that there is a difference between 'society as it *appears* to itself' and 'society as it is or is really becoming'. 'The consciousness which society may have of itself which is expressed in general opinion . . . may be an inadequate view of the underlying reality.' Social knowledge can contain 'errors'. Not only is there a possible distinction between 'the state of the society' and 'social opinion', between 'society as it is' and 'society as it sees itself', but the latter view 'may produce an erroneous picture'.[40]

THE NATURE OF COLLECTIVE IDEOLOGY

A collective subject, then, is liable to 'collective preconceptions', to the production of illusion rather than truth. What is the nature of these false collective representations, these collective deceptions which masquerade as collective truths? In the first place, they are formed of necessity. Humans necessarily conceive of the physical and social world which surrounds them. They eternally and universally produce mental representations, conceptions, of their environment. External reality is always and everywhere depicted internally by ideas. This inevitable tendency, this 'faculty of ideation', is partly attributable to the unique symbolic propensities of the human species. Conceptualization is an inherent aspect of human specificity, determined by the singular social and intellectual nature which characterizes human beings and constitutes their humanity. Conceptualization is also necessitated by the exigencies of survival. It is a natural response mechanism, a technique of adaptation. These necessities – the demands of human nature, and the demands of adaptation – are concomitant with human existence. Yet the methods of scientific inquiry are not. Knowledge in the form of conception precedes and exceeds knowledge in the form of truth.

At the practical level, humans are driven to *react* to the environment. This reaction first takes the form of representations.

> So that we can cope satisfactorily with the things of the tangible world, we evolve certain *représentations*. In our minds we portray (*nous nous représentons*) the wind as a breath, the sun as a flat disc a few centimetres wide, and light as a tenuous, intangible body which passes through the air like an arrow, and so on.[41]

These representations or ideas, which constitute the primary, mental reaction, condition and mediate the secondary, behavioral reaction. 'Man cannot live in an environment without forming some ideas about it according to which he regulates his behavior.'[42] At the intellectual level, humans are driven to *understand* their own behavior in the social world, as well as the phenomena of the physical world. 'Man needs to understand what he does, though often he is easily satisfied; this is often the reason lying behind a myth.'[43] Thus, every rite corresponds to 'a more or less organized system of representations that will explain and justify it'. The same is true in the case of religion, for example. 'Men have long been obliged to make for themselves a notion of what religion is, long before the science of religions started its methodical comparisons.'[44] This intellectual, conceptual 'need' extends to all of human conduct.

> As we feel the need of understanding, or of believing we understand, the reasons for our conduct, thought is applied to ethics before the latter has become the object of science. A certain manner of representing and explaining to ourselves the principal facts of the moral life has thus become habitual.[45]

In general, with respect to all reality, physical and social, there is a corresponding mental universe, a universe of representations, which predates the niceties of science: 'phenomena are already represented in the mind not only by rather definite perceptions but also by some kind of crude concepts . . . *thought and reflection are prior to science*'.[46] Collective preconceptions, then, exist as the conceptions of the world which are formed, of necessity, and prior to science. Collective preconceptions are *prescientific* collective conceptions.

For Durkheim, prescientific conceptions are those which are formed directly through experience, without the intervention of method. It is characteristic of 'preconceived ideas' that they are formed 'by chance and without method' . . . 'without any method, according to the circumstances and chances of life'.[47] They are '"representations"' of reality 'which we have been able to make in the course of our life'. The thought and reflection which operate prior to science result in 'ideas or concepts' which are simple products of everyday experience. 'They are created by experience and for it.' These are concepts of 'everyday life . . . formulated without the discipline of science'.[48] Preconceptions are capricious rather than methodical, and they are experiential rather than experimental. They are mundane and spontaneous, reflexive and not reflective. Though they are called concepts, they are specified as *pre*concepts. They are somehow intermediary between sensations and concepts. In fact, they are more like sensations than like concepts. To Durkheim, this means that they are *empirical* in nature.

Collective thought can be 'spontaneous' rather than reflective, empirical rather than rational.[49] Primitive social thought, for example, operates in 'sensations and movements of sensibility, not in concepts'. While social thought tends to become more rational and logical, it begins in the realm of the sensate, as perception of the particular and concrete.[50] The pre-eminent

form of primitive, collective, social thought, religion, is likened
by Durkheim to individual sensation. Religions are social
preconceptions.

> *They are in the social order what sensation is in the individual.* We
> might ask why it is these religions distort all things as they do
> in their processes of imagery. But is it not true that sensation,
> equally, distorts the things it conveys to the individual?[51]

Preconceptions not only *pre*-exist science in primitive society and
religion; they also *co*-exist with science in modern society, as
common knowledge or 'lay ideas'. These 'common, average
conceptions', also resemble individual sensations. 'They are
made from day to day, *empirically*, devoid of all logic and
method.'[52]

In addition to being empirical, preconceptions tend to be
practical in nature. Just as they are, in a sense, true empirically,
an empirical form of knowledge, they are true practically, a
practical form of knowledge. Their 'primary function' is 'to put
our action in harmony with our environment'. Representations
formed prior to science 'may successfully fulfil this function'.
Preconceptions are concepts of things 'as everyday life finds it
useful to conceive them'. The conceptions of 'lay or practical
knowledge' begin with perceptions of objective reality, but differ
from science in their 'manner of elaboration'.[53] Which is to say
that there is a difference between what is true practically and
what is true theoretically: the 'divergences' between practical
knowledge and science mean for Durkheim that there is a
divergence between practical knowledge and truth. There are
such conceptual creatures as 'false but useful notions'. For
example, the representation that 'the common man' has of
something 'cannot correspond to the reality'. 'It may well meet
the needs of everyday practice, but it does not convey the
essence of things.'[54]

Preconceptions are representations of reality which are
'illusions', but illusions which are 'necessary in practice'.[55] They
are 'errors', but errors which are *'true practically'*.[56] For Durkheim,
there is a difference – a positive contradiction – between
empirical, practical truth and rational, theoretical truth. There
is an opposition between empirical knowledge and scientific
knowledge, between practical and speculative knowledge. There
is a relation of distinction and enmity which ideally separates

and divides 'representative functions' from 'practical functions'. Hostility and mutual exclusion cleave 'understanding' from 'the practical faculties': 'understanding is only one of our faculties. It can increase beyond a certain point only to the detriment of the practical faculties'.[57]

Of course, since these forms of knowledge are antithetical, only one can claim to be true. And that is, predictably, scientific, speculative, representational knowledge. Preconceptions may well be 'true' empirically and practically. But with respect to truth, they are false.

COLLECTIVE IDEOLOGY VERSUS COLLECTIVE TRUTH: METAPHOR OF PRECONCEPTION, DICHOTOMY OF KNOWLEDGE

The possibility of 'a positive contradiction between the actual state of a thing as it is and as it appears in the mind' is realized in the form of preconceptions. As noted, despite their empirical and practical truth, they are apodictic 'illusions' and 'errors'. Epistemologically, preconceptions, or 'preconceived ideas', have 'no right to any credit whatsoever'.[58] The representations characterized as 'false but useful notions' are only related to truth as 'so-called truth'.[59] They do not 'correspond' to, do not 'convey the essence' of reality. While they may be adequate to practice, they do not *adequate reality*. Common sense, one type of 'collective preconception', exists both consciously and unconsciously as 'error'. Facts are originally, before science, 'necessarily unknown'. Therefore, 'any "representations" which we have been able to make of them in the course of our life . . . are devoid of scientific value and must be distinguished from the scientific mentality'.

The 'ideas or concepts' formed by prescientific thought and reflection 'are not legitimate substitutes for things'. They are empirical – 'created by experience' – and practical – created 'for' experience, 'their primary function is to put our action in harmony with our environment'. 'Now, a representation may successfully fulfil this function while theoretically false.' In fact, 'such ideas' obscure rather than translate, express, reflect or represent reality: 'they are like a veil drawn between the thing and ourselves, concealing them [*sic*] from us the more successfully as we think them more transparent'.[60] Science, like the truth it is designed to find, needs concepts that adequately express things as they actually are, and not as everyday life finds it useful to conceive them. Now those concepts formulated without the discipline of science do not fulfil this condition.[61]

All of the inadequacy and illegitimacy, error and illusion, all of the falseness of preconceptions, creates an absolute distance, a radical separation, between them and truth. And therefore science, in its quest for truth, must move away from preconceptions, from ideology. This is the meaning of the first corollary rule of sociological method: *All preconceptions must be eradicated.*[62] To study religion, for example, 'it is necessary to begin by freeing the mind of every preconceived idea'. The preconceived ideas of religion formed of necessity but without method 'must be rigorously set aside'.[63] In general, science must be 'free' from 'ready-made judgements'. Science requires 'complete freedom of mind'. 'We must rid ourselves of that habit of seeing and judging which long custom has fixed in us.'[64]

Preconceptions might appear to be true, but that illusion is only another dimension of their deception. Genuine reason requires 'release from the suggestions of "reason" thus understood'.[65] The scientist necessarily 'divests himself of this so-called truth'.[66] The sociologist, for example:

> ought . . . to repudiate resolutely the use of concepts originating outside of science for totally unscientific needs. He must emancipate himself from the fallacious ideas that dominate the mind of the layman; he must throw off, once and for all, the yoke of these empirical categories, which from long continued habit have become tyrannical.[67]

The sociologist, as a scientist, 'has to disregard the preconceptions which he had of facts'.[68] In fact,

> as a condition of their acceptance into the sociological fraternity, we ask men to discard the concepts they are accustomed to apply to an order of facts, in order to re-examine the latter in a new way.[69]

This process of divestiture, the repudiation and eradication of preconceptions, the emancipation from them, may be quite difficult. While there is a tendency to 'see only what our prejudices permit us to see', nonetheless 'we are unaware of them'.[70] Yet, however difficult, it remains possible. Humans, or scientists at least, can control and negate even the unconscious machinations of preconceptions.

> The impulses of common sense are so deeply ingrained in us that it is difficult to eradicate them from sociological discussion. When we consciously free our thoughts of them, they still mold our unconscious judgements; and against such error we have no defense. Only long and special training can teach us to avoid it.[71]

Science must painstakingly eliminate *pre*conceptions, prescientific and extra-scientific conceptions, for a reason. And that is in order to construct *new*, scientific, true conceptions. Social science must not 'paraphrase the traditional prejudices of the common man' because 'the aim of all science is to make discoveries'. When the members of the sociological fraternity 'discard' their customary concepts, it is to 're-examine' the facts 'in a new way'. Instead of 'lay concepts' and 'lay terms', science must devise scientific concepts and scientific terms. These are necessarily new, necessarily different. 'We need . . . to formulate entirely new concepts, appropriate to the requirements of science and expressed in an appropriate terminology.' Science 'must dismiss all lay notions and the terms expressing them' because it 'has to create new concepts'.[72] The scientist who 'divests himself' of 'so-called truth' then 'replaces these false but useful notions with others, arrived at by quite different methods'.[73]

A renunciation and replacement of collective preconceptions must occur if science is to exist. This is, in effect, a renunciation and replacement of collective *ideology*. The 'sphere of ideology' has a complex, dual, meaning for Durkheim. Its two, inter-related aspects are as follows. The term 'ideology' refers first to the study of ideas as opposed to the study of things, objects, reality. This is the sense in which Durkheim contrasts the ideological, subjective method ('introspection') with the scientific, 'objective' method. Through introspection, it is only possible to discover pre-existing ideas, preconceptions about things. The objective method, on the other hand, is a method characterized by externality. It is necessary to look at phenomena from the outside, as facts or things. And it is equally necessary to look outside of oneself, away from one's latent conceptions of things. The object of ideology is *ideas*. The object of science is *objects*.

The second, more conventional meaning of 'ideology' refers to the characteristic, essential falsehood of the preconceived ideas from which science must turn away. Preconceptions are prescientific and extra-scientific, which means that they are anti-scientific. They are inherently untrue. For example, a scientific understanding of religion must not proceed from preconceived ideas of religion. It must proceed from religion itself. 'It is not from our prejudices, passions or habits that we should demand the elements of the definition . . . it is from the reality itself.'[74] Similarly, the study of ethics must proceed *away from* preconceptions about ethics, must proceed *to* ethics themselves, in order to proceed *from* ethics themselves:

> as our ideas of physical things are derived from these things themselves and express them more or less exactly, so our idea of ethics must be derived from the observable manifestation of the rules that are functioning under our eyes . . . Consequently, these rules, and not our superficial idea of them, are actually the subject matter of science, just as actual physical bodies, and not the layman's idea of them, constitute the subject matter of physics.[75]

Science must start, 'not with concepts', but with direct perceptions of objects, which is to say it must start with objects. It must 'dismiss all lay notions and the terms expressing them', to 'return' to 'sense perception', to 'the primary and necessary substance underlying all concepts', which is to say it must return to objects.[76]

Despite the fact that the phenomena science addresses 'are already represented in the mind', science must turn away from the representations, and return to the phenomena themselves. However, this is difficult, since 'these ideas are nearer to us . . . than the realities to which they correspond'. Despite the fact that these preconceived 'ideas or concepts' are 'not legitimate substitutes for things', they are in fact 'substituted' for reality, 'mistaken' for it.

> Instead of observing, describing, and comparing things, we are content to focus our consciousness upon, to analyze, and to combine our ideas. Instead of a science concerned with realities, we produce no more than an *ideological analysis*.[77]

An ideological analysis is one which mistakenly moves 'from ideas to things'. 'By elaborating such ideas in some fashion, one will never therefore arrive at a discovery of the laws of reality.' Ideas, specifically prescientific ideas, ideological ideas, are 'illusions', a 'veil drawn between the thing and ourselves, concealing them [sic] from us the more successfully as we think them more transparent'. On the other hand, a scientific analysis is one which necessarily moves 'from things to ideas'.[78] The scientist must, in essence, *displace ideas* to *face facts*: 'the sociologist must disregard the preconceptions which he had of facts, in order to *face the facts* themselves'.[79] To discover truth, as opposed to ideology, a scientist must turn a deaf ear to pre-existing, conventional ideas, and listen instead to facts. There must be a 'release', from preconceived, ideological '"reason"' in order '*to allow the things themselves to speak*'.[80]

Durkheim goes even further than an identification and critique of ideology. He goes beyond the location and rejection of ideology, as preconceptions. He insists that preconceptions must not constitute the content of science, of knowledge, because preconceptions are untrue. In addition, he suggests that preconceptions should themselves be examined, as social facts in their own right. Ideology is not to be accepted or believed. Its relation to science and truth is a negative one, a relation of opposition and contradiction. Yet there is another form the relation should take. Ideology must not be mistaken for reality, nor misidentified as truth. Ideological analysis must not pose as scientific analysis. Science must turn away from, and in a sense turn on, ideology. But it must also turn *to* ideology; not as knowledge, but as an object of knowledge. Science must study ideology. Ideology is not truth, but it is a fact: 'these conceptions in turn are additional facts which must be properly identified and studied objectively'.[81] Preconceptions, or the 'sentiment' which pre-exists science, is: 'a subject for scientific study, not the criterion of scientific truth'.[82]

The antagonism between preconceptions and science works in two directions. Science encounters preconceptions as an obstacle to truth, as an enemy already occupying a certain territory, the territory of knowledge, and lying in ambush. It must seek them out, however insidiously they are hidden, as apparently transparent illusions, as unconscious prejudices. And then it must destroy them, it must perform the negative task of eradication before it can commence the positive task of exploration and discovery. It must destroy false knowledge before it can create true knowledge. Preconceptions are problematic for science.

Conversely, science is problematic for preconceptions. The inroads which science makes into established knowledge are troublesome, troubling. Science disturbs and disrupts accepted ideas. The project of eradication then confronts an active resistance on the part of preconceptions. The aim of all science is to make discoveries, and 'every discovery more or less disturbs accepted ideas'. 'Current thought' can be 'shaken out of itself', for example by Durkheim's own work, and it resists.[83]

> The ideas we form of things have a vital interest for us, just as the objects, themselves, and thus assume an authority which brooks no contradiction. Every opinion that disturbs them is treated with hostility.[84]

As 'the system of accepted ideas' must be 'modified', to 'make room for the new order of things and to establish new concepts', minds 'resist' the discoveries of science through 'inertia'.[85] Durkheim himself intends to advance some propositions 'which will disrupt certain accepted ideas'.[86] He wishes to promote scientific understanding, and scientific understanding runs counter to preconceptual understanding.

> It can increase beyond a certain point only to the detriment of the practical faculties, disrupting sentiments, beliefs, customs, with which we live, and such a rupture of equilibrium cannot take place without troublesome consequences.[87]

The collective preconceptions of collective ideology are disturbed and disrupted by science and the truth it engenders. But they do not give up without a fight. Science is troublesome for them, and they in turn prove troublesome for science. They meet the encroachments of science with resistance. This is true for science in general. It is 'every science' which 'encounters analogous resistances at the outset', resistances of 'sentiments' and 'prejudice'. This is true even for the physical sciences which appropriate the physical world as their object.[88] 'The same antagonism breaks out each time a new science is founded.' The natural sciences, applied to the material world, are not immune.[89] Universally, 'science has encountered incredulity whenever it has revealed to men the existence of a force that has been overlooked'.[90] Science eventually triumphs over this resistance, and effects a double conquest, in one, vast domain: it vanquishes ideological knowledge about nature, and it vanquishes nature itself, as true knowledge of the natural world.

Ideology concedes hegemony to science with respect to the nonhuman realm. However, it then concentrates its forces to mount a massive resistance against scientific advances into its last bastion, the empire of the human and the social. 'As far as social facts are concerned, we still have the mentality of primitives.'[91] While Durkheim wants to 'extend scientific rationalism to human behavior', and divest 'common sense' of its authority on social matters, people are 'little accustomed to treat social phenomena scientifically'. In fact, Durkheim must caution the audience of the *Rules*. 'The reader must bear in mind that the ways of thinking to which he is most inclined are adverse, rather than favorable, to the scientific study of social phenomena.' The sentiments and prejudices which resist every science find their 'last retreat' in sociology.[92] The scientific innovation, according to which social facts are objective, naturally 'offends common sense'. Sociology, like all the sciences which precede it, introduces 'a world hitherto unknown'. It discovers a new 'system of realities', the conception of which inevitably 'encounters traditional prejudices'.[93]

In one sense, then, the science of society is resisted for the same reasons that all science is resisted, because it is new. Preconceptions necessarily exist about social phenomena. Social science necessarily makes new discoveries, creates new concepts, and upsets the pre-existing ones. Minds necessarily resist novel ideas, through 'inertia'. However, more importantly, there are unique dimensions of the resistance to human or social science, objections which are specific to its object. There is a particular unwillingness to view society scientifically, as part of nature. 'There are only a small number of minds which are strongly penetrated with this idea that societies are subject to natural laws and form a kingdom of nature.'[94] More specifically, it is the scientific treatment of human beings, their inclusion in the natural world, that is opposed by human thought. It is 'especially when man became an object of science' that the 'antagonism' or 'resistance' to science became 'fierce'. Such 'collective sentiments', under 'different forms', have effectively 'hindered the development of psychology and sociology'.[95]

Collective sentiments, or preconceptions, are created about

all aspects of the universe, the social as well as the natural world.

> Sentiments pertaining to social things . . . have been formed in the course of history; they are a product of human experience . . . They result from all sorts of impressions and emotions accumulated according to circumstances, without order and methodological interpretation . . . these sentiments are simply strong but confused states of mind.[96]

Yet preconceptions about social things are distinguished from their counterparts, preconceptions about physical things, by their relative intransigence. 'In sociology, especially, these prejudices or "idols" . . . are likely to . . . be substituted for the study of facts.'[97]

It is harder to displace social preconceptions with scientific conceptions, for several reasons. In the first place, social phenomena appear to be self-evident, transparent, visible to the naked eye. 'The sociologist seems to move in a sphere perfectly transparent to his view.'[98] If people are 'so easily contented', with prescientific explanations of social facts, 'it is because social events seem to them the clearest thing in the world';

> it is because they have not yet realized their real obscurity; it is because they have not yet recognized the necessity of resorting to the laborious methods of the natural sciences to gradually scatter the darkness.[99]

Durkheim takes issue with the view that social phenomena are manifestly clear and obvious to the observer. He sides with science, which maintains that 'things are complex and difficult to understand'.

This is especially true of social things. 'If we had really only to open our eyes and take a good look in order to perceive at once the laws of the social world, sociology would be useless or, at least very simple.'[100] To the rhetorical question, 'is it not enough to observe social phenomena as they are given to us in our everyday experience?' Durkheim responds: 'This last method . . . is full of illusions. One does not know social reality if one has seen it only from the outside and has ignored its foundations'.[101] Social reality is more complex than physical, or even psychological reality, and therefore more difficult to fathom without recourse to science. Consciousness is 'helpless' in knowing social facts, 'even more helpless in knowing them than in knowing its own life'. The necessity of studying social facts scientifically, or 'objectively', is especially acute, 'since they result from syntheses which take place outside us and of which we have not even the confused perception which consciousness can give us of internal phenomena'.

Social facts are the products of former generations and collectivities of individuals, and therefore 'we can only with difficulty obtain even a confused and inexact insight into the true nature of our action and the causes which determined it'. Even simple, individual, internal phenomena are 'known only imperfectly'. Social phenomena are complex, collective and external.[102] Thus, there is a particular 'incompetence of consciousness' in relation to the laws of the social world.[103] In effect, 'there are forces at play in society that the vulgar observer is unable to perceive, but which are none the less real'.[104] Humans are not predisposed to be 'able to see' social facts. Social facts naturally tend to escape their view.

> But social action follows ways that are too circuitous and obscure, and employs psychical mechanisms that are too complex to allow the ordinary observer to see when it comes. As long as scientific analysis does not come to teach it to them, men know well that they are acted upon, but they do not know by whom.[105]

Social facts are particularly resistant to scientific cognition because they are particularly complex. But there is another factor, besides their apparent simplicity and actual complexity, which accounts for the relative persistence of preconceptions concerning social life. The scientific mandate, according to which all preconceptions must be eradicated, is hardest to realize in social science. 'The frequent interference of sentiment makes this emancipation from lay ideas particularly difficult in sociology.' There is an 'emotional character' which 'infects' social as opposed to physical objects.[106] What is the nature of this sentiment and emotion? Why does human/social life have a special affinity with ideological, prescientific thought, and a special hostility to science? Collective preconceptions are inordinately tenacious when their subject matter happens also to be their subject. The human subject refuses the status of scientific object, because it refuses the status of object. It thinks, and therefore it thinks itself free. Underlying the problematic nature of social or human science is the problematic nature of social or human determinism.

Science is inextricably linked with determinism, in fact it is wholly identified with determinism: science and determinism are one and the same thing. And this is why the continuous expansion of the scientific approach meets its staunchest resistance at the threshold of human existence.

> If the principle of determinism is solidly established today in the physical sciences, it is only a century ago that it was first introduced into the social sciences, and its authority there is still contested.[107]

The ideological preconception which is endemic to the human, social world, and which militates against the establishment of science there, is the 'ideology' of human individualism. Thus the pair determinism/science is opposed, resisted, by the pair individualism/ideology, which appears as anti-science.

One aspect of 'the sphere of ideology' is the tendency of thought according to which 'social things . . . appear to be nothing but the overt manifestation of ideas . . .'.[108] If the first *corollary* rule of sociological method is to eradicate all preconceptions, the first *rule* of sociological method is to consider social facts as things. This concept, the basis of social science, is given the following meaning by Durkheim: '. . . the most important characteristic of a thing is the impossibility of its modification by a simple effort of the will'.

> Far from being a product of the will, they determine it from without; they are like molds in which our actions are inevitably shaped. This necessity is often inescapable.[109]

Social facts are not 'our own personal constructs'.[110] In fact, it is a 'dangerous illusion' to imagine that morality, for example, is a 'personal artifact'. Society is 'a product of innumerable forces', just as 'we are the product of things'. Individuals produce or determine neither society nor themselves.[111] To view the individual as the cause of social phenomena is 'in flagrant contradiction to the fundamental principles of thought'. Nonetheless, despite the compelling logic of social determinism, it 'offends common sense' to consider social facts objectively, as real things and real forces.[112]

> There is only a very small number of individuals who feel that their duties have a social origin. The majority see it quite differently, and it is from this difference that all the opposition to my idea has arisen.[113]

The tendency to individualism produces the tendency to reduce social facts to 'the individual mind'. It is this tendency, which Durkheim attributes to the 'psycho-sociologist', that he labels 'ideology'. To this tendency, as well as to the tendency to place social facts 'beyond the realm of nature', Durkheim opposes his theory, the theory of sociological naturalism.[114] Society is part of the natural world. It is a natural kingdom; subject to natural laws, and therefore subject to science. Yet it is a natural kingdom with its own specificity and autonomy from the rest of nature. It is specific and transcendent with respect to other natural realms, which means that it is not reducible to other natural realms.

Notably, society is not reducible to human individuals. It has a real existence, above and beyond individuals. It is more than the sum of its parts. Emerging from the association of individuals, it rises up and turns back on them to dominate them. Individuals are the elemental cells. Society is the holistic organism which deploys and determines them. Society is the summit of nature: not an ethereal summit which is beyond scientific scrutiny or which evaporates as its concrete base is revealed. Society is a real, effective, determinative entity at the summit of nature. With respect to individuals, society is god.

One characteristic form of the individualist ideology is anarchism. Anarchism is a 'social and moral blindness', the result of 'that disposition of the mind that prevents certain individuals from seeing social things as they are'; in other words, from seeing that 'there does exist something empirically demonstrable outside the individual and which transcends him'.[115] In order to move from ideology to science, it is necessary to move from anarchistic individualism to sociological social determinism. It is necessary to move from the individualistic appearance to the deterministic reality of social life.

> Instead of stopping at the exclusive consideration of events that lie at the surface of social life, there has arisen the need for studying the less obvious points at the base of it – internal causes and impersonal, hidden forces that move individuals and collectivities.[116]

RELIGION AND SOCIALISM AS COLLECTIVE IDEOLOGY

Durkheim acknowledges the existence of collective preconceptions, collective as opposed to individual false thought, collective ideology. Given the foregoing characteristics of these collective errors or mistakes, there are many examples, numerous instances of lapses in collective wisdom. The most exemplary instance, however, which serves as a perfect illustration of collective ideology, is religion. In the first place, religion is collective as opposed to individual thought. In fact, it is the pre-eminent form of collective thought, social thought par excellence. In the beginning, religion uniformly inhabits and propels every individual consciousness in the collective consciousness, of which it is the primary component.

This is the second characteristic of collective ideology which religion epitomizes. Religion is associated with primitive, as opposed to modern, social thought. In fact, initially, religion and social thought are essentially co-extensive. Over time, however, religion recedes from the collective consciousness. And again, as the foremost example of collective ideology, its recession is necessary to, and necessitated by, the rise of science. Religion is the major ideological foe of science, the major form of resistance against its advances. Religion first opposes the scientific, or non-theological, understanding of nature. But 'hard' science, with its demonstrated successes and practical applications, wins out, and unseats religion from the throne of knowledge. The primitive hegemony of religion over collective thought slowly gives way, through bitter struggle and ultimate defeat, to the hegemony of science . . . with respect to the physical world.

The battle lines are redrawn, with more at stake, around the contested field of humanity. If religion is innately hostile with respect to natural science, it is virulently so with respect to human and social science. This is both the last and the most important domain to which religion makes a claim, over which it claims epistemological, as well as legislative and judicial, authority. Religion persists in the modern world. It survives the advent of modernity and the eclipse of its absolute monarchy over human life and thought. In particular, it survives its banishment from the material world. Religion survives, but it survives in a limited sphere, in exile as it were. In the modern world, religion is confined to the spiritual realm, to the realm where the divine and the natural co-exist, as the human soul. Thus, like the collective ideology which it exemplifies, religion is especially antagonistic to the science of human individuals and human society. But science challenges religion even on the human front. In fact science establishes itself in the human world, it takes the human world as its object.

But the scientific mentality is still not the common or general mentality. The scientific position is an élite or minority position. Conversely, religion, representative of all collective ideology, is popular thought, the thought of the crowds or masses. Ironically, religion is typical of lay, as distinct from scientific, thought.

Finally, religion, like all collective preconceptions, is false. It is ideological and anti-scientific because it is untrue. Religion, like science, constitutes a system of collective representations. Religion represents the universe. But, unlike science, religion represents the universe falsely. Religious thought exists as erroneous thought. Religion pretends to truth, but it is in reality the antithesis of truth. Religion, Durkheim repeats, is a 'delirium'.[117] The reasons with which the faithful justify their rites and myths are, simply, 'erroneous'. In the idea of the soul, which is 'a product of history and mythology', 'men find themselves prisoners of this imaginary world of which they are, however, the authors and the models'.

Religious thought 'transfigures' and 'disfigures' the world as it attempts to translate it. It 'transforms' its object, until the latter is 'unrecognizable'. Religion is a 'veil with which mythological imagination has covered' the realities of 'nature, man, society'. It is true that primitive religion is 'the most disconcerting for reason', as it reflects the greatest contrast 'between reason and faith'. Nonetheless, even modern religion, 'even the most rational and laicized' religion, is inextricably linked to 'speculation', and 'cannot really be scientific'. With respect to religion, science is a 'rival power'.[118] The 'popular imagination' conceives of god. 'Science certainly could waste no time over this conception, of which it does not even take cognizance.' Religion consists of symbols and explanations which, while 'satisfying the crowd' are 'not adequate to reality'.[119]

Truth only proceeds from free inquiry, and free inquiry only proceeds in the absence of the 'yoke' of tradition and custom.

Light is sought only as the darkness of ideology is pierced, as its inadequacy is revealed. Reality is examined only as the veil of religion is lifted. This means that philosophy and then science only ascend to the extent that the force of religion declines. 'This is why philosophy, the first, synthetic form of knowledge, appears as soon as religion has lost its sway, and only then; and is then followed progressively by the many single sciences.'[120] Philosophy, the precursor of science, 'is possible only when religion has lost something of its hold'. In general, 'free thought ... supposes ... a preliminary regression of ... religious beliefs'.

There is a fundamental antagonism between all religion and all science. 'The same antagonism breaks out each time a new science is founded.' This antagonism emerges even between the Christian religion, which 'gave individual reflection a larger place than any other religion', and science. It emerges even between religion and the science of 'the material world': 'the natural sciences themselves found an obstacle in faith'.[121] But again, it is the science of human beings which is most anathema to religion.

> But it is especially when man became an object of science that the resistance became fierce. The believer, indeed, cannot but find repugnant the idea that man is to be studied as a natural being, analogous to others, and moral facts as facts of nature ... these collective sentiments, under the different forms they have taken, have hindered the development of psychology and sociology.[122]

Religions 'do not express the things of the physical world as they are'. On the other hand, religions do represent the social world. But only in a misrepresentative way. Religions:

> are in the social order what sensation is in the individual. We might ask why it is these religions distort all things as they do in their processes of imagery. But is it not true that sensation, equally, distorts the things it conveys to the individual?[123]

The difference between religion and sensation is that one has a collective, one an individual subject. 'The distortion, however, is not the same in both instances, because the subjects differ.' Religion and sensation are united in their identity as forms of ideology. They are both illusions. 'It is for the thinkers to rectify these illusions that are necessary in practice.' Religious beliefs are an attempt to express social realities, as sensations are an attempt to express physical realities. However, in actuality, they only 'conceal' them.[124]

There is one factor which differentiates religion from other forms of collective ideology. It is not individualistic in nature. Religion is an exceptional form of ideology in that it recognizes the forces of society. It recognizes them, but it translates them into theological terms, and they lose everything in the translation. Through religion, humans express the transcendence and determinative power of society. They represent the superior social being, which Durkheim insists is a natural being, as a supernatural being, as god.

> As long as scientific analysis does not come to teach it to them, men know well that they are acted upon, but they do not know by whom. So they must invent by themselves the idea of these powers . . . they were led to represent them under forms that are really foreign to their nature and to transfigure them by thought.[125]

'Men' imagine 'an abstract entity' in place of 'a concrete object of whose reality we are vividly aware'. They conceal 'a concrete and living reality', society, under the veil of god.[126] The 'common conceptions by which men have tried to represent this sensed supremacy', the supremacy of society, as 'a personal being' or an 'abstract force' are mystical, metaphorical, ideological.[127]

> The gods are no other than collective forces personified and hypostatized in material form . . . when these phantom deities vanish into air and the reality they represent appears by itself alone, it is to this society that . . . annual tributes will be offered.[128]

There is one other classic example of collective ideology cited by Durkheim, in addition to those *bêtes noires* of science, especially social science, which he opposes as a matter of course: individualism, anarchism, pragmatism, utilitarianism, empiricism, and of course, religion. And that is socialism. As religion is inspired by a reality, the reality of social forces, socialism is inspired by a reality, the reality of social problems. Socialism is a conception of the social crisis of transition occasioned by the division of labor. But it is a false conception, and as such it is wrong, both intellectually and practically. Socialism is an example of collective thought which takes the form of 'practical social doctrines', based on 'emotions'. The collective subject of socialism is not the rational, enlightened scientific community but the 'masses', 'interest groups' and 'parties'. Its aim is not knowledge but 'reform' of the social organization.[129] It is an example of the 'confused aspirations' of particular segments or 'parts' of society: 'each only expresses one aspect and not always very faithfully'.[130]

Socialism is heresy because it contradicts the organicism which Durkheim equates with science. Durkheim dismisses it as a lie. Socialism, according to Durkheim, divides society against itself, into opposing interest groups, rather than unifying society and representing the common interest of the entire collective being. It represents the interests of a part of society, at the expense of the interests of society as a whole. Socialism fails to recognize the truth, which is the essential unity of the social organism.

Socialism is additionally unscientific because it fails to recognize the necessity of extant social reality, which is as necessary and beneficial as any natural reality, because it *is* a natural reality. The social organism is, like other, lesser organisms, immutable, except through evolution. Socialism wrongly seeks to change society rather than to describe society. It bases its knowledge on practical objectives, rather than basing its practice on scientific knowledge. It ignores the principle according to which 'practical results' can only be 'derived from facts'.[131] The mission of science is 'to express' 'what is', namely the natural and universal 'laws' of reality. The mission of socialism and other 'practical doctrines' is 'to modify' 'what exists' by way of 'reforms'.[132]

Socialism does not study society 'as it is', with the sole legitimate and realizable practical aim, the aim of the social scientist, which is to restore the social organism to health, to 'make it more like itself'. Durkheim is a social biologist, statesmen are social physicians; socialism is a social symptom.

Socialism is not a science . . . it is a cry of grief, sometimes of anger, uttered by men who feel most keenly our collective malaise. Socialism is to the facts which produce it what the groans of a sick man are to the illness with which he is afflicted, to the needs that torment him.[133]

The correct diagnosis and 'remedies' for 'illness' in the social organism are not those of the 'feverish patient', those which 'the suffering masses of society have spontaneously and instinctively conceived of'. Socialism is 'unscientific'. It 'refracts' rather than 'reflects' its conditions. Like all collective misconceptions, it is a 'social fact' rather than social truth. It is, properly taken, as an 'object of science', rather than mistaken, for knowledge.[134]

Chapter 6

Collective truth

There is an impossibility in some way physical of not recog-
nizing the truth . . . from the truth emanates a light which is
irresistible.[1]

COLLECTIVE IDEOLOGY AND COLLECTIVE TRUTH: METAPHOR OF PERCEPTION, CONTINUUM OF KNOWLEDGE

Durkheim sets collective knowledge against individual knowledge as the unmistakable and unmistaken domain of truth. The
collective consciousness generally appears, unproblematically, as
the infallible producer and guarantor of absolute knowledge.
Conversely, ideology generally appears, unproblematically, as
co-extensive with asocial, individual, empirical and experiential
'knowledge'. Yet, paradoxically, Durkheim sometimes allows the
possibility of collective preconception, error, falsehood. He sets
this collective form of untruth against collective truth, thereby
rendering the latter problematic, calling it into question. The
collective consciousness produces the incorrect alongside the
correct. It contains mistakes, and therefore it contains conflict,
between truth and untruth. Ideology can be a collective and
conceptual, rather than an exclusively individual and perceptual,
phenomenon. Thus Durkheim creates a whole series of dichotomies, between various forms of collective wisdom – rationality,
science, the state – and various forms of collective falsehood –
public sentiment, lay ideas, the unreflected beliefs of the masses.

Collective falsehood tends to be spatially diffuse, common or
vulgar; and temporally diffuse, historically pervasive. Collective
wisdom tends to be spatially localized, the exclusive province of

an élite; and temporally localized, the exclusive province of modernity. The logic of history is expressed in the progressive expansion of the collective, as opposed to the individual, consciousness and its representations. But, moreover, within the collective consciousness, it is manifest in the progressive expansion of collective wisdom, at the expense of collective falsehood. The superior thought and knowledge of the minority and of modernity, understood as science, will gradually eclipse and supplant the inferior, ideological preconceptions of the majority and of tradition. Truth will become collectively predominant as error is defeated within the social mind.

Despite the consistency of this position, both internally, within Durkheim's thought, and externally, within his intellectual milieu, it is a difficult one for him to sustain. The truth/falsehood dichotomy is troublesome for Durkheim, because it contradicts the tenets of rationalism and objectivism which inform his epistemology. The polarity: collective truth/collective ideology ultimately breaks down, just as the polarity: collective truth/individual ideology ultimately breaks down. Inferior social knowledge stands in the same relation to superior social knowledge as individual knowledge does to collective knowledge. But in each case, it is a dual relation.

On the one hand, the relation individual knowledge: collective knowledge, as well as the relation social fallacy: social fact, is a relation of falsity and truth. On the other hand, it is a relation of lesser truth and greater truth. Durkheim prefers to think in terms of continuities, of inferior and superior forms of knowledge, of the less true and the more true; rather than in terms of an essential and radical opposition between the true and the ideological. Because knowledge for Durkheim is finally a representation of reality, it cannot finally be 'wrong'. It can only exist as a greater or lesser, clearer or dimmer, reflection. Knowledge, in all its forms, responds to reality, and is therefore more or less determined by it.

Collective ideology is like individual ideology. They are both negated/surpassed by collective truth. The contrast between ideology, collective or individual, and collective truth, is like the contrast between the sensation and the concept. In comparison to the concept, the sensation is unequivocally an inferior form of knowledge. If in one sense the sensation is false knowledge, in another sense it is only less true knowledge. This is because the sensation, like all ideology, individual and collective, shares a common property with collective truth, the property of relating to reality.

Ironically, while Durkheim is an anti-empiricist, his basic model of knowledge is that of perception. Thus all knowledge, whether right or wrong, whether produced by a collective or an individual subject, is grounded in an object: the real, natural and ideational, physical and social, world. All knowledge is a subject/object relationship, and therefore all knowledge is valid, to a greater or lesser degree. Perception can be more or less true. But because it is always the response by a subject to a stimulus, always an observation by a subject of a real thing, it is never entirely untrue.

Falsity is meaningless when knowledge is categorically understood as an object presenting itself to a subject, or as a subject regarding an object. Knowledge for Durkheim is such a presentation, such a regarding, such a process of perceiving. Knowledge for Durkheim is essentially vision; knowing is essentially seeing. Seeing is more or less perfect: vision is clearer or more obscure, deeper or more superficial, more or less revelatory, more or less complete. Nonetheless, it is impossible to fail to see that which, in reality, is there; just as it is impossible to see that which, in reality, is not there. Vision is limited, and its limitation contains the guarantee of its truth.[2]

In this way, all of the oppositions Durkheim establishes, between false and true forms of collective knowledge, must be reconstructed; reestablished on a truth continuum, rethought as more or less adequate versions/visions of the objective world. False collective thought is rehabilitated, and reappears as representation: less or mis-representative vis-à-vis true collective thought, but a representation of reality nonetheless. Ideas, or 'représentations' of things 'are derived from these things themselves and express them more or less exactly . . .'.[3] In general, 'all internal life draws its primary material from without. All we can think of is objects or our conceptions of them'.[4] Consciousness, individual or social, merely 'clarifies' an external, autonomous, immutable reality.[5]

Thus the difference between common knowledge and the truth held by science and the state, between lay mass thought and expert élite thought; the difference between the knowledge of delimited social groups and the social subject in its entirety, between the partial perspective of one society and the global perspective of humanity itself; the difference between primitive and modern thought ... are actually differences of degree rather than differences of kind. Ideology as illusion or deception does not exist at the collective level any more than it exists at the individual level. Ideology, collective or individual, only exists as crude knowledge, as rough approximation, as less-than-adequate adequation, as superficial or dim perception.

Ideology cannot mean untruth, or falsity. It is not the negation of truth and knowledge. 'Ideology' simply indicates, like the empirical knowledge to which it is so closely related, an alternative and inferior, but nonetheless knowing, form of knowledge, a lesser and perhaps even worthless, but nonetheless somehow true, form of truth. Just as collective representations and knowledge are more true than individual representations and knowledge, some collective representations and knowledge are more true than others. At the collective as well as at the individual level, there are misunderstandings, but no mistakes. Durkheim unifies the world of knowledge by banishing falsehood from it, by making the world of knowledge and the world of truth one.

The first premise under which Durkheim operates to deny the possibility of collective error, is that collective thought, like individual thought, is essentially a response to reality. The collective subject is transcendent with respect to the individual subject, and the representations it effects are therefore epistemologically preferable. But the formation of knowledge by the collective subject is no less a process of subject/object relations, mediated by reflective perception. 'Among peoples as well as individuals, mental representations function above all as an expression of a reality not of their own making; they rather spring from it.'[6]

Collective thought does not produce reality; collective thought reproduces reality. Conceptual thought is elaborated by society, but not arbitrarily. Collective ideas or representations are, precisely, representations, of the object world.

> Now it is unquestionable that language, and consequently the system of concepts which it translates, is the product of a collective elaboration. What it expresses is the manner in which society as a whole represents the facts of experience. The ideas which correspond to the diverse elements of language are thus collective representations.[7]

Between a subject and an object linked by the act of perception, there is no room, or margin, for error.

Concepts are, definitionally, collective representations ('. . . concepts are collective representations . . .'). This formulation serves to distance them, on the one hand, from the individual: *collective* representations. On the other hand, it serves to distance them from absolute creativity on the part of the collective subject. It delivers conceptual thought simultaneously from relativism and from falsehood: collective *representations*. Collective concepts are not radically, heterogeneously, different from individual percepts:

> they are as concrete representations as an individual could form of his own personal environment: they correspond to the way in which this very special being, society, considers the things of its own proper experience.[8]

The difference between collective, conceptual, representations and individual, perceptual representations, is due to the difference in nature of the collective subject and its object. The collective subject and its object have specificity. But they are no less subject and object, connected in a relation where, epistemologically speaking, the object is determinative. Collective concepts are apodictically superior to individual percepts, but they are not radically 'other' in genesis. Individual representations consist of sensations and percepts. Conversely, sensations and percepts are individual representations: representations, necessarily, of things. Likewise, 'concepts express the manner in which society represents things'.[9]

The collective subject, like the individual subject, then, is constrained to consider things, and to represent things. Collective and individual knowledge differ only to the extent that the particular subject and the particular object of the act of perception productive of knowledge differ. Collective representations are nothing more than 'the way in which the group conceives itself in its relation to objects which affect it . . . the way in which a society thinks of itself and of its environment'.

> The group differs from the individual in its constitution, and the things that affect it are therefore of a different nature. Representations or concepts that reflect neither the same objects nor the same subjects cannot be traced to the same causes.[10]

Nonetheless, the social subject, like the individual subject, can only think of itself and of its environment. It can only conceive itself and its relation to objects. Objects and things affect it. Its ideas and concepts are representations which reflect these things and objects. The states of the collective consciousness, its 'mentality', may be 'different' from individual mentality and the states of the individual consciousness. Collective consciousness may contain '"representations" of another type'. Yet collective consciousness, no less than individual consciousness, contains only representations. Social representations may 'reflect a reality different from the individual's reality'.[11] But social subjects and their representations, no less than individual subjects and representations, do in fact reflect reality. The world expressed by the entire system of concepts is not the world which society constructs or creates, but the world which society 'regards'.[12]

Of course, 'society alone' (and not the individual) 'can furnish the most general notions' with which the world can be represented.

> Such an object can be embraced only by a subject which contains all the individual subjects within it. Since the universe does not exist except in so far as it is thought of, and since it is not completely thought of except by society, it takes a place in this latter; it becomes a part of society's interior life, while this is the totality, outside of which nothing exists.[13]

Society may be a unique subject, an inimitable subject. It may have a unique, illimitable object, the universe. The absolute total subject and its absolute total object may together comprise absolute totality. But society, however transcendent with respect to individual subjects, is ever a subject itself, a subject contemplating an object.

> If society is something universal in relation to the individual, it is none the less an individuality itself . . . it is a particular subject and consequently particularizes whatever it thinks of.[14]

It is in the nature of the social subject 'to *see* things in large and under the aspect which they ordinarily have'.[15] The collective consciousness '*sees* things only in their permanent and essential aspects'. 'At the same time that it *sees* from above, it *sees* farther; at every moment of time it embraces all known reality'.[16] There are thus several quite different guarantees of truth implicit in the collective thought process. The collective subject, specifically, uniquely, unlike the individual subject, is a perfect subject of knowledge. Collective representations – specifically, uniquely, unlike individual representations – are rational, essential, abstract conceptions rather than superficial, particularized, concrete sensations. But the universal, general, guarantee of truth, uniting the collective subject with the individual subject on the terrain of true knowledge, is that the subject/object relation is one of sight.

The second premise about collective knowledge under which Durkheim operates is that it is true because it is collective. This position has less to do with the transcendent faculties of a collective subject than it has to do with the spatial and temporal extensiveness of collective knowledge. The collective subject of consciousness contains all of the individual subjects of consciousness within it, and it persists over time. Thus, not only is the knowledge it acquires different and better, it is also infinitely verified.

Collective knowledge cannot be false, because it is knowledge held collectively. Knowledge held by a multitude, and a succession, of discrete individuals cannot plausibly be untrue. It cannot possibly be divorced from the objective reality which is witnessed by all individuals in their individual existences as well as in their collective existence. The reality-testing of collective knowledge is unlimited and incessant. Collective knowledge is confirmed knowledge.

> A collective representation presents guarantees of objectivity by the fact that it is collective: for it is not without sufficient reason that it has been able to generalize and maintain itself with persistence. If it were out of accord with the nature of things, it would never have been able to acquire an extended and prolonged empire over intellects . . . the men who accept it verify it by their own experience. Therefore it could not be wholly inadequate for its subject.[17]

Collective thought is always, necessarily and automatically, objective; always, necessarily and automatically, in accord with the nature of things. It is never, it could not be, wholly inadequate for its subject/object.

Collective thought is always true, never false, by definition. 'It is impossible . . . that so general an error be a simple illusion and correspond to nothing in reality.'[18] 'A sentiment so general *cannot* be a pure illusion, but must express, in confused fashion, some aspect of reality.'[19] Generality is the guarantee of collective knowledge. Collective, social illusion, delusion or deception – collective, social ideology – is impossible, it cannot exist. Conversely, the very existence of social thought proves its truth. Its persistent existence places it beyond all doubt and enshrines it, hallows it, haloes it, in unquestionable veracity:

> when a collective sentiment has persistently asserted itself throughout history, one may rest assured that it has a factual basis ... Such widespread ideas could not result from a simple aberration or deception under which men have laboured for centuries.[20]

Durkheim believes, on the basis of these two premises, that collective ideas, representations, thought and knowledge are all true. Yet he doesn't believe that collective thought is all equally true. Therefore, while he refuses to distinguish between true and false social discourse, he frequently invokes the distinction between collective beliefs which are less true, and those which are more true. Again, he rejects an oppositional dichotomy in favor of a progressive continuum. The terminology he employs to demarcate greater truth and lesser truth is the terminology of perception. Essentially, reality is seen more or less clearly. The object remains constant, but the eye of the beholder varies. It is more or less acute, its vision more or less refined.

Durkheim's favored metaphorical contrast involves the relative obscurity or clarity of knowledge. The word 'obscure', indicating knowledge which is less true, is common in Durkheim's work. It is laden with meaning, connoting at one and the same time the different dimensions of darkness, vagueness, and unawareness.

Darkness: an object is more or less hidden from view because the subject/object relation of perception is interfered with. Its natural medium of 'light', 'illumination', 'enlightenment', is insufficiently present. An object is bathed in shadowy dimness and murkiness, in the dark black night of ignorance, rather than in the cold grey dawn of reason. The subject has less knowledge of the object, because it cannot (yet) be fully seen. This is partly due to circumstances of time and place, but also partly due to the nature of the subject, and the nature of its particular mode of inquiry. Human history is a gradual process of enlightenment.

And within that historical progression, there are certain subjects which especially shed light on things, certain methods of investigation which especially illuminate them.

Vagueness: an object presents itself, or is perceived, only vaguely. It appears 'indistinct', 'indefinite', 'ambiguous'. The object is present, clear and immutable. But the subject has only weak powers of perception, and the subject/object relation is distant and unsystematic. The subject is merely glancing at an object, from afar or with faulty eyesight, and passively receives 'vague' 'impressions' from it. There is no probing scrutiny, no visionary revelation of the object in all its crystalline truth and meaning. Additionally, since the object appears only vaguely, conceptions of the object are likewise vague; 'confused', 'unintelligible', 'inarticulate', 'implicit'.

Unawareness: the obscure object is one partially hidden from view, cloaked or veiled in secrecy, mystery, or ignorance. The obscure object is partially concealed as an object of clear, precise and exhaustive knowledge. It is also partially concealed as an object of consciousness. It is 'non-conscious', 'unconscious', 'sub-conscious'. It is fully present objectively, but either there is no knowledge of it (non-consciousness); or whatever knowledge of it which exists is submerged or buried in the depths of con-sciousness. The object is absent from the clear surface of the subject's conscious awareness.

Durkheim describes the less true in terms of the relative obscurity of the object and knowledge of it. Durkheim also portrays less true knowledge as more 'immediate' knowledge. Like obscurity, immediacy is a very dense, significant concept. In the first place, temporally, it signals knowledge which is unrefined or unprocessed; 'crude' or 'crudely formed'. Know-ledge of this sort is immediate in the sense that it is instantaneous. It is 'spontaneous', 'automatic', 'unconsidered', 'unreflective', 'instinctive'. It is formulated 'without method', 'without disci-pline'. The subject is subjected to knowledge. Knowledge is not subjected to operations by the subject which would render it more complete, more accurate, more incisive. Immediate knowledge is raw knowledge.

In the second place, topographically, immediacy evokes super-ficiality. Immediate knowledge is knowledge of the 'superficial', of the surface of objects. The immediate object is not only the object which initially and simply presents itself, or is initially and simply perceived. It is also the object which proximately presents itself, which is proximately perceived. And the aspect of the object which is most proximate, which is immediately adjacent to the subject is its external aspect, its outside, which simultaneously contains and conceals its internal truth and meaning.

Immediate knowledge is knowledge of 'appearance'. It is knowledge which is unmediated, which is not subjected to rigorous conceptual labor aimed at capturing the 'essence' of the object: its internal nature; its abstract, general, universal nature; and its relational nature, the relations linking it to other objects giving it its sense, its meaning and direction. Immediate knowledge is surface knowledge of external appearance, and not deep knowledge of internal essence. It is devoid of 'understanding', 'reason', 'explanation'; of 'patient', 'deliberate', 'considered', 'reasoned', and laborious 'analysis'. It is basically 'reflexive' rather than 'reflective'.

It is clear that Durkheim understands 'less true' collective knowledge as analogous or parallel to individual knowledge, in two ways. First, lesser social thought is more like sensation than like rationality. Durkheim explicitly compares less sentient collective representations to 'sensations', knowledge of the 'senses'. Second, like individual, perceptual knowledge, collective knowledge is not untrue. It is 'inferior': 'imperfect' knowledge, knowledge which is to some extent 'inadequate' to its object. It is knowing less, but it is not knowing falsely. Therefore, in this mode of thinking, Durkheim revalidates the same sorts of knowledge that he elsewhere calls 'false', 'erroneous', 'delirious' 'deception'. He redefines 'primitive', 'lay', 'popular', 'common', 'vulgar', 'mass', 'crowd' or 'public' opinions, sentiments, and preconceptions: 'myths, dogmas, traditions, currents . . . legends' et cetera. They are not wrong, here; not ideological. They reflect actual, true knowledge. But it is only knowledge 'to a certain point'.[21]

Durkheim is forced to admit, and does so freely and explicitly, that the difference between collective ideology and collective truth is a quantitative, and not a qualitative, difference. The wisdom of primitives, the laity, the masses, is not pure folly. It has something in common with, it bears a resemblance to, it is connected with and related to the wisdom of modernity, science and the state. With respect to primitive thinking, Durkheim says, in *Primitive Classification*: 'Primitive classifications . . . seem to be connected, *with no break in continuity*, to the first scientific classifications.'[22] Primitive classificatory thought is itself actually 'scientific', as it represents 'a first philosophy of nature'. Again, with respect to the mentality of primitives, Durkheim says, in *The Elementary Forms of Religious Life*:

> So it is far from true that this mentality has no connection with ours. Our logic was born of this logic. The explanations of contemporary science are surer of being objective because they are more methodical and because they rest on more carefully controlled observations, but *they do not differ in nature* from those which satisfy primitive thought. Today, as formerly, to explain is to show how one thing participates in one or several others.[23]

What can be said of the relationship between primitive thought and modern thought,[24] can also be said of the relationship between contemporary non-scientific thought and science. Between those concepts which are 'scientifically elaborated and criticized' and those which are merely collective, '*there are only differences of degree*'. This is because, on the one hand, an unscientific collective representation 'presents guarantees of objectivity by the fact that it is collective'. Scientific concepts are 'methodically controlled' but collective representations are experientially controlled and verified. A collective representation 'could not be wholly inadequate for its object'. Even if unscientific, it has 'object value'.

On the other hand, science itself is not perfect. While laic collective concepts are only 'imperfect symbols', scientific symbols are themselves only 'approximative'. And while common knowledge derives authority from its object value as well as from popular sentiment, conversely science derives authority from 'faith' and 'opinion' as well as from its adequation to reality.[25] Scientific knowledge is abased, and unscientific knowledge elevated in this construction of similarity and continuity, of difference within equivalence. What is crucial here, however, is the elevation of unscientific knowledge, its redemption from the status of error, falsehood, and untruth to the status of lesser truth. And again, this is based at least in part on the relation to the object world which it shares with science: the relation of observation.

All collective thought/representation/knowledge is similar in that it all has 'objective value'. For example, with respect to non-scientific beliefs about suicide, Durkheim says that 'in spite of the crudeness of the popular formula the conception nevertheless has objective value'. There are objections to the common conceptions, criticisms of 'the reasons satisfying the crowd' because of their unscientific, inadequate, nature; but 'the process they symbolize is nonetheless real' and the imperfect form of its representation 'cannot lessen its reality'.[26]

Durkheim is suggesting less a negative relation of enmity, diametrical opposition and mutual exclusion, between false ideology and true science, than a positive relation of affinity, similarity and peaceful co-existence, between unscientific and scientific thought. Scientific knowledge is a subset of collective thought in general, deriving from a specialized, expert, élite subset of the collective consciousness. It is superior to common knowledge, but not substantially different. Collective concepts which are 'scientifically elaborated and criticized' are 'always in the very slight minority'. However this superior minority does not completely invalidate the inferior majority. The minority of knowledge of the minority is better, but not essentially in conflict with, the mass of knowledge of the masses.

In fact, scientific knowledge necessarily co-exists with other forms of knowledge. 'At each moment of history . . . there is a determined place for clear ideas, reflected opinions, in short for science, beyond which it cannot normally extend.' There is an 'equilibrium' in every society between 'understanding' and 'the practical faculties . . . sentiments, beliefs, customs, with which we live'. Since science is 'nothing other' than the collective consciousness 'carried to its highest point of clarity', it is, definitionally, only a part of the collective consciousness. To increase society's adaptability, that portion of collective intelligence which is 'guided by science' must 'take a larger part in collective life'. Science (like the state, the social brain or 'organ of collective thought') must continuously expand, as society advances into complexity. But it can never totally displace and replace the common, everyday, practical, preconceptual, ideological/ knowledge of the collective consciousness. Even as it automatically expands, it causes disruption, rupture, and 'troublesome consequences'.[27]

Superior, scientific knowledge never disposes of its inferior, ideological/knowledge counterpart. The two are in a sense comparable and in a sense compatible. Science does not destroy or eliminate ideology/knowledge, but it can transform it. The false cannot be transformed into the true. But the inferior can be improved. The obscure can be enlightened, illuminated, and clarified. The less-than-adequate can be made more adequate, the imperfect perfected. Scientific concepts constitute that sub-set, or 'minority' of collective representations which have been worked, which have been 'elaborated and criticized'. They are not different in nature from common ideas, but they are different. And the difference amounts to elaboration/transfor-mation. Common ideas are the crude, raw material which science refines. The phenomena taken as an object by a new science:

> are already represented in the mind not only by rather definite perceptions but also by some kind of crudely formed concepts ... thought and reflection are prior to science, which *merely uses them more methodically*.[28]

Science, or 'speculative knowledge', and 'lay', or practical knowledge, begin at the same place. Their shared 'point of departure' is perceptions or sensations of the objective world. 'It is only beyond this point, namely in the manner of elaboration of these common data, that divergences begin.'[29] Science is merely more objective, more systematic and methodical; and it 'speaks' of objects 'in a different language from that of the layman'.[30] The 'system of accepted ideas' must merely be 'modified', must merely 'make room' for the new concepts of science. Preconceived ideas are different from, but modifiable and hospitable, with respect to scientific ideas. The difference is that the former consists simply of 'ordinary perception', while the latter consists of 'devious and complicated paths'.

Science is other than non-science in the sense that it is more than non-science. The gap is the gap between 'opening our eyes and taking a good look to perceive at once the laws of the social world', on the one hand; and sociology on the other. To open the eyes and take a good look, to perceive something at once, does not generate false knowledge. It merely generates insufficient knowledge. The 'popular imagination' is beset by nothing worse, nothing more epistemologically suspect, than its own 'customary over-simplicity'.[31] And in fact, the 'common conceptions' of the popular imagination, the 'reasons satisfying the crowd' 'need only be *transposed* into another idiom to be given their full import'.[32] It is only the 'definite *form* in which we usually clothe these ideas' which is 'without scientific value'.

Science is defined as '*clear* ideas, *reflected* opinions'.[33] Scientific and unscientific ideas and opinions are differentiated solely by the relative clarity, and reflection, afforded to one and the same vision of one and the same object. Knowledge is produced through the process of discovering/uncovering reality. Unscientific knowledge is knowledge which comes first, knowledge which is 'prior to science'. It uncovers less of reality. Durkheim describes the progressive, cumulative process ('investigation') of the quest for reality:

> In order to discover it, external signs are first used which most clearly reveal it. Then, as the investigation proceeds, these outward tangible signs are replaced by others. Only when one has gone beyond the level of tangible appearances does it become possible to discover the innermost characteristics of the thing, which pertain to its very essence.[34]

Understood in this way, the appearance/essence dichotomy is recast. No longer representing the false/true distinction, it here stands for the outward/inward, less true/more true distinction, where 'there are only differences of degree', and ideas 'do not differ in nature'. There is *first* knowledge, separated from science only by the procedure of investigation. Science is only *beyond* non-science. Science digs deeper, sees further, than non-science. Science is a 'deeper analysis' of reality.

While it cannot be said that knowledge of the outward tangible appearance is false knowledge, it cannot be denied that the greater truth, the momentous truth, the eternal and ideal truth, or 'essence' of reality, always lies deeper and further, at one remove, on the other side of an 'investigation', from the physical senses and from common sense. Alternatively, since it is 'founded in reality', this inferior, first knowledge (like sentiment, 'only a confused expression of the real'), can be reformulated, processed, 'expressed in intelligible terms'.[35] In the study of morality, for example, the 'method' which creates science out of non-science requires nothing more than 'to transform the confused, popular notions of morality into precise and clear-cut notions'. The 'layman's confused notions', are no more adequate than 'auditory and visual sensations'. Neither are they any more false than such sensations. These 'ill-articulated *impressions*' do not need to be *negated*, as they themselves are not the negation of truth. They need only be *transformed*, into better ideas, into superior knowledge . . . into 'scientific *expressions*'.[36]

THE TRUTH OF COLLECTIVE IDEOLOGY: SOCIALISM AND RELIGION REVISITED

There are two examples of inferior collective thought which Durkheim treats extensively, and which illustrate the tension between his tendency to speak of 'untrue' ideas and his tendency to speak of 'less true' ideas. The first example is that of socialism. Durkheim does not believe in the tenets of socialism (except as he redefines it beyond recognition).[37] And so in some sense, he believes it is ideology, false social doctrine. But in another sense, he is unprepared to call even an opposing, hostile theory strictly and absolutely wrong. He doesn't describe socialism as a system of incorrect ideas which portray reality erroneously and deceptively. On the contrary, he concedes that socialism is a response to society itself and its actual ills.

Socialism is a perception of reality. It is an inferior perception of reality, in that it is a spontaneous, experiential, empirical and non-expert perception. But it is in no way divorced from the objective, material world. It is intimately bound up with social truth. It is neither a fabrication nor a hallucination. It is a sincere view of an undeniable object. Socialism is not science. But it is not pure untruth.

> Socialism is not a science . . . it is a cry of grief, sometimes of anger, uttered by men who feel most keenly our collective malaise. Socialism is to the facts which produce it what the groans of a sick man are to the illness with which he is afflicted, to the needs that torment him.[38]

Socialism is a diagnosis and set of remedies for social ills, but a diagnosis and prescription formulated by the 'feverish patient' itself. It is a response to a sick society, but which 'the suffering masses of society' have themselves 'spontaneously conceived of'. Socialist ideas are themselves 'symptoms' of a genuine social condition.[39]

Socialist theory, then, is produced by 'facts'. It is caused by 'collective malaise'. It is a perception, in fact a perception by those 'who feel most keenly' the objective stimulus in question.

It is no more false, arbitrary or deceitful than any other perception of any other object. Like all perceptions, it is essentially an effect, and determined in its nature by reality itself. Socialism is an empirical sensation rather than a rational science. Like a sensation, it is inferior to rationality and science. But like a sensation, it is a form of knowledge.

Religion, of course, is a centerpiece in Durkheim's work.[40] His study of religion can be understood as his definitive study of social or collective ideology. And, based on his exhaustive focus on religion, it can be concluded that Durkheim denies the existence of ideology, repudiates the concept of ideology, when ideology is understood as erroneous collective representation, as false social thought.

By rights, religion should be the mortal enemy of the science Durkheim champions. As a scientist, Durkheim should logically desire to defeat and demolish religion, to negate and nullify it, to eliminate and replace the ideas it propounds. Religion should die, in order that science should live. This is all the more the case because of the fact that Durkheim is a social scientist, battling for 'men's' souls, for the right to depict human reality and determine their behavior, with an alternative and compelling ideological system. It is one of the greatest ironies of Durkheim's oeuvre that he both destroys and redeems religion, in one and the same movement.

Unlike other scientists and social scientists of his day, Durkheim neither turns his back on religion, nor dismisses it, simply, as untrue. Instead, he critically appropriates it, sublates it, and enlists it in the service of his own ideas. Durkheim provides not a scientific denunciation, but a scientific explanation of religion. Durkheim's science provides a justification of religion, and in return, religion provides a justification of Durkheim's science. Iconoclastically, Durkheim proclaims that religion, the *bête noire* of other scientific attitudes, is not essentially false but essentially true. Its truth is not unqualified. Religion sees, as it were, through a glass darkly. But nonetheless it sees.

Religion is a view or vision of reality. In fact it is a view of the same reality which is the object of Durkheim's vision. It is the specific nature of this common object, its peculiar status as an object of knowledge, which forges the unholy Durkheimian alliance between science and religion, sociology and theology. Religion is actually the only ally Durkheim can claim, as he faces the unenviable task of declaring the very existence, the very reality, of the object of his scientific attentions. The burden of proof is, so to speak, on him. In attesting to the truth of the primitive popular religious beliefs, Durkheim is effectively attesting to the truth of his own scientific theories. And he simultaneously claims the legions of religious believers as witnesses to his scientific revelations. The weight of the masses, and of historical tradition, are on his side.

In avowing the truth of religion, Durkheim assumes the right to explain that truth. Religion is true, it is actual knowledge, he says, because it is knowledge of a true reality. Religious ideas are true because they relate to, represent, translate, symbolize, express a REAL TRUE OBJECT. But of course the real, true, extant, redoubtable object heralded, established and worshipped by religion is the same object which Durkheim is attempting to herald, establish, and study scientifically: society. Religion, as it understands itself, is not completely true. There is no god, strictly speaking. On the other hand, religion, as Durkheim understands it, is completely, if crudely true. There *is* a god, because god and society are one and the same. In proving, in a sense, the existence of god, Durkheim proves, in a sense, the existence of society. The former 'proof' serves as a camouflage or smokescreen for the latter.

Religion, like all ideas, represents truth because it *represents*. Religious representations are nothing more or less than collective representations, 'which express collective realities'.[41] In fact, 'religion expresses nothing which does not exist in nature'.[42] There is a certain 'reality', which is neither physical nor individual in nature, in relation to which religion 'has a significance and an objective value'.[43] Religion is not mere superstition, because 'religious forces are real'.[44]

Religion corresponds to 'a concrete object of whose reality we are vividly aware' . . . 'a concrete and living reality'. There is a 'thing itself' which motivates and inspires religion.[45] Within the framework of Durkheim's science:

> Religion ceases to be an inexplicable hallucination and takes a foothold in reality. In fact, we can say that *the believer is not deceived* when he believes in the existence of a moral power upon which he depends and from which he receives all that is best in himself . . . *he is not the dupe of an illusion*; this

exaltation is real and is really the effect of forces outside of and superior to the individual.[46]

Religious beliefs 'contain a truth which must be discovered'.[47] Durkheim, the scientific explorer, believes that he has made such a discovery. And in discovering/uncovering the 'truth' of religion, he finds that religion is somehow even more true, more scientific, than the science of his contemporaries. The primitive pagan and the common Christian recognize a true reality which the modern scientific atheist denies three times. The religious sensibility contains a profound knowledge of which the pseudo-scientific mentality is profoundly ignorant. This is because religion recognizes and knows god. And Durkheim recognizes and knows that god is society, and that society exists. Religion's 'foothold in reality' consists in the fact that the moral power around which it revolves is not a hallucination: *'this power exists, it is society'*.

In one short phrase heard 'round the world, Durkheim overturns the conventional relationship between science and religion. He discredits religion, as it is, and substantiates it, as he sees it. He discredits science, as it is, and substantiates the science of his own vision. Religion, above all, is like Durkheimian sociology. And, above all, both are true.

> Before all, it is a system of ideas with which the individuals represent to themselves the society of which they are members, and the obscure but intimate relations which they have with it. This is its primary function; and though metaphorical and symbolic, this representation is not unfaithful. Quite on the contrary, it translates everything essential in the relations which are to be explained: *for it is an eternal truth that outside of us there exists something greater than us, with which we enter into communion.*[48]

Religion has 'a meaning and a reasonableness' because 'the god is only a figurative expression of the society'. The 'sacred principle' acknowledged and venerated by religion is simply 'society transfigured and personified'.[49] The 'sacred forces' acknowledged and feared by religion are nothing other than 'collective forces'.[50]

> The first power which men have thought of as such seems to have been that exercised by humanity over its members . . .

the first powers of which the human mind had any idea
were those which societies have established in organizing
themselves.

Ultimately, Durkheim maintains that '*religious thought is something
very different from a system of fictions*'. Religion 'corresponds' and
'expresses' a certain 'reality' – society – and certain 'forces' –
collective forces. These realities serve as the 'foundation' of
religion, which translates them into 'language' and 'symbols'.[51]
Thus, the impressions of the faithful '*are not imaginary*'. They are
to collective knowledge what sensations are to individual knowledge. But they are knowledge nevertheless, knowledge which
has a special affinity with the science of society:

> *this reality, which mythologies have represented under so many
> different forms, but which is the universal and eternal objective cause
> of these sensations sui generis out of which religious experience is
> made, is society.*[52]

Religion is the primordial way in which individuals represent
the realities which they see and feel, acutely and yet obscurely:
society, social forces, and social relations. 'Before all, it is a
system of ideas with which the individuals represent to themselves the society of which they are members, and the obscure
but intimate relations which they have with it.' Individuals
develop mythological interpretations of the social forces which
they 'feel'. Originally, 'men know well that they are acted upon,
but they do not know by whom'.[53] Religion is the first form of
social self-consciousness:

> *religions, even the most uncouth, are not merely fantasies that have
> no basis in reality* ... they ... interpret in a symbolic form
> social needs and collective interests. They represent the
> various connexions maintained by society with the individuals
> who go to make it up, as well as the things forming part of
> its substance. And these connexions and interests are real ...
> Religions are the primitive way in which societies become
> conscious of themselves and their history. They are in the
> social order what sensation is in the individual.[54]

If religion is the first form of social self-consciousness, the
awareness on the part of individuals/society that society itself
exists, then Durkheim's science is *not* a revolutionary departure

from religion, but only an evolutionary development of it. 'The gods are no other than collective forces personified and hypostatized in material form.' Durkheim is himself a believer in collective forces, in fact a worshipper of collective forces. He finds them not only necessary – real and powerful, terrible – but also beneficial – good, goodly, godly.

Durkheim makes occasional oblique references to the secular religious practice implied by his sociological scientific theory. Accordingly, he finds no difference between a religious ceremony and 'a reunion of citizens commemorating the promulgation of a new moral or legal system or some great event in the national life'. In fact, these national, secular activities are the 'feasts and ceremonies of the future', of the desirable future, beyond the 'moral mediocrity' occasioned by the fact that 'the old gods are growing old or already dead, and others are not yet born'.[55] Durkheim is helping to bury the old gods. Yet he is simultaneously helping to deliver the new ones. He wishes to unveil the new, real god, society, behind the old idolic god, god. He is the messiah of the 'new faith': 'when these phantom deities vanish into air and the reality they represent appears by itself alone, it is to this society that these annual tributes will be offered'.[56]

In addition to its basic objectivity, religion is both pervasive and persistent. For Durkheim, these characteristics are indicative of truth value. Religious beliefs find easy and widespread acceptance because they stand the test of experience, as well as the test of time.

> It is *inadmissible* that systems of ideas like religions, which have held so considerable a place in history, and to which, in all times, men have come to receive the energy which they must have to live, should be made up of a tissue of illusions . . . How could a vain fantasy have been able to fashion the human consciousness so strongly and so durably?[57]

Against the other scientists of his day, Durkheim argued that if religion is 'explained' as erroneous, then it remains 'incomprehensible', because it is '*incomprehensible* that humanity should have remained obstinate in these errors through the ages, for experience should have very quickly proven them false'.[58] What Durkheim concludes is that 'the unanimous sentiment of the believers of all times *cannot* be purely illusory'.[59] Social knowledge is definitionally, tautologically, legitimate.[60]

Armed with these proofs of the essential veracity of religion, Durkheim must nevertheless qualify his convictions. Religion is true, but it is less true than science. It is knowledge, specifically knowledge of society, but it is knowledge which is inferior to that of science, specifically the science of sociology. Religion is not the 'error', 'delusion', 'illusion', or 'delirium' Durkheim labels it elsewhere. But neither is it pure, unadulterated, perfect truth either. Religion represents or adequates reality, but it does so inadequately. There is a 'gap' or 'distance' between the religious representation and the corresponding reality. This space, the space of difference between ideology and science, Durkheim understands as a space of imperfection, transformation, transfiguration, disfiguration, distortion. But he does not understand it as an intraversable gulf, radically separating fact from fiction.

The true cause of religious thought, which is social reality, is transformed by religion. The true nature of religious sentiments, which are actually social sentiments, can only 'appear very imperfectly' through the lens of religion.[61] The mythological interpretation of social forces is one in which 'men' are 'led to represent them under forms that are really foreign to their nature and to transfigure them by thought'.[62] Society is a circuitous, obscure, and complex reality which is necessarily portrayed, but in a necessarily 'simple' manner, by the popular imagination, in its 'customary over-simplicity'.[63] The concrete, objective, living reality of society is portrayed figuratively, in 'figures and metaphors', in 'metaphorical conceptions', as an 'abstract entity', 'a personal force', an 'abstract force', as god.[64] Religion creates the 'illusion' of 'anthropomorphism'. It correctly identifies society as the greatest super/natural power. But, as 'science . . . did not yet exist' when religion was conceived by society, and society conceived by religion, a partial 'error' was committed, which consisted in mystifying the social reality discovered by religion. 'It was only a metaphor, but it was taken literally.'[65]

Religion represents 'the sentiment inspired by the group in its members', but in a 'projected' and 'objectified' guise.[66] Religious thought corresponds to actual, social realities. But these realities: 'express themselves religiously only when religion transfigures them. Between society as it is objectively and the sacred things which express it symbolically, the distance is considerable'.[67]

Mythical explanations 'translate' reality, though they are actually 'disfiguring it in doing so'.[68] Religious explanation has a foundation in reality, but: 'it does not follow that the reality which is its foundation conforms objectively to the ideas which believers have of it . . . none of these conceptions express it adequately'.[69] There is 'reality' in mythologies and theologies, but it appears 'only in an enlarged, transformed and idealized form'.[70] The 'delirium' of religion amounts to the fact that the collective mind 'adds to the immediate data given by the senses'. In this sense, 'nearly every collective sentiment is . . . delirious'.[71]

Durkheim feels the same ambivalence toward collective religious sentiments as he does toward individual empirical sensations. They are both consigned to the same epistemological limbo: they are neither completely false nor completely true.

> If a scientist states it as an axiom that the sensations of heat and light which we feel correspond to some objective cause, he does not conclude that this is what it appears to the senses to be. Likewise, even if the impressions which the faithful feel are not imaginary, still they are in no way privileged intuitions; there is no reason for believing that they inform us better upon the nature of their object than do ordinary sensations upon the nature of bodies and their properties. In order to discover what this object consists of, we must submit them to an examination and elaboration analogous to that which has substituted for the sensuous idea of the world another which is scientific and conceptual.[72]

On the one hand, since religions 'are in the social order what sensation is in the individual', they are subject to the same element of 'distortion'. Religions 'distort all things . . . in their processes of imagery'.

On the other hand, religious beliefs 'express' social realities. But they do so 'in metaphor'. And they 'conceal' and 'veil' the same realities which they reveal, presenting them crudely, 'personified and hypostasized in material form', as 'phantom deities'.[73] Durkheim is capable of criticizing religion, of exposing its shortcomings as a system of knowledge. Yet, conversely, the same religious symbolic reality can be viewed in a different light, seen from a different, more positive perspective. 'It may be that the religious symbol conveys the corresponding moral reality imperfectly; but this does not mean that it is devoid of all reality.'[74] Consistent with his basic ambivalence about the truth value of religion, Durkheim expresses an unresolved ambivalence about the relationship between religion and science. In some moments, he indicates that in the modern world, science – collective truth and wisdom – should displace religion – collective falsehood and mysticism – as society's consensual, guiding belief system. However, elsewhere, and predominantly, he posits an essential unity, compatibility, and complementarity between the scientific and the religious modes of thought. In the first place, Durkheim sees religion as the point of origin of science: as a precursor or progenitor of science; even as a first, archetypal instance of science. 'If philosophy and the sciences were born of religion, it is because religion began by taking the place of the sciences and philosophy.'[75] Scientific thought, along with law and morality, 'were born of religion, were for a long time confounded with it, and have remained penetrated with its spirit'.[76]

At the most basic level, the 'principal categories . . . are born in religion and of religion; they are a product of religious thought'. The categories are of social origin, but only *because* they are of religious origin:

> religion is something eminently social. Religious representa-
> tions are collective representations which express collective
> realities . . . So if the categories are of religious origin . . . they
> too should be social affairs and the product of collective
> thought.[77]

Since the categories are of religious origin, and since reason is 'nothing more than all the fundamental categories taken together',[78] then Durkheim establishes a religious as much as a social theory of reason: for him the two are equivalent. At a more elaborate level, religion utilizes categories to classify, to order the universe. Religions are 'systems of ideas which . . . give us a complete representation of the world'. Within religious thought, all the elements of the world are 'arranged' in a 'systematic classification embracing the whole of nature'.[79]

Religion is also the original source of the idea of force. The idea of physical forces 'is very probably derived from that of religious forces'.[80] The totemic principle is 'of interest for the history of scientific thought' because it is 'the first form of the idea of force'.[81] 'So the idea of force is of religious origin. It is from religion that it has been borrowed, first by philosophy, then by the sciences'.[82] Ultimately, 'all the forces of the universe have been conceived on the model of the sacred forces'. The social explanation of the idea of force is also, in actuality, a religious explanation. The entire conception 'of efficacy, of productive power, of active force' is said to depend on 'social causes' because the first idea of force was 'the mana, wakan, orenda, the totemic principle'.[83]

Crucially, religion initiates the practice of thinking in terms of rational relations among empirically discrete objects.

> The essential thing was not to leave the mind enslaved to visible appearances, but to teach it to dominate them and to connect what the senses separated; for from the moment when men have an idea that there are internal connections between things, science and philosophy become possible. Religion opened up the way for them.[84]

Primitive religion contains a belief in 'contagion', an unseen, mystical relationship linking various material things together. Religion confuses and confounds apparently unrelated entities. The confusions and interpenetrations it imputes to things,

> have played a role of the highest utility in logic; they have served to bind together things which sensation leaves apart from one another . . . contagion, the source of these confusions . . . has opened the way for the scientific explanations of the future.[85]

In the intersection of the concept of force, and the concept of interconnection, the concept of causality emerges. The law of causality is religious and social in two ways. First, collective religious thought first identifies the causal relation, the power and mutual participation which unite objects causally. Second, the first causal agent perceived by the social mind is the collectivity itself. Religion is the organized recognition by society of the causal power of its own causal might.

Like science, religion conceives of categories and classifications, connections and causality. It is true that religion is guilty of 'immoderate confusions as well as sharp contrasts'. 'When it connects, it confounds; when it distinguishes, it opposes.' But it is true that religion is implicated as a fundamentally logical system of thought. Religion 'employs logical mechanisms with a

certain awkwardness, but it ignores none of them'.[86] As the
matrix of non-empirical, rational, logical thinking, religion is the
prototype of scientific thinking. Religion is related to science
because it precedes science and gives birth to it, but also
and more fundamentally because it is itself the first science.
Originator of science, religion is also the original science. In a
more indirect way, by a more circuitous and lengthy route,
religion is also the predecessor/ancestor of social science.
Religion leads naturally and logically to a science of society,
because it inaugurates science in general, and also because it is
the first consciousness/self-consciousness of the social entity, of
the existence of the object/subject society.

Durkheim poses the unity of religion and science as a historical
unity, as a continuity between the two. And yet he also poses
their unity as a synchronic unity in terms of a peaceful co-
existence between the two within one time-frame. There is, he
claims, no necessary 'antinomy' between science on the one
hand, and morals and religion on the other.[87] Specifically, he
notes that there is only a delimited space within any collective
consciousness for pure scientific understanding. And secondly,
he believes that science and religion can carve out separate
spheres of influence, can share the territory of the social mind,
because they each perform different, differentiated functions.

Certainly, science can perform an integrative function as well
as a knowledge function, and a practical function as well
as a theoretical function. Conversely, religion can serve in a
theoretical-epistemological capacity, as well as in its primary,
integrative and practical capacities. But science is a specialized,
superior structure for the production of speculative, theoretical
knowledge. And religion is specialized and superior in integrative and practical matters, matters of action. Durkheim expects
religion to 'progressively retire' before science, as science 'becomes
better fitted to perform the task'; specifically, the 'cognitive and
intellectual functions'.[88] He further expects the 'secular religion'
of the state to supplant religion in the integration of society, as
he expects the secular education of the state to supplant religion
in the practical matter of providing norms for behavior.

Nonetheless, despite the allocation of its basic roles to science
and the state, Durkheim anticipates the long-term persistence
or 'survival' of religion. Religion, he says, 'seems destined to
transform itself rather than to disappear . . . there is something

eternal in religion'.[89] Science is unparalleled at producing facts, but the facts of science 'are not enough': 'in so far as religion is action, and in so far as it is a means of making men live, science could not take its place'.[90]

Durkheim redefines the conflict between religion and science as a conflict between 'faith' and 'science'. The struggle between religion and science is effectively displaced. Science and religion co-exist with each other; science and faith contend with each other for influence over religion. While no longer combative with respect to religion, science assumes a critical and controlling position over it, and thereby usurps the position traditionally held by faith.

> From now on, the faith no longer exercises the same hegemony as formerly over the system of ideas that we may continue to call religion. A rival power rises up before it which, being born of it, ever after submits it to its criticism and control ... this control will constantly become more extended and efficient, while no limit can be assigned to its future influence.[91]

This situation is eventuated because, in its apotheosis as social science, science is transformed from the enemy of religion into the defender of religion. Modern science first grants religion its right to exist.

> That which science refuses to grant religion is not its right to exist, but its right to dogmatize upon the nature of things and the special competence which it claims for itself for knowing man and the world.[92]

The faith which is the essence of religion is gradually displaced by science, as science, beyond passively granting religion its right to exist, begins to actively substantiate it. And a religion based on science is no longer a religion based on faith. The strange bargain which Durkheim's science strikes with religion is that, on the one hand, science will henceforward seek to justify religious faith. On the other hand, henceforward, faith 'must be justified':

> a theory must be made of it which must undoubtedly be founded upon the different sciences ... first of all, upon the social sciences, for religious faith has its origin in society; then

upon psychology, for society is a synthesis of human consciousnesses; and finally upon the sciences of nature, for man and society are a part of the universe and can be abstracted from it only artificially.[93]

Religion and science co-exist in a peaceable kingdom. Religion becomes secular, 'rational and laicized'. It renounces its 'right to dogmatize' about the nature of reality. It becomes a handmaiden to science, as an 'impetus to action', a theory 'destined to make men live and act'. This, the final function of religion, is itself increasingly assumed by a rapidly expanding state. The future of religion may be without end. But it is progressively restricted, kept in its place; and its place is continuously eroded by the inroads of science and government.

Durkheim draws unlikely parallels between science and religion, based on his sociological theory of knowledge. Religion is not 'ideology' but the bedrock of science itself. He also prefigures an unlikely relationship between science and religion. He envisions their eventual détente and even mutual support. But his most striking statements about science and religion are those which lift religion out of the realm of ideology; which, in fact, effectively obliterate the realm of ideology itself. Durkheim eviscerates the concept of ideology as untruth, renders its meaning as falsehood meaningless. If ideology is understood as the opposite of, as different from science and truth, then for Durkheim ideology does not exist. For, in the final analysis, he claims that the pre-eminent form of ideology, religion, is essentially *the same as* science.

Ultimately, Durkheim claims that 'there are only differences of degree between science and religion'.[94] Between 'the logic of religious thought and that of scientific thought' he believes that 'there is no abyss'. Science and religion are, finally, 'made up of the same elements'.[95] Religious beliefs rest on a specific experience, 'whose demonstrative value is, in one sense, not one bit inferior to that of scientific experiments, though different from them'.[96] Religion's objective is to translate reality into intelligible language, an intelligible language 'which does not differ in nature from that employed by science'. Science and religion are the same, in that 'the attempt is made by both to connect things with each other, to establish internal relations between them, to classify them and to systematize them'.[97]

What then is the difference between science and religion? How can they be distinguished? How is it determined that science has greater truth value than religion? The only difference is that while their respective elements are the same, they are 'inequally and differently developed' by science and by religion.[98] While 'the essential ideas of scientific logic are of religious origin' science 'gives them a new elaboration'. Nevertheless, these 'perfectionings of method' which distinguish science from religion 'are not enough to differentiate it from religion'. Both science and religion 'pursue the same end'. They are not opposed to one another, but merely at different ends of a continuum, the infinite continuum of knowledge. In the beginning 'there are no religions which are false'.[99] In the end: *scientific thought is only a more perfect form of religious thought*.[100]

THE HISTORY OF KNOWLEDGE:
THE PERFECTION OF THE SUBJECT/OBJECT/
RELATION

It is Durkheim's theory of material history, the progressive division of labor in society, which is generally considered to be the center of gravity in his oeuvre. Yet it is his theory of nonmaterial history which is arguably his own central focus. Certainly he thinks it important to provide a descriptive anatomy of the material basis of society, the collective body or social organism. But this is more a prerequisite than a preoccupation. *The Division of Labor*, his most materially oriented work, is largely a morphology, an elaboration of the two definitive social structures located at either end of an evolutionary continuum. But it is also, and equally, a study of the mental and moral transformation undergone by society as a result of the division of labor.

Durkheim is keenly interested in the transformation from mechanical solidarity and collective consciousness to organic solidarity and a hybrid individual/occupational/collective consciousness. In fact, he may be more interested in this than in the actual process of specialization occurring in the base economy, the material basis of solidarity and consciousness. And after the pro forma *Division of Labor*, he increasingly turns his attention to the psychic life of society, to the mental and moral life, not less real than the physical life of individuals or collectivities, but more complex, a higher stage of nature.[101] Sociology, he says, is essentially the study of public opinion. His own work, he says, is essentially the study of morality.

Against this background, his theory of knowledge assumes greater significance. The history of ideas and ideals is more important, to him, than the history of social organization. With society, as with individuals, it is the life of the mind that interests him. The psychology, not the physiology, of society, is paramount. The development of its supra-organic summit, over and above the development of its substrative base, is crucial. For Durkheim, the moral, ideal aspect of the social mind takes precedence over its mental, ideational aspect. But his chronicle of ethics lies at the surface of his work, in plain sight, while his epistemology remains more implicit.

The history of knowledge, like the history of its social foundation, is one of progress. Like a biological or social organism, knowledge changes over time in a movement of development and evolution. Knowledge continuously increases and improves; gradually, inexorably. The history of knowledge is a process of *enlightenment*. Enlightenment is a concept used by Durkheim in specific instances of *claircissement*. But it is a good summary concept for his theory of the history of knowledge. Enlightenment is education: the illumination and clarification of an object, the solving of a mystery, the growth and dissemination of truth. It is the slow but steady perfection of primally imperfect knowledge. And this more than anything else is the meaning of history for Durkheim: the perfection of knowledge over time. This overarching process of perfection actually encompasses several processes. According to Durkheim, knowledge moves closer and closer to omniscience as its three components move closer and closer to perfection. The *subject* of knowledge evolves to perfection. The *object* of knowledge evolves to perfection. And the *relation* between the subject and the object of knowledge evolves to perfection.

The subject of knowledge is, originally, the human/animal *individual subject*. It is simply capable of knowledge in its most inferior form: knowledge as perception or sensation, and therefore knowledge of the tangible appearance of apparently isolated physical objects. The amalgamation of a plurality of individual human animals into one collective social being marks the creation of human beings *qua* human beings, as well as THE quantum leap in the history of knowing. With the advent of human society, the collective consciousness emerges, and with it rational knowledge and its linguistic accoutrements.

Rational knowledge is conceptual, categorical, classificatory, connective, causal knowledge. It is *ideal* knowledge, knowledge which conceives the eternal laws of the universe, the eternal essence of things, and the eternal relations which unite them.

> Since the world expressed by the entire system of concepts is the one that society regards, society alone can furnish the most general notions with which it should be represented. Such an object can be embraced only by a subject which contains all the individual subjects within it. Since the universe does not exist except in so far as it is thought of, and since it is not completely thought of except by society, it takes a place in this latter; it becomes a part of society's interior life, while this is the totality, outside of which nothing exists.[102]

Concepts 'express the manner in which society represents things' and therefore 'conceptual thought is coeval with humanity itself'.[103] Collective representations may be 'crude in the beginning' but:

> with them the germ of *a new mentality* was given, *to which the individual could never have raised himself by his own efforts*: by them the way was opened to *a stable, impersonal and organized thought* which then had nothing to do except to *develop its nature*.[104]

The institution of society is inevitable, and therefore so is the revolutionary epistemological transformation effected by transformation of individual consciousnesses into a collective consciousness. It is inevitable that a *social subject* of knowledge is born of individual subjects, and replaces them.

Just as inevitable is the subsequent metamorphosis of the social subject: the evolutionary development of the social body, and the attendant evolutionary development of its mind. The society/subject can be more or less inclusive, more or less total, and therefore its knowledge can be more or less perfect. A small society is more particularized, less general, less encompassing than a large society, and therefore its knowledge reproduces some of the limitations of individual knowledge.

> In a small society, since everyone is clearly placed in the same
> conditions of existence, the collective environment is essen-
> tially concrete . . . The states of consciousness representing it
> then have the same character . . . they are related to precise
> objects . . . The collective impressions resulting from the
> fusion of all these individual impressions are then deter-
> mined in form as well as in object . . . the nearer the common
> conscience is to particular things, the more it bears their
> imprint, the more unintelligible it also is.[105]

Conversely, as society expands to include diverse things, environments and consciousnesses, it comprehends a generalized object,
a totalized object, and therefore comprehends the abstract, the
essential and the relational. The collective consciousness of a
small society has a 'defined' character.

> But it changes its nature as societies become more voluminous.
> Because these societies are spread over a vaster surface, the
> common conscience is itself obliged to rise above all local
> diversities . . . and consequently to become more abstract . . .
> The more differences among individual portraits serving to
> make a composite portrait, the more indecisive the latter is.[106]

Durkheim equates the tendency to abstraction, generality and
indecisiveness, which are concomitants of size and volume, with
the tendency on the part of civilization 'to become more rational
and more logical'. He can make this equation based on the
following argument.

> That alone is rational which is universal. What baffles the
> understanding is the particular and the concrete. Only the
> general is thought well . . . when civilization is developed over
> a vaster field of action, when it is applied to more people and
> things, general ideas necessarily appear and become pre-
> dominant there. The idea of man, for example, replaces . . .
> that of Roman, which, being more concrete, is more refractory
> to science.[107]

It is natural, and therefore unavoidable, that the primitive,
simple and undifferentiated social structure should become the
modern, complex and organic social structure. It is natural, and
thus unavoidable, that the religious collective consciousness
should become the scientific collective consciousness:

scientific thought is only a more perfect form of religious thought. Thus it only seems natural that the second should progressively retire before the first, as this becomes better fitted to perform the task.[108]

As primitive society is the collective subject of religious thought, modern society is, in a sense, the collective subject of scientific thought. In another sense, the subject of science is a modern, specialized, rational individual: the scientist. Most accurately, the subject of science is a specialized collective consciousness within the general collective consciousness.

Individual scientists are partial subjects with partial knowledge, and they must combine their subjectivities and knowledges to form an objective subject and objective knowledge:

> each scientist has, nonetheless, his own intellectual and moral individuality. Each sees the world – or better, a given part of the world – from his own perspective; but *all of these various points of view, far from being exclusive, mutually correct and complement one another.*[109]

The subject of science is a collective, complementary, cumulative subject. Similarly, sociology is a combination of specific, limited, partial sciences which each grasp only portions of a total reality. General sociology is a '*synthesis*' of 'particular' or 'special' sciences. The aggregation of 'specific and *mutually supplementary* works' is the means to reconstruct 'the nature of collective reality' in toto, in all of its complexity, in all of its diverse aspects.[110] Science and social science are collective enterprises, modelled on the ultimate collective subject, society.

Primitive and simple knowledge becomes modern and complex knowledge. Obscure social intuition, more like individual sensation than collective wisdom, is enlightened, and approaches pure rational truth. This process, the gradual effacement of religion by science, occurs within one society, as the growth and development of a specialized region within a particular, complex, social mind. However, there is a limit to the amount of truth which can be seen by a single subject, even a single collective subject. Even a collective subject is subjective, and subjectivity is antithetical to truth. Complete and perfect truth is only attainable by a complete and perfect subject. And a complete and perfect subject is not a specific social subject but a general *human subject.*

Rationality requires an interindividual, *transcendent* collective subject. Truth requires an intersocietal, *universal* collective subject. Society is universal and divine with respect to individuals. But above society, universal and transcendent and divine in relation to society, is humanity, the *perfect* subject. And Durkheim feels, in optimistic moments, that the march of progress is toward the further evolution of an incipient internationalization of societies and their sciences.

Attributing social origins to logical thought . . . is relating it to a cause which implies it naturally. *But this is not saying that the ideas elaborated in this way are at once adequate for their object.* If society is something universal in relation to the individual it is nonetheless an individuality itself, which has its own personal physiognomy and its idiosyncrasies; *it is a particular subject* and consequently particularizes whatever it thinks of. Therefore collective representations also contain subjective elements, and these must be progressively rooted out, *if we are to approach reality more closely* . . . logical thought tends to rid itself more and more of the subjective and personal elements [as] a social life of a new sort is developing . . . international life. As it extends, the collective horizon enlarges; the society ceases to appear as the only whole, to become part of a much vaster one . . . Consequently things can no longer be contained in the social moulds according to which they were primitively classified; *they must be organized according to principles which are their own,* so logical organization differentiates itself from the social organization and becomes autonomous. Really and truly *human thought* is not a primitive fact; it *is the product of history*; it is the ideal limit towards which we are constantly approaching, but which in all probability we shall never succeed in reaching.[111]

Like the subject of knowledge, the object of knowledge changes over time. It changes in a manner not unlike evolution. In fact its changes mirror the evolutionary process. The object of knowledge proceeds from the simple to the complex, following, as it were, the evolutionary sequence. Or, in another figure, the search for knowledge begins at the bottom of the hierarchy of nature, and moves to its apex. These two figures are interchangeable because Durkheim's familiar hierarchy of nature resembles the evolutionary chain, stood on its side, a perpendicular version of the linear model.

The hierarchy of nature, like the straight line of evolution, begins with simple, inanimate elements of matter. It proceeds to combinations of inanimate elements, culminating in animate phenomena. It moves upward, toward ever more complex combinations of inanimate/animate elements until it reaches the human individual. There it begins with the material substratum, and advances to the transcendent psychical product of that most complex and fortuitous combination of elements, the human mind. Science, established after a struggle in the lower spheres of nature – the spheres of 'material things' and 'matter' – is tolerated. But in the world of 'psychic life', in 'the world of souls', science is still regarded as a 'profanation'. Nevertheless, 'science will establish herself as mistress even in this reserved region'.[112] The human individual itself becomes an element of unprecedented complexity in the formation of the being at the crown of creation: the social being.

There is still reluctance to view society as an object of knowledge. 'As far as social facts are concerned, we still have the mentality of primitives.' But this is only because humans do not yet realize that 'societies are subject to natural laws and form a kingdom of nature'. They have 'not *yet* recognized the necessity of resorting to the laborious methods of the natural sciences to *gradually scatter the darkness*'.[113] Society itself is not an undifferentiated object of knowledge. Society's lower, physical side or substratum is the combination of individual bodies. Its higher, mental side arises out of this combination, as the consciousness of consciousnesses. Additionally, society is lower or higher on the scale of natural/evolutionary hierarchy, depending on its simplicity or complexity, on the nature and number of its constituent elements, and the manner of their combination.

Modern society is the most complex object which can be contemplated. Simultaneously it is the most sentient subject. With sociology, Durkheim sets the supreme subject to reflect on the supreme object, in a movement of nascent self-consciousness. Knowledge will be perfect when the pinnacle of nature, society, knows itself perfectly.[114] With one qualification. If the apogee of nature is not society but humanity, and the ultimate subject is not the social but the human subject, then even sociology can be eclipsed. Perfect knowledge is, in fact, the self-knowledge of humanity by humanity, the self-consciousness of humanity, the totalizing re/unification of the total subject and the total object, which are, after all, one and the same:

> each country represents, or at least may represent a special point of view toward mankind; these various ways of conceiving the same object, far from being antagonistic, call forth one another because of their differences. For they are only different perspectives on the same reality – a reality whose infinite complexity can be expressed only through an infinity of successive or simultaneous approximations . . . this supra-societal ideal is too rich in its variegated elements to be expressed and realized in its totality through the character of any one such state.[115]

The final dimension of the perfection of knowledge is the perfection of the relation between its subject and object. This is accomplished in two ways, by two separate mechanisms. Society knows itself and its world best through two means: through science and through the state. Science consists in the perfecting of rationality. It represents the institution of objectivity and the infusion of systematic method into the quest for truth. And of course science is destined to be born, to grow and to mature. Its domain is progressively extended, as is the sophistication of its technique. Science literally knows no bounds, neither as to the nature of the subject matter it explores nor the competence with which it searches for knowledge. Therefore, the truth which science can produce, or find, is unlimited. Science is capable of infinite perfection.

Unexpectedly, however, Durkheim designates the state, and not science, as the specialized organ of collective thought, as the 'brain' of society. The state is the clear, focused, illuminated and illuminating, reflective center of the collective consciousness. It is to the social mind what consciousness itself is to the individual mind. The form and content of its knowledge is as superior to the public opinion of the masses as conscious knowledge is to the murmurs of the unconscious. Like science, the state is on the ascendancy, replacing religion as the collective vehicle of thought, and replacing god as the symbol of society and object of collective worship. Like science, the state has an infinite capacity for ascertaining truth. Its procedures are progressively refined, as its empire over social life is progressively extended. Durkheim describes the state, 'the organ of social thought', in the following way. 'This is truly an organ of reflection: although still in a rudimentary stage, it has a future of progressive development.'[116]

If science can procure perfect knowledge in a speculative way, if it can undertake the pure pursuit of truth, the state can produce perfect knowledge toward practical ends. The collective consciousness is in fact bicentric, in deference to the exigencies of social life. Absolute truth is the ideal end of the perfection of knowledge, and it is to this end that science is dedicated. But in the interim, during the process of the enlightenment, the social subject, which is an actor as well as a knower, must act.

> Science is fragmentary and incomplete; it advances but slowly and is never finished; but life cannot wait. The theories which are destined to make men live and act are therefore obliged to pass science and complete it prematurely.[117]

It is to the enlightened action of the collective social subject that the modern state is dedicated. But while the state specializes in practical theory, even scientific theory can be used for practical ends.

> But if in some measure we are the product of things, we can, through science, use our understanding to control both the things that exert an influence upon us and this influence itself. In this way, we again become our masters. Thought is the liberator of the will.[118]

The means of enlightenment are science and the state. The ends of enlightenment are total knowledge, and total control. This is no 'less true of the moral world' than of the physical world.

Notes

INTRODUCTION

1 Paraphrase of Crane Britton's question, cited by Parsons (1949, p. 3).
2 Actually, it is more of an 'eternal return' within philosophy, and contains implicit ontological and philosophical assertions, however 'negative' they may be. See note 3, below.
3 For a discussion of the relations between pre-structuralism (structural functionalism); structuralism (critical, egalitarian, multi-cultural/ feminist/Marxist structuralism); and post-structuralism (deconstruction) see Lehmann (1993). See also Agger (1991). For a trenchant critique of Durkheimian structural functionalism, see Agger (1989).
4 See Lehmann op. cit. and Derrida (1988).
5 See Brantlinger (1990). Brantlinger is critical of both structuralism and deconstruction (his criticisms of Althusser are problematic − Althusser is much more Gramscian, for example, than Brantlinger allows), but he sees that both activities are forms of cultural studies. See also Agger (1992).
6 I am grateful to Roslyn Bologh for pointing out Durkheim's total neglect, in his thousands of pages of sociology, of the issue of sexuality. The dual social system he describes and advocates is predicated on heterosexuality (the ultimate form of sexual interdependence, 'integrating' not only the patriarchal family but also linking the private sphere of patriarchy to the public sphere of capitalism), and he takes it for granted. For an incisive feminist analysis of Weber, see Bologh (1990).
7 On Durkheim's theory of race, see also Fenton (1980, 1984), and Lehmann (Forthcoming).
8 Lehmann (1990, 1991, Forthcoming).
9 Lehmann (1993).

1 THE 'STRUCTURE' OF INDIVIDUALS

1 Durkheim's organicism is treated by Giddens (1971a); Lukes (1985); Nisbet (1952, 1965); Szacki (1979); Tiryakian (1978); Wallwork (1972); Zeitlin (1981); most often as a 'metaphor', analogy, or image. See Hirst (1973, 1975); Pearce (1989); Therborn (1976) for indirect recognition of Durkheim's organicism. Gane (1988) refers to Durkheim's 'evolutionism' as the foundation for his focus on social morphology and physiology; structure and function; normality and pathology, etc. Alpert (1939) denies Durkheim's organicism, as a variant of 'realism' (see below).

2 *Rules*, p. 142.

3 *Division*, p. 72.

4 *Rules*, p. 126.

5 *Ibid.*, pp. 144–5.

6 *Suicide*, p. 320.

7 See, for example, the discussions in *Professional Ethics and Civic Morals*, pp. 45–7; *Rules*, pp. 80–7; *Division*, pp. 174–93.

8 *Division*, p. 127.

9 The debate continues over whether Durkheim's theory is essentially synchronic and static, unable and unwilling to deal with social change. From a Marxist perspective, Bottomore (1981) critiques Durkheim's focus on order at the expense of change. Coser (1967) and Poggi (1972) point out Durkheim's relative inattention to social change from a Conflict Theory perspective. Bellah (1959); Giddens (1971a); Tiryakian (1978); and Wallwork (1972), for example, see Durkheim as a fundamentally 'historical' thinker. Pope (1973) claims that Parsons (1949) has misleadingly de-emphasized social change in Durkheim's theory. Giddens (1971b, 1976) argues against the sharp dichotomy and mutual exclusion of conflict and change theory (represented by Marx) on the one hand, and order and stability theory (represented by Durkheim) on the other. Durkheim's evolutionary model of social change has been touched on by Giddens (1971a); Lukes (1985); Nisbet (1965, 1975); and Pope (1973). Gane (1988) sees 'evolutionism' as central to Durkheim's thought; Fenton (1984) sees it as both incorrect and dispensable. Szacki (1979) notes that Durkheim focuses on species of societies, of which there are two. The argument of the present work is related to Szacki's position. There is a theory of social change in Durkheim's work, but it is so restricted as to exclude all forms of change except one: evolutionary differentiation; and all forms of society except two, which collapse into one: simple (undifferentiated) and complex (differentiated) versions of the same thing.

10 *Division*, pp. 71; 137; 174–7.

11 *Rules*, p. 103.

12 *Division*, p. 41.

13 *Ibid.*, pp. 190–2.

14 *Ibid.*, p. 181.

15 *Règles*, p. 12.

16 *Sociology and Philosophy*, p. 31.
17 'Sociology', pp. 360–1.
18 *Division*, p. 262.
19 *Ibid.*, pp. 337–8.
20 *Ibid.*, p. 270.
21 *Ibid.*, p. 350, note.
22 *Philosophy*, p. 24.
23 *Ibid.*, p. 30.
24 *Education*, pp. 60–1.
25 *Division*, pp. 276–7.
26 *Education*, p. 59.
27 'Sociology', p. 360.
28 *Suicide*, p. 320.
29 *Education*, p. 62.
30 *The Elementary Forms of the Religious Life*, p. 389.
31 *Education*, p. 62.
32 *Essays on Morals and Education*, p. 147.
33 *Ibid.*, p. 142.
34 The argument here is that Durkheim's organicism is *not* 'merely' a metaphor. The metaphor *is* the theory. This is true not only because, in general, metaphors operate as theories; but also because in this specific instance, Durkheim has a literalist conception of the social organism. Durkheim's notion of social 'structure' distances him from the problematic of structuralism, which is tendentially incompatible with even metaphorical organicism, and absolutely opposed to literal organicism. Durkheim's concretist, substantialist, view of the social body is similarly antithetical to structuralism. Therborn (1976) implicitly recognizes this aspect of Durkheim's thought. Alpert (1939) and Gane (1988) explicitly deny it.
35 There is no agreement on this fundamental point. Ritzer (1988, p. 83) says that Durkheim 'put to rest once and for all the group mind thesis'. Alpert (1939) denies the group mind thesis, as a Hegelian form of 'realism'. Conversely, Lukes (1985) says that Durkheim is a social realist, because he conceives of 'society' as a collective mind. Benoit-Smullyan (1948); Hirst (1975); and Therborn (1976) also see a collective mind in Durkheim's theory. Those who do acknowledge Durkheim's collective mind concept usually do so disparagingly; his supporters are prone to defend him by denying his ideas.
36 *Philosophy*, p. 59.
37 *Ibid.*, p. 91.
38 Durkheim, *Les Formes Elementaires de la Vie Religieuse*, p. 633.
39 *Philosophy*, p. 34.
40 'Sociology', p. 365.
41 *Philosophy*, p. 26.
42 *Forms*, p. 29.
43 'Duality', p. 335.
44 Bellah (1959) says, in opposition to the usage of '*conscience*' as conscience, and '*idéals*' as ideals or values, that 'the original

conception was broader than these terms suggest'. Lukes (1985) and Zeitlin (1981) state that *'conscience'* means both consciousness and conscience.

45 Both critics and supporters of Durkheim have imputed this identification of 'society' with ideas, norms, beliefs and values, collective representations, culture, etc. to him. They include Alexander (1986); Benoit-Smullyan (1948); Hirst (1975); Mestrovic (1988); Parsons (1949); Poggi (1973); Szacki (1979); Therborn (1976); Wallwork (1972); Zeitlin (1981).

46 *Philosophy*, p. 59.
47 *Ibid.*, p. 96.
48 *Suicide*, p. 302.
49 *Ibid.*, p. 312.
50 *Rules*, p. xli.
51 *Ibid.*, p. xliv, note.
52 *Ethics*, p. 69.
53 Durkheim, *Le Suicide*, p. 361.
54 *Forms*, p. 283.
55 *Ibid.*, p. 479.
56 *Ibid.*, p. 495.
57 *Rules*, p. 103, note.
58 *Forms*, p. 487.
59 *Philosophy*, pp. 96; 34, note.
60 *Suicide*, p. 312.
61 *Philosophy*, pp. 30–1.
62 *Rules*, p. lv.
63 *Forms*, pp. 254; 260.
64 'Dualism', p. 335.
65 *Philosophy*, p. 93.
66 *Ibid.*, p. 89.
67 *Education*, p. 123.
68 *Forms*, p. 260.
69 *Division*, p. 97.
70 *Philosophy*, p. 73.
71 *Forms*, pp. 238; 239, note; 408.
72 *Philosophy*, p. 93.
73 *Education*, p. 92.
74 'Sociology', p. 367.
75 *Education*, p. 92.
76 *Division*, p. 14.
77 *Suicide*, pp. 314–15.
78 The conclusion suggested by the present argument is that Durkheim is both (and therefore in a sense neither) a materialist and an idealist. The material social body (structure, morphology, milieu) conditions and determines the ideal, the social mind and its contents: like the individual mind and its contents, they are both dependent and relatively autonomous with respect to their material substratum. The social mind and collective representations in turn condition and determine individual minds and ideas. Individual

minds and ideas in turn produce material individual behavior. This analysis, as well as being faithful to the meaning of Durkheim's work, resolves the either/or problem by transcending it. The confusion engendered by an either/or question is indicated by Lukes' (1985) statement that the answer is 'inconclusive'. He understands this as a manifestation of Durkheim's indecisiveness over 'society' as *either* morphological structure *or* collective consciousness. Some try to periodize the issue, seeing the early Durkheim as more of a materialist and the later Durkheim as more of an idealist or as a voluntarist. See especially Alexander (1986) and Parsons (1949). Although Bellah (1959) mistakenly sees the early Durkheim as a simple materialist, he sees the later Durkheim as both or neither, due to the reciprocal relations and relative autonomy of ideas with respect to structure. Giddens (1971a) correctly understands that Durkheim is both an idealist and a materialist, that he sees the relation of the collective consciousness to its social structural base as comparable to the relation of the individual mind to the individual body. Giddens also correctly notes that Durkheim is not as far from Marx on the idealism/materialism issue as is commonly thought. Mestrovic (1988) believes that Durkheim transcends all such dichotomies. Hirst (1975); Pearce (1989); and Therborn (1976) see Durkheim as an idealist, because of his emphasis on collective consciousness/representations.

79 *Forms*, p. 260.
80 The issue of social realism or emergence in Durkheim's theory is rife with confusion, equivocation, and debate on the part of secondary interpreters. Those who claim or imply that Durkheim is a social realist include: Benoit-Smullyan (1948); Giddens (1971a); Hirst (1975); Nisbet (1952); Pearce (1989); Pope (1973); Szacki (1979); Therborn (1976); Tiryakian (1978); Wallwork (1972); Zeitlin (1981). Lukes (1985) relates the social realism issue to Durkheim's supposed ambiguity over whether the collective mind is immanent or independent of individuals. (This is a false opposition: Durkheim is clearly a social realist, but he also clearly takes the immanentist position.) He criticizes Durkheim's 'reification' of the abstraction 'society', by which is apparently meant his social realism. Alpert (1939); Bellah (1973); Fenton (1984); Gane (1988); and Parsons (1949) also equate social realism with the 'reification' or 'hypostatization' of an abstraction – society – but deny that Durkheim is guilty of it. Alpert (1939) identifies Durkheim with 'relational' or 'associational' realism, as opposed to either 'ontological' (organicist or Hegelian) realism or nominalism. (Relational realism sounds like, but is not, structuralism.) Mestrovic (1988) echoes the claim that Durkheim is neither a realist nor a nominalist, transcending the dichotomy. Nye and Ashworth (1971) contend that the nominalism/realism dilemma remains unresolved in Durkheim's writings and that he vacillates between the two positions rather than dialectically synthesizing them.
81 *Forms*, p. 471.

82 *Philosophy*, pp. 90–3.
83 Durkheim, *L'Education Morale*, p. 140.
84 *Education*, p. 89.
85 *Philosophy*, p. 52.
86 *Suicide*, p. 305.
87 *Ibid.*, p. 322.
88 *Rules*, pp. 103–4.
89 *Ibid.*, p. 106.
90 *Ibid.*, p. 123.
91 *Règles*, p. 122.
92 *Forms*, p. 29.
93 *Ibid.*, p. 237.
94 *Ibid.*, p. 493.
95 *Ibid.*, pp. 495–6.
96 *L'Education*, pp. 68–9.
97 *Ibid.*
98 *Ibid.*, p. 86.
99 *Ibid.*, pp. 100; 76; 101; 104; 119; 130.
100 *Suicide*, p. 310.
101 *Rules*, pp. xlix; 104.
102 *Education*, pp. 62; 65.
103 *Philosophy*, p. 26.
104 'Sociology', p. 363.
105 *Philosophie*, p. 42.
106 *Philosophy*, p. 37.
107 *Philosophie*, pp. 58–9.
108 *Philosophy*, pp. 51–2.
109 *Rules*, p. xlix, emphasis added.
110 *Forms*, p. 493, emphasis added.
111 *Ibid.*, p. 490, emphasis added. Others who contend or imply that Durkheim is a collective subjectivist include: Benoit-Smullyan (1948); Hirst (1973, 1975); Pearce (1989); Therborn (1976). Hirst's arguments are particularly compatible with the present work, as he also opposes collective subjectivism to structuralism, claiming that Durkheim has no concept of social structure. Gane (1983a, 1988) refutes this contention, equating subjectivism with ego, will, telos and unity, which he claims Durkheim does not impute to society. However, Gane recognizes Durkheim's treatment of society as 'body and soul'; 'collective consciousness and morphology'; an 'emergent individuality'; a 'unique intelligence'; a 'being' etc. Alpert (1939) similarly denies Durkheim's collective subjectivism (as 'realism'), while admitting that Durkheim views society as a distinct, independent, effective 'personality' or existence. Alpert inadvertently points out one reason for the neglect of Durkheim's collective subjectivism. Many commentators focus *either* on Durkheim's collective body ('organicist' realism; positivism, etc.) *or* his collective mind ('Hegelian' realism; idealism, etc.). Few put the two aspects of his ontology together as a collective subject. Lukes (1985) cites Durkheim's alleged ambivalence over whether

'society' means *either* collective representations *or* morphological structure.
112 *Rules*, p. 59.
113 *Division*, p. 286.
114 *Philosophy*, pp. 30–1.
115 *Ibid.*, pp. 24–5.
116 *Philosophie*, p. 100.
117 *Suicide*, p. 387.
118 *Rules*, p. 124.
119 *Forms*, p. 471.
120 *Suicide*, pp. 364–5.
121 *Ibid.*, p. 373.
122 *Ibid.*, p. 369.
123 On the centrality of the study of morality to Durkheim's sociological mission, see e.g. Giddens (1971a); LaCapra (1985); Lukes (1985); Poggi (1972); Tiryakian (1978); Wallwork (1972).
124 *Division*, p. 14.
125 *Ibid.*
126 *Ibid.*, p. 33.
127 *Ibid.*, pp. 432–5.
128 *Ibid.*, p. 239.
129 *Ibid.*, p. 409.
130 *Ibid.*, pp. 398–9.
131 *Ibid.*, pp. 408–9.
132 *Ibid.*, pp. 42–3.
133 *Rules*, p. 40.
134 *Ibid.*, p. 70.
135 *Ibid.*, pp. 60–1.
136 *Philosophy*, p. 38.
137 *Ibid.*, p. 60.
138 *Ibid.*, p. 61.
139 *Ibid.*, p. 66.
140 *Essays*, p. 34.
141 *Ibid.*, pp. 31–2.
142 *Ibid.*, p. 35.
143 *Ibid.*, pp. 35–41.
144 *Ibid.*, p. 75.
145 *Ibid.*, p. 84.
146 *Ibid.*, p. 131.
147 *Education*, p. 87.
148 *Ibid.*, pp. 113; 111.
149 *Division*, p. 366.
150 *Education*, p. 47.
151 *Rules*, p. 7.
152 *Philosophy*, p. 77.
153 *Suicide*, p. 315.
154 *Philosophy*, p. 77.
155 *Division*, p. 426.
156 *Suicide*, pp. 371–2.

157 Others who recognize Durkheim's 'social structure' as an 'expressive totality', in the Hegelian sense critiqued by Althusser, include: Besnard (1983); Filloux (1977); Hirst (1975); Lacroix (1981); and Pearce (1989). Gane (1988) refutes this contention.

2 THE SOCIAL DETERMINATION OF 'INDIVIDUALS'

1 This tends to be the view of Durkheim's critics, or the aspect of Durkheim's work which is viewed negatively. Durkheim's supporters tend to deny or minimize his social determinism. Durkheim is unpalatable as a social determinist, as social determinism is unpalatable (alternatively 'Marxist' *or* 'conservative'). Thus e.g. Alexander (1986) and Munch (1988) follow Parsons (1949) in finding voluntarism in Durkheim's writings, or in re-writing Durkheim's writings to bring out the voluntarism that he 'really' intended, despite what he wrote. (This practice is criticized, with Parsons clearly in mind, by Jones, 1977.) Parsons claims that Durkheim began as a materialist/determinist, positing a utilitarian/Marxian individual which instrumentally and mechanically adapts to a social environment. Then, he matured into a voluntarist, his true self, before lapsing ultimately into idealism. This interpretation is based on a notion of voluntarism as the determination of behavior by internalized norms and therefore by individual subjective states (normative 'self-control'). It also derives from an abstract emphasis on Durkheim's theory of autonomy and free consent as aspects of morality. Pope (1973) sees this perspective as a distortion of Durkheim's thought. Mestrovic (1988) adopts a view similar to Parsons' by describing Durkheim's theory as 'representationalism', and claiming that as such it transcends the dualistic alternatives, subjectivism/objectivism; individual voluntarism/social determinism, etc. Mestrovic's 'representationalism', like Parsons' 'voluntarism', is a form of idealist social determinism. Actually, Durkheim is consistently and unambiguously scientific and deterministic in his thinking, which revolves around social realism and social determinism. He is not a voluntarist, and he moves progressively further from the voluntarist position and 'action theory' throughout his work. Hirst (1973, 1975) and Pearce (1989) have contrasting positions on the significance and value of Durkheim's work, but both seem to acknowledge his social determinism.
2 *Division*, pp. 287; 131; 179; 279; 302; Durkheim, *De La Division du Travail Social*, p. 288; Durkheim, *Le Suicide*, pp. 221; 217.
3 *Formes*, pp. 7–8; *Division*, pp. 105; 134; 287–8; *Suicide*, p. 221; *Division*, p. 135; *La Division*, p. 205.
4 *Suicide*, p. 221.
5 *La Division*, p. 170.
6 *Suicide*, p. 221.
7 *Division*, p. 198.

8 *La Division*, pp. 288; 205; *Formes*, p. 8.
9 *Suicide*, p. 221; *Ethics*, p. 56.
10 *La Division*, p. 99.
11 *Ibid.*, p. 100; *Suicide*, p. 221.
12 *La Division*, p. 100.
13 *Division*, pp. 194; 202–3.
14 *Ibid.*, p. 404.
15 *La Division*, pp. 100, 155.
16 *Division*, pp. 130; 166, note.
17 *La Division*, p. 171, original emphasis.
18 Bellah (1959) and Giddens (1971a) note that Durkheim advances a conception of the individual in general, and individuality, individualism, even egoism, as social and historical in nature.
19 *Division*, pp. 279–80.
20 *Ibid.*, p. 131.
21 *Ibid.*, p. 226.
22 *Ibid.*, pp. 279–80.
23 *Rules*, pp. xlviii–ix.
24 *Education*, p. 119.
25 *Rules*, pp. lvi; 1; 3; 5; 90; 28; lviii. There is almost universal agreement among secondary interpreters that Durkheim renounced utilitarianism, egoism and methodological individualism. Nisbet (1965), who sees Durkheim as a conservative, says that his theory developed in dialectical opposition to atomism, reductionism, analytical individualism and utilitarianism. Durkheim's work thereby constitutes 'a massive attack upon the philosophical foundations of liberalism'. On the other hand, Giddens (1971a), sees Durkheim as a liberal, but understands his work (specifically *The Division of Labor*) as a polemic against utilitarian individualism as well as against traditionalism. Likewise, Tiryakian (1978) identifies Durkheim as a liberal, but sees in him an anti-psychological and anti-utilitarian understanding of social solidarity. Many supporters of Durkheim, however, attribute some form of 'individualism' (as opposed to social determinism and/or collectivism) to his work. Alexander (1986) and Parsons (1949) find both utilitarianism (the early works) and a putative individualism (the mature, 'voluntaristic' works) in Durkheim. Alexander speculates that one reason Durkheim's theory evolved into voluntarism was that he wanted to distance himself from the 'utilitarian' materialism and determinism of Marx. (Parsons et al. mistakenly conflate materialism and determinism; idealism and voluntarism.)
26 Durkheim, 'Cours de science sociale: leçon d'ouverture', p. 26.
27 'Cours', p. 26.
28 *Division*, p. 344.
29 *Rules*, p. liv, note.
30 *Ibid.*, p. 123.
31 *Forms*, pp. 236–7.
32 *Ibid.*, pp. 239, note; 239; 257; 461.
33 *Suicide*, p. 252.

34 *Ibid.*, p. 335.
35 *Rules*, p. 101.
36 *Education*, pp. 33; 110.
37 *Ibid.*, p. 118.
38 'Sociology', pp. 364–5.
39 *Division*, p. 197.
40 *Ethics*, p. 61.
41 *Division*, pp. 420; 427.
42 Discussion in *Education*, pp. 24–41.
43 *Socialism*, p. 202.
44 *Division*, p. 348.
45 'Sociology', p. 367.
46 *Division*, pp. 325; 342–4.
47 *Forms*, p. 83.
48 *Rules*, pp. 116–18.
49 'Prefaces', p. 348.
50 *Division*, pp. 348–9.
51 *Suicide*, p. 151, emphasis added.
52 Takla and Pope (1985) see force, and the conception of reality as a system of forces, as the core of Durkheim's theory.
53 *Suicide*, pp. 38–9; 51.
54 *Forms*, p. 495.
55 *Suicide*, p. 252.
56 *Division*, pp. 345–6.
57 'Cours', p. 26; *Rules*, p. 18.
58 'Cours', p. 43.
59 *Ibid.*, p. 30.
60 Wallwork (1972) recognizes Durkheim's theory of a natural hierarchy. He calls it 'emergent evolution'. Others refer to Durkheim's *Naturphilosophie*, naturalism, positivism, evolutionism, etc.
61 *Philosophy*, p. 33.
62 'Cours', p. 27.
63 *Division*, p. 349.
64 *Règles*, p. xiv.
65 *Rules*, p. 29.
66 *Ibid.*, pp. xxxix-xl.
67 *Ibid.*, pp. lvi-ii, note.
68 The following discussion is in *Education*, pp. 114–19, emphasis added.
69 *Rules*, p. lvi.
70 *Forms*, p. 260.
71 *Suicide*, pp. 309–10; 325, note.
72 *Rules*, p. 126.
73 'Cours', pp. 25–7.
74 *Ethics*, pp. 60; 91.
75 *Rules*, p. 141.
76 *Suicide*, p. 252.
77 *Ibid.*, p. 325, note.
78 *Ibid.*

79 *Philosophy*, p. 3.
80 *Rules*, p. lviii, emphasis added.
81 *Ibid.*, p. 5.
82 'Cours', p. 28, emphasis added.
83 This interpretation of Durkheim's internalization concept remains in contradistinction to that of Alexander (1986) and Parsons (1949) who see internalization as Durkheim's way of effectively dissolving society and the individual into each other, and effectively dissolving determinism into voluntarism. Hirst (1973, 1975) e.g. sees internalization as social determinism.
84 *Rules*, p. 102.
85 *Forms*, p. 240.
86 'Sociology', p. 369.
87 *Forms*, p. 240.
88 *Division*, p. 99.
89 'Dualism', p. 326.
90 *Leçons*, pp. 74; 109.
91 'Dualism', p. 325.
92 *Forms*, p. 282.
93 'Dualism', p. 326.
94 *Forms*, pp. 240; 408; 30.
95 'Dualism', p. 325.
96 *Rules*, pp. 101–2.
97 *Essays*, p. 79.
98 *Ibid.*, p. 127.
99 *Rules*, p. 6, emphasis added. Cf. Althusser, esp. 1971.
100 Coser (1967); Nisbet (1952); and Zeitlin (1981) identify the idea of the social constitution of the individual as a conservative element in Durkheim's thought. Hirst (1973, 1975) and Therborn (1976) both acknowledge Durkheim's theory of social constitution but find Durkheim conservative for other reasons. His theory of positive social determinism actually seems to anticipate more 'radical' work such as Althusser's and Foucault's versions of structuralism.
101 *Education*, p. 108.
102 Present references to the religious inspiration of aspects of Durkheim's thought focus on Judeo-Christian or specifically Christian imagery and ideas. This is because Durkheim's thought itself often seems to operate in the Christian philosophical domain. Filloux (1976), however, points out the significance of Durkheim's rabbinical heritage, and sees a relationship between the Judaic concept of god in terms of creativity, life, and goodness, and Durkheim's concept of society.
103 *Forms*, p. 243.
104 *Essays*, p. 31.
105 *Division*, pp. 345–6; 349.
106 *Essays*, pp. 54; 127.
107 *Education*, p. 68.
108 Durkheim, 'Pragmatism and Sociology', p. 429.

109 *Division*, pp. 338; 350.
110 Genesis 2:7.
111 *Essays*, pp. 127; 150.
112 *Rules*, p. 106.
113 *Ibid.*
114 *Forms*, p. 465.
115 *Essays*, p. 150.
116 *Rules*, p. 102.
117 'Dualism', p. 325; citation of Genesis 1:26.
118 *Suicide*, p. 323.
119 *Rules*, p. 107.
120 *Division*, p. 338.
121 *Ethics*, pp. 90; 60.
122 'Dualism', p. 328.
123 *Education*, p. 70.
124 *Ibid.*, p. 119, emphasis added.
125 Giddens (1971a) recognizes the body/soul duality as part of a series of dualities separating body, sensation, the personal, individual and egoistic from soul, concepts, morality, the impersonal, social, collective and altruistic. Lukes (1985) recognizes the body/soul split as a manifestation of Durkheim's penchant for dualism. Coser (1967) and Poggi (1972) see conservative implications in the opposition of the individual as body and bad as against society as spirit and good. Mestrovic (1988) relates Durkheim's body/soul dualism to Schopenhauer's will/idea dualism, and identifies the body, the insatiable and irrational will, and the 'id' with the 'egoistic' 'biological individual'; ideas or 'representations' with society. Through the individual internalization of collective representations, the society/individual duality is transcended and the social psychological approach of Durkheim reflects this unified subject/object. Again, representationalism appears not to transcend dualisms, but to stand for an idealist form of social determinism. Further, the obvious parallel between Durkheim and Freud is more likely to be the result of Freud's influence on Durkheim (who knew German and studied in Germany) than the influence of *Durkheim* on *Freud,* as Mestrovic claims.
126 *Division*, pp. 135; 166, note; 198.
127 'Dualism', pp. 337–8.
128 *Ibid.*, p. 334.
129 *Philosophy*, p. 73.
130 *Division*, p. 350, emphasis added.
131 *Education*, p. 92, emphasis added.
132 *Essays*, p. 127, emphasis added.
133 *Forms*, pp. 298; 388.
134 *Ibid.*, p. 306.
135 'Dualism', pp. 337–8.
136 Durkheim says that there are two classes of consciousness: social representations which are conceptual, and individual representations, which express the organism (*Forms*, pp. 298; 388; 'Dualism', p. 337).

137 *Suicide*, p. 212.
138 *Forms*, p. 297.
139 *Ibid.*, pp. 283; 298–9; 305.
140 Those who view Durkheim as a conservative tend to compare his theory to Hegel's; those who view him as a liberal tend to contrast the two. Nisbet (1952), as an example of the former position, places Durkheim's thought in the tradition of German Romanticism. Giddens (1971a), exemplifying the latter position, dissociates Durkheim from German Romanticism in general and Hegel in particular. He compares Durkheim instead to Marx, and sees them both as aiming to transcend German Romanticism as well as utilitarian individualism. Knapp (1986) writes about the Hegelian origins common to Marx, Durkheim and Weber.

3 THE 'INDIVIDUALISM' OF DURKHEIM

1 Some recent commentators have acknowledged or emphasized Durkheim's 'individualistic' tendencies. They include: Benton (1977); Fenton (1984); Gane (1988); Mestrovic (1988); Pearce (1989). However, much of this analysis involves interpreting the interaction of biological and social determinism, and/or ideational, internal, normative self-control as individual autonomy, freedom, and voluntarism; and/or interpreting Durkheim's concepts ('the cult of the individual', 'personality', 'enlightened assent', 'moral autonomy', 'the dualism of human nature', social determinism as freedom from physical determinism, etc.) as representing actual or ideal individualism. These interpretations are problematic (see below, 'Recuperation'). Hirst (1973, 1975) provides a brilliant analysis of Durkheim's 'individualism' as the corollary of his essentialist conception of society as unified, given and necessary. Contradictions, problems, deviance, etc. must be external to society; hence, the necessity of a humanist, asocial, extra-social individual. Fenton (1984) notes ambiguities in Durkheim's 'unique' conception of individualism, especially concerning anomie and egoism as biological; 'enlightened assent' as individual autonomy; and social restraint as freedom.
2 *Rules*, p. 8.
3 *Forms*, pp. 305–6. The parallel between this conception of individuality and the monad is not lost on Durkheim; he explicitly cites the Liebnizian model.
4 *Division*, p. 302.
5 *Ibid.*, p. 131.
6 *Ibid.*
7 *Ibid.*, p. 137.
8 *Ibid.*, pp. 302–3.
9 *Ibid.*, p. 303.
10 *Ibid.*, pp. 299; 430.
11 *Ibid.*, pp. 131; 329–30.

12 *Ibid.*, pp. 105–6.
13 *Ibid.*, pp. 99–100.
14 *Ibid.*, p. 310.
15 *Ibid.*, pp. 131; 79.
16 *Ibid.*, pp. 167–8.
17 *Ibid.*, pp. 171–2.
18 *Ibid.*, pp. 172–3.
19 *Ibid.*, p. 424.
20 Durkheim, 'Individualism and the Intellectuals', p. 26, emphasis added.
21 *Divison*, pp. 305; 320–1.
22 *Ibid.*, p. 167.
23 *Ibid.*, pp. 403–4.
24 *Ibid.*, pp. 299; 131; 220.
25 *Ibid.*, pp. 429; 197–8; 347; 403–4.
26 *Ibid.*, pp. 297–300.
27 *Rules*, p. 94.
28 *Ethics*, p. 61.
29 'Prefaces', p. 532.
30 *Division*, pp. 130–1; 179; 194.
31 *Ibid.*, pp. 153; 167–8; 228–9; 283–4; 299; 347; 'Prefaces', p. 533.
32 *Division*, p. 131; 403; *Forms*, p. 471.
33 *Ethics*, pp. 56–7.
34 *Division*, p. 130; 'Prefaces', p. 533; 'Individualism', p. 26; *Suicide*, p. 319; *Division*, pp. 403; 179; emphasis added.
35 Gane (1983a) imaginatively probes Durkheim's implication that various groups have differential relations to 'society' (morality, norms, etc.). Fenton (1984) claims that, for Durkheim, internalization and conformity are not automatic; thus egoism, anomie, crime and deviance are 'normal'. Giddens (1971c) emphasizes that Durkheim doesn't account for individual non-adherence to norms, varying individual degrees of attachment to norms, or varying individual interpretations of norms; nor for the social causation of such phenomena as conflicts of interest. Hirst (1973, 1975) notes that the normal/pathological distinction tends to individualize and de-socialize the pathological. Lukes (1985) takes issue with the fact that Durkheim explains egoism and anomie, for example, as an absence of society, a lack of social goals and rules, rather than as the realization of egoistic, anomic social goals and rules. Poggi (1972) points out the fact that since Durkheim equates or conflates the normative and the social, he is led to consider the non-normative as non-social or anti-social in nature. Zeitlin (1981), on the other hand, stresses that Durkheim does put forward a theory of crime and deviance as social, socially caused, and normal. Durkheim has two theories of deviance which are not mutually exclusive: (1) it is individual (biologically determined); (2) it is social (socially determined). The second theory is articulated in Durkheim's discussions of suicide and sexual anomie.
36 *Suicide*, pp. 373; 281; 214–15; 209.

37 There is a vast amount of secondary writing and argumentation on the meaning of anomie. This is somewhat inexplicable, given the extraordinary simplicity and clarity with which Durkheim explains the concept. It actually has two usages in Durkheim's work, corresponding respectively to a general and a specific meaning. The first is the general meaning, the meaning given prominence in *The Division of Labor*. Here, anomie is the temporary lack of rules, patterns and habits to regulate and harmonize the new organs and functions of society and their interrelations. The second, specific meaning is that found in *Suicide, Socialism and Saint-Simon, Professional Ethics* and *Civic Morals*, etc. Here, anomie represents the absence of a particular type of rules, those which set limits on individual aspirations; notably, stratified limits on material aspirations, as well as monogamous limits on sexual aspirations.

38 *Suicide*, p. 258.

39 *Socialism*, pp. 119; 204.

40 Despite their common foundation, an absence of society; and their frequently common occurrence, in periods or spheres characterized by social absence, egoism and anomie are distinct concepts: Durkheim makes this distinction explicitly and patently and unambiguously clear, and his whole theoretical edifice supports two distinct conceptual dualities: anomie/regulation and alienation/integration. Nonetheless, Parsons (1949) confuses and conflates the two, as do those who speak in terms of Durkheim's 'one cause of suicide'. Giddens (1971a) and Lukes (1985) recognize the distinction, and Parsons' error.

41 *Suicide*, pp. 382; 288; 389; 258.

42 *Rules*, p. 97.

43 *Suicide*, p. 308.

44 *Rules*, p. lv.

45 *Division*, p. 305.

46 *Forms*, pp. 239; 239, note.

47 *Rules*, pp. 69; xxxviii; 71.

48 *Division*, pp. 429; 73–4; 79; 106.

49 *Suicide*, p. 319.

50 'Prefaces', pp. 532–3.

51 *Ethics*, p. 61.

52 *Forms*, p. 30.

53 *Education*, p. 42.

54 *Division*, p. 380.

55 'Sociology', pp. 365; 368.

56 Hirst (1973, 1975) stresses this line of thinking in Durkheim's work; while it is antithetical to the interpretation of Alexander (1986) and Parsons (1949). According to them, Durkheim's early work is 'positivist', materialist, and determinist; his final work is idealist; and in his prime he is a voluntarist. In none of these alleged phases does socialization appear as problematic. Socialization supposedly is not part of his early, materialist, determinist, 'utilitarian' phase. And in his voluntarist period, socialization is perfect, simple, and

untroubled, uniting individual and society in the intercourse of internalization, making one of two.

57 *Division*, p. 28.
58 *Suicide*, pp. 373–4.
59 'Cours', p. 48.
60 *Forms*, p. 240.
61 *Education*, p. 108, emphasis added.
62 *Ethics*, p. 56.
63 *Division*, pp. 386–7.
64 *Philosophy*, p. 56.
65 *Suicide*, p. 336.
66 *Division*, pp. 297–302.
67 *Ibid.*, pp. 283–4.
68 *Ibid.*, pp. 287; 321; 283; 404.
69 *Ibid.*, p. 400.
70 *Ethics*, p. 63.
71 *Suicide*, p. 159
72 The argument here is that Durkheim's 'individualism' and 'voluntarism' can best be understood as biological, and especially social, determinism. The reverse is argued by Alexander (1986); Parsons (1949); Mestrovic (1988) and Munch (1988) who, in Habermasian fashion, would conflate Durkheim and Weber, and superimpose voluntarism and consensus over determinism and coercion in theory and reality.
73 Giddens (1971a); Mestrovic (1988) and Zeitlin (1981) e.g. focus on this theme in Durkheim's work. Zeitlin notes the conservative import of the social bargain in which the individual submits to society in exchange for the benefits of civilization, and in which freedom is equated with self-mastery and duty; happiness is equated with regulation and limitation.
74 *Philosophy*, p. 56.
75 *Division*, pp. 386–7.
76 *Philosophy*, pp. 72–3.
77 *Education*, pp. 54; 124.
78 *Essays*, p. 153.
79 *Education*, p. 124.
80 *Ibid.*, p. 51.
81 *Ibid.*, p. 54.
82 *Suicide*, p. 127.
83 *Philosophy*, p. 3.
84 *Rules*, p. 123.
85 *Essays*, p. 133.
86 *Philosophy*, pp. 74; 3.
87 *Ethics*, p. 91.
88 *Education*, pp. 115–18.
89 *Ibid.*, pp. 118–20.
90 *Ibid.*, p. 125.
91 Alexander (1986) follows Parsons (1949) in singling out this third element of morality, misinterpreting it as voluntaristic, and

mistaking it for Durkheim's entire theory of morality. Moral autonomy is not the same as voluntarism, but merely a form of determinism in which the determinism is understood and accepted. Tiryakian (1978) identifies Durkheim's notion of individual autonomy and enlightened consent as Kantian. According to Fenton (1984, 230–1), 'there is . . . a conception of liberty and individualism in Durkheim's work which is quite at variance with common understandings', especially in relation to the concept of 'enlightened assent' as 'individual autonomy'.

92 *Education*, p. 120.
93 'Individualism', p. 24.
94 *Ethics*, p. 91.
95 *Philosophy*, p. 56.
96 *Forms*, p. 306.
97 *Essays*, p. 153.
98 *Education*, p. 73.
99 *Ibid.*, p. 118.
100 *Ibid.*, p. 73.
101 *Forms*, p. 30.
102 *Ethics*, p. 60.
103 *Philosophy*, p. 56.
104 *Education*, p. 69.
105 *Ethics*, p. 90.
106 *Education*, pp. 108; 119.
107 *Essays*, p. 150.
108 *Forms*, p. 306.
109 *Ibid.*, pp. 307–8, emphasis added.
110 *Philosophy*, p. 59.
111 'Individualism', p. 28, footnote, emphasis added.
112 *Suicide*, p. 337.
113 'Individualism', p. 24.
114 *Forms*, p. 472.

4 IDEOLOGY AND TRUTH: INDIVIDUAL AND COLLECTIVE KNOWLEDGE

1 Durkheim's *dominant* epistemological tendencies are extrapolated here. The complexity and/or contradiction in his epistemology is explored below, in the discussion of his theory/theories of the relation/s between perceptions and concepts.
2 Relationality is only one tendency in Durkheim's thought. Substantialism is another (see above, Chapter 1). He might better be called a social psychological realist, as he argues, in effect, for the real existence of a social mind and socially produced ideas as opposed to the real existence of social relations and structures. Therborn (1976) rightfully points out Durkheim's idealist (social) psychologism; or, in Hirst's terms, 'mentalism'.
3 *Classification*, p. 87.

4 Within his own discussions, Durkheim fails to adequately separate epistemology from ontology, society as subject of thought from social thought as object of knowledge.

5 *Forms*, p. 28.

6 *Division*, pp. 348–9.

7 *Philosophy*, p. 33.

8 *Forms*, pp. 31–2, note.

9 *Ibid.*, p. 27.

10 Durkheim and Mauss, *Primitive Classification*, pp. 4; 7.

11 *Ibid.*, p. 8.

12 There is wide agreement on Durkheim's rationalism. See: Bellah (1959); Coser (1971); Giddens (1971a); LaCapra (1985); Lukes (1985); Richter (1960); Tiryakian (1978). The sociological nature of Durkheim's theory of knowledge is also widely recognized. See e.g.: Benoit-Smullyan (1948), Fenton (1984), Hamnett (1984), Hirst (1975), Mestrovic (1988). On his sociological rationalism see especially Tiryakian. Alpert (1939) cites Durkheim's 'relational realism'. Benoit-Smullyan describes Durkheim's synthesis of 'positivism' (scientism) and 'agelicism' (social realism) into 'sociologism' and 'scientific rationalism'. Nisbet (1965) argues that Durkheim's methodology is a rationalist form with an anti-rationalist content. Recent commentators have pointed out Durkheim's self-contradiction, between explicit rationalism and apparent empiricism (i.e. his admonitions to examine 'things themselves'). Benton (1977) sees 'realism' (objectivist, relational rationalism and theoretical constructivism) as well as 'positivism' (empiricism) in Durkheim's work. Hirst opposes his own 'rationalism' (theoretical constructivism) to Durkheim's 'anti-theoretical realism' (empirical positivism) and 'essentialism'. Keat and Urry (1975) oppose their own 'realism' (materialist, objectivist rationalism) to Durkheim's 'positivism' (empiricism), and critique his apparent realism as essentialist, but point to his anti-reductionism as an anti-positivist tendency. Pearce (1989) approves of Durkheim's 'scientific rationalism', 'realist' and representationalist tendencies, and epistemological critiques; but objects to his empiricist, positivist, essentialist, and metaphysical tendencies. Some claim that Durkheim synthesizes empiricism and rationalism (as well as materialism and idealism; objectivism and subjectivism, etc.) into 'scientific rationalism' (Gane 1988), 'voluntarism' (Munch 1988), or 'representationalism' and 'empirical' or 'renovated' 'rationalism' (Mestrovic). Mestrovic and Willer (1968) deny Durkheim's crude empiricism, claiming that he recognizes a theoretical/conceptual as well as an empirical dimension of reality and knowledge.

13 *Forms*, pp. 27–8.

14 *Ibid.*, p. 27. One of the most important controversies surrounding Durkheim is the issue of periodization: whether his work is unified, forming a consistent whole; or whether it is divided, forming distinct theoretical stages. The debate over the continuity or discontinuity of Durkheim's thought was brought to prominence by

Parsons' (1949) four-stage thesis, and often centers on the relation of the later *Forms* to the rest of Durkheim's writings. Parsons argues that Durkheim's thought constitutes two separate structures, or syntheses, which are internally unified and consistent, but which are opposed to one another and demarcated from one another by a 'radical break'. Durkheim's early theoretical synthesis, positivism, is replaced by a second theoretical synthesis, voluntarism, in *Forms*. Alexander (1986) largely accepts this formulation. Besnard (1982) sees evidence of a rupture in Durkheim's work circa the concept anomie, related to conditions in Durkheim's life. Coser (1971) and Poggi (1972) see evidence of a transformation from materialism to idealism. The argument of the present work is that Durkheim's work constitutes a single unified structure, but that it is a structure characterized by contradictions, tendencies, and countertendencies. There are divisions in Durkheim's work, but they run throughout its extent, and are neither chronological nor textual divisions. Hirst (1975) takes this position. The present work examines Durkheim's writings as a corpus in contradiction, and not period-by-period or text-by-text. The reason for the inordinate emphasis on *Forms* in this section is simply that Durkheim focuses inordinately on epistemology in that text. Most commentators agree that there is a basic continuity in Durkheim's work, that it is consistent over time, albeit with changes in focus or emphasis. They include Alpert (1939); Benoit-Smullyan (1948); Coser (1967) (implicitly); Fenton (1984); Gane (1988); Giddens (1970, 1971a); LaCapra (1985); Mestrovic (1988); Munch (1988); Nisbet (1965); Pope (1973); Therborn (1976); Tiryakian (1978). Others are more equivocal, citing 'shifts' or 'developments' over time in Durkheim's work. They include Bellah (1959); Lukes (1985); and Wallwork (1972). Fenton, Gane and Wityak and Wallace (1981) do see a break in Durkheim's view of primitive thought (see below, note 78, and Chapter 5).

15 *Forms*, p. 482.
16 'Dualism', p. 327.
17 *Forms*, p. 26.
18 *Ibid.*, p. 28.
19 *Forms*, p. 482; 'Dualism', p. 327. The body functions as 'an individualizing factor' (*Forms*, p. 305).
20 *Forms*, p. 29.
21 *Ibid.*, p. 23, note.
22 *Ibid.*, pp. 26, emphasis added; 411; 485.
23 *Ibid.*, pp. 487–9; 494.
24 'Dualism', p. 338.
25 *Ibid.*, pp. 327–9.
26 'Pragmatism', p. 430.
27 *Forms*, p. 26.
28 'Dualism', p. 329.
29 *Forms*, p. 28.
30 *Ibid.*, p. 481.
31 'Dualism', pp. 327; 337.

32 *Forms*, pp. 22–3.
33 *Ibid.*, p. 171.
34 *Ibid.*, pp. 411–12.
35 *Ibid.*, p. 23.
36 *Ibid.*, p. 259.
37 *Ibid.*, p. 469.
38 *Ibid.*, p. 270.
39 *Ibid.*, p. 465.
40 *Philosophy*, p. 95. The seemingly more appropriate translation of 'ideaux', 'ideas', is used here, rather than the overly narrow translation used in the text, 'ideals'.
41 *Forms*, p. 270.
42 *Ibid.*, p. 412.
43 *Ibid.*, p. 410.
44 This formulation certainly recalls some of the themes of post-structuralism and the whole irrationalist tradition.
45 *Forms*, p. 270.
46 *Ibid.*, p. 31.
47 Additionally, thought is social because society *imposes* thought. Thought is social on the one hand because it originates in society, and on the other hand because it is common to society's individual members: the two features are related. Because the collective consciousness creates thought, thought is inevitably uniform. The thought of individuals is first created by society as a whole, and then necessarily and forcibly penetrates and constitutes their consciousnesses. Since individuals do not create thought, they therefore necessarily receive it from without, from society. And since thought is a social fact, it therefore automatically has the power of social forces, the power of obligation. Others also point out Durkheim's focus on society as an imposer, endorser, or authority, instead of (Worsely, 1956) or in addition to (Benoit-Smullyan, 1948) society's role as subject, origin, creator, producer of thought.
48 *Forms* pp. 493; 490; 495; 479; 482; 492.
49 *Ibid.*, pp. 485; 494; 'Dualism', p. 327.
50 *Forms*, p. 269.
51 *Ibid.*, pp. 28; 492–3.
52 *Ibid.*, pp. 480; 492–3; 494.
53 'Pragmatism', p. 430.
54 'Dualism', p. 338.
55 *Forms*, pp. 26; 27; 480; 487.
56 *Ibid.*, pp. 482–7.
57 *Ibid.*, pp. 482; 484.
58 *Ibid.*, p. 26.
59 'Dualism', p. 338.
60 *Forms*, pp. 487; 482; 488.
61 *Ibid.*, pp. 22; 32; 172.
62 *Ibid.*, pp. 406; 411.
63 *Ibid.*, pp. 28; 483.
64 *Ibid.*, p. 29.

65 *Ibid.*, p. 482.
66 'Dualism', p. 327.
67 *Philosophy*, p. 96.
68 *Forms*, pp. 481–2.
69 *Ibid.*, p. 486.
70 'Dualism', p. 94.
71 *Forms*, p. 482.
72 *Ibid.*, pp. 32; 32, note; 172.
73 *Ibid.*, pp. 22; 492, emphasis added.
74 'Dualism', p. 327.
75 *Philosophy*, p. 96.
76 *Forms*, p. 482.
77 The 'mental states of society' also include sentiments, moods and emotions. In fact, these affective states of mind can influence the formation of categories: 'It is thus states of the collective mind which give birth to these groupings, and these states moreover are manifestly affective. There are sentimental affinities between things as between individuals, and they are classed according to these affinities . . . things change their nature because they affect the sentiments of groups differently' (*Classification*, 85–6).
78 Durkheim substantiates his understanding of rational thought as social thought in several ways. For example, religion, the 'eminently collective' phenomenon, the 'eminently social' fact, is seen as the primal source of all non-empirical thought: concepts and categories, logic and reason, philosophy and science. Philosophy and the sciences were 'born of religion'. Religion functioned as the original medium of ultra-sensory knowledge, predating and precursing philosophy and science. As such, religion contributed 'to forming the intellect itself'. The 'form' as well as the substance of human knowledge can be traced to it; notably, the 'essential ideas' and 'categories of the understanding'. Since religion is 'eminently social' and religious representations are collective representations, the categories, which 'are of religious origin' are also, necessarily, 'social affairs and the product of collective thought' (*Forms*, 21–2). Religion 'opened up the way' for science and philosophy by supplanting the individual, empirical ways of knowing. It was able to do so precisely because it is 'a social affair' (*Forms*, 270). The fact that religious thought is both conceptual and primitive leads Durkheim to re-define primitive thought as conceptual in *Primitive Classification* and *Forms* according to Fenton (1980, 1984); Gane (1983a, 1983b, 1988); Wityak and Wallace (1981). Conversely, Worsely (1956) sees Durkheim identifying primitive religious thought as anti-scientific, and Hamnett (1984) sees Durkheim's view of religion and science as social relativizing both.
79 *Forms*, p. 490, emphasis added.
80 *Ibid.*, pp. 482–8.
81 *Ibid.*, p. 490.
82 *Division*, p. 287.
83 'Pragmatism', p. 430.

84 *Forms*, p. 492.
85 *Ibid.*, p. 26.
86 *Ibid.*, pp. 489–90.
87 *Ibid.*, p. 481.
88 *Ibid.*, p. 172.
89 *Ibid.*, pp. 487–8.
90 *Ibid.*, p. 492.
91 *Ibid.*, p. 491, emphasis added.
92 *Ibid.*, pp. 489; 172, emphasis added.
93 *Ibid.*, p. 22.
94 *Ibid.*, p. 26.
95 *Ibid.*, pp. 28–9.
96 *Ibid.*, p. 470.
97 *Ibid.*, p. 488.
98 Again, in pursuing the implications of Durkheim's relationalism, I am confining myself to one of two conflicting tendencies in his thought. His relationalism is more pronounced in his epistemology; while his substantialism is more pronounced in his ontology.
99 *Forms*, pp. 483–4.
100 *Philosophy*, p. 96.
101 *Forms*, p. 485.
102 'Conceiving something is both learning its essential elements better and also locating it in its place.' (*Ibid.*, p. 484.)
103 *Ibid.*, pp. 30–1; note, 32.
104 *Rules*, pp. 18–19.
105 *Forms*, p. 41, emphasis added.
106 *Ibid.*, pp. 269–70.
107 *Ibid.*, p. 270.
108 *Ibid.*
109 *Ibid.*, p. 407.
110 *Rules*, p. xliv.
111 *Suicide*, p. 311.
112 *Rules*, pp. xlvi; xliv.
113 *Suicide*, pp. 311–12.
114 *Forms*, pp. 491–3.
115 *Ibid.*, p. 488.
116 *Ibid.*, p. 31.
117 *Essays*, p. 88.
118 *Ibid.*, p. 54, emphasis added.
119 *Forms*, p. 27, emphasis added.
120 *Rules*, pp. 14; 31.
121 *Ibid.*, pp. 14–15.
122 *Ibid.*, p. 14.
123 *Ibid.*, p. 17.
124 *Ibid.*, p. 32.
125 *Ibid.*, p. 33.
126 *Ibid.*, p. 34.
127 *Ibid.*, p. 33.
128 *Forms*, pp. 484–5.

129 *Ibid.*, pp. 492–3.
130 *Philosophy*, p. 96.
131 *Rules*, p. xliv.
132 'Dualism', p. 329.
133 *Forms*, p. 490.
134 *Ibid.*, p. 465.
135 *Ibid.*, p. 484.
136 'Dualism', p. 329.
137 *Forms*, pp. 30–1.
138 *Ibid.*, pp. 488–9.
139 *Ibid.*, pp. 480; 487.
140 'Dualism', p. 338.
141 *Forms*, p. 26.
142 *Ibid.*, p. 484.
143 'Pragmatism', p. 430.
144 *Forms*, p. 27.
145 *Rules*, p. 33; *Philosophy*, pp. 67–73.
146 *Division*, pp. 290–1.
147 'Prefaces', p. 347.
148 *Socialism*, p. 9.
149 *Forms*, p. 494.
150 *Rules*, p. xliv.
151 *Forms*, p. 465.
152 *Philosophy*, p. 75.
153 *Forms*, p. 486.
154 *Ibid.*, p. 465.
155 *Education*, pp. 22; 116.
156 *Essays*, p. 88.
157 *Rules*, p. xliv.
158 *Ibid.*, p. 44.
159 *Forms*, p. 465.
160 There are clear parallels between certain tendencies in Durkheim's theory of knowledge and ideology, and Althusser's epistemology. On the other hand, there are clear contradictions. Strawbridge (1982) e.g. provides a preliminary exploration of this subject. Hirst (1975) implicitly compares Durkheim's and Althusser's identification of ideology with spontaneous humanism, voluntarism, idealism, individual subjective experience, and the misrecognition of the social; and acknowledges Durkheim's non-Althusserian identification of rationality and truth with the social subject. Hirst and Benton (1977) approve of Durkheim's distinction between science and ideology, as well as his conceptualization of the latter; but find that he lapses into ideology himself.
161 *Forms*, p. 490.
162 On Durkheim's sociological theory of language, see Gane (1983a).
163 *Rules*, p. xlix.
164 *Ibid.*, p. 1.
165 *Forms*, p. 484.
166 'Pragmatism', p. 430.

167 *Forms*, p. 29.
168 *Philosophy*, pp. 67–73.
169 'Prefaces', p. 347.
170 *Forms*, p. 483.
171 *Ibid.*, p. 484.
172 *Ibid.*, p. 489.
173 *Ibid.*
174 *Ibid.*, pp. 493–4.
175 *Forms*, pp. 495–6.
176 *Ibid.*, p. 483.
177 Zeitlin (1981), for example, criticizes Durkheim's neglect of individual motives, as others, e.g. Lukes (1985) criticize his general neglect of individual psychology; while Pope (1973) defends this practice in terms of Durkheim's theoretical anti-individualism and anti-psychologism, and the impossibility of ascertaining individual motives. Fenton (1984) sees parallels between Durkheim's and Marx's conception of thought as social, and individuals as incapable of perceiving social structural causation. Durkheim himself discusses the deceptive nature of individual motives, the fact that they are tendentially different from and even contrary to genuine causes, and even genuine individual motives.
178 *Rules*, p. xilv.
179 *Ibid.*, p. xlv.
180 *Forms*, p. 297.
181 *Suicide*, p. 43.
182 *Philosophy*, pp. 20–2.
183 *Forms*, p. 407.
184 *Ibid.*, pp. 411–12.
185 *Ibid.*, p. 491, emphasis added.
186 *Rules*, p. xliv, emphasis added.
187 *Ibid.*, p. xlvi.
188 *Ibid.*, p. liii, emphasis added.
189 *Suicide*, pp. 311–12, emphasis added.
190 *Ibid.*, p. 151.
191 *Philosophy*, p. 79.
192 *Forms*, p. 483.
193 *Ibid.*, pp. 492–3.
194 *Ibid.*, p. 484, emphasis added.
195 *Ibid.*, p. 485.
196 *Ibid.*, pp. 31–2.
197 *Ibid.*, pp. 492–3, emphasis added.
198 *Ibid.*, p. 490, emphasis added.
199 'Pragmatism', p. 430.
200 *Ibid.*, p. 433.
201 *Ibid*, p. 434.

5 COLLECTIVE IDEOLOGY

1 On Durkheim's sociological theory of knowledge see e.g. Lukes (1985) and Tiryakian (1978). Mestrovic (1988) calls Durkheim's sociological theory of knowledge 'representationalism': collective representations are both the means and the object of knowledge.
2 *Suicide*, pp. 226–7; 387.
3 *Classification*, p. 88.
4 *Forms*, p. 412.
5 'Pragmatism', pp. 433–4.
6 *Classification*, pp. 86–7.
7 *Forms*, p. 493.
8 *Ethics*, p. 161.
9 The debate over whether Durkheim is a materialist or an idealist usually occurs on ontological ground. Those inclined to see him as a materialist point to the relative weight he assigns social 'morphology', or social structure. Those who label him an idealist point to the significance he attributes to collective representations. Epistemologically he is primarily an objectivist and therefore a materialist. Reality precedes and determines ideas. There are other, ontological, senses in which Durkheim is a materialist (social structure determines ideas); and also ontological senses in which he is an idealist (social/individual ideas determine individual behavior). Fenton (1984) recognizes this complexity, identifying Durkheim as both a materialist (ideas are superstructural reflections of the social structure) and an idealist (collective representations are relatively autonomous and the essence of social life).
10 *Forms*, pp. 31–2; 32, note.
11 *Ibid.*, p. 483.
12 *Ibid.*, p. 485.
13 *Ibid.*, p. 487.
14 *Philosophy*, pp. 95–6.
15 *Essays*, p. 54.
16 *Forms*, p. 486.
17 *Ibid.*
18 *Suicide*, pp. 226–7.
19 *Forms*, p. 485.
20 'Pragmatism', p. 433.
21 *Philosophy*, p. 31.
22 On the relation between Durkheim's concept of the relative autonomy of collective representations and his escape from categorization as either a materialist or an idealist see Bellah (1959), Lukes (1985) and Mestrovic (1988).
23 Bellah (1959) discusses Durkheim's opposition to the relativism of extreme pragmatism. Benoit-Smullyan (1948), Hamnett (1984) and Worsely (1956) see Durkheim as a relativist, because of his sociological theory of knowledge (society as subject or object of knowledge). According to Benton (1977), Durkheim's science/ideology distinction saves him from relativism. Fenton (1984), Gieryn (1982),

Hamnett (1984) and Hirst (1975) point to a contradiction in Durkheim's thought, between scientism and sociologism – the implicit relativism of his sociological theory of knowledge. Mestrovic (1988) believes that Durkheim combines relativism/pragmatism (knowledge is explained, as social) and absolutism/rationalism (knowledge is valid, as social). Lukes (1985) contends that Durkheim combines a relativistic approach to mythological 'knowledge' with an objective approach to science. Tiryakian (1978) sees Durkheim as opposing skepticism. Wallwork (1972) says, on the issue of moral relativism, that Durkheim argues for the variability of morality, but attributes that variability to structural causality rather than to arbitrariness.

24 According to Lukes (1985) Durkheim fails to distinguish between ideas that are true and ideas that are believed to be true. Munch (1988) ascribes this view to Durkheim as a strength: he sees validity as a matter of consensus.

25 Contrary to the criticism that Durkheim ignores individual thought (e.g. Lukes, 1985; Zeitlin, 1981), Durkheim actually discusses it a great deal. He simply believes that it is inferior to social thought.

26 On Durkheim and ideology see Larrain (1980) and Schmid (1981). Lukes (1985) highlights Durkheim's conceptualization of the co-existence of mythological and scientific truth in every society. Benton (1977) and Hirst (1975) both find a science/ideology distinction, a theory of collective ideology, and a lapse into ideology (empiricism) in Durkheim's theory. The relativist interpretation of Durkheim would imply his reduction of all thought to 'ideology', e.g. Hamnett (1984, p. 206).

27 *Ethics*, p. 79, emphasis added.

28 *Philosophy*, p. 64.

29 *Rules*, pp. 142–3.

30 *Essays*, pp. 89; 136.

31 *Ethics*, p. 79.

32 *Ibid.*, p. 92.

33 *Ibid.*, p. 93.

34 *Forms*, p. 486.

35 *Division*, p. 280.

36 This is similar to the way in which he becomes the arbitrary arbiter of the 'normal'.

37 *Ethics*, p. 161.

38 *Division*, pp. 290–1.

39 *Classification*, p. 88.

40 *Philosophy*, p. 63.

41 *Essays*, p. 89.

42 *Rules*, p. 14.

43 *Philosophy*, p. 77.

44 *Forms*, p. 38.

45 *Division*, p. 36.

46 *Rules*, p. 14, emphasis added.

47 *Division*, p. 36; *Forms*, p. 38.

48 *Rules*, p. xliv; 15; 43.
49 *Ethics*, p. 79.
50 *Division*, pp. 290–1. Gane (1988), Fenton (1984), and Wityak and Wallace (1981) find in early Durkheim an asocial conception of primitives and a view of their thought as individual, sensate and antithetical to collective, modern, scientific thought.
51 *Ethics*, p. 160, emphasis added.
52 *Socialism*, p. 11, emphasis added.
53 *Rules*, pp. 15; 43–4.
54 *Essays*, p. 89.
55 *Ethics*, p. 161.
56 *Forms*, p. 98.
57 *Division*, p. 280.
58 *Forms*, p. 38.
59 *Essays*, p. 89.
60 *Rules*, pp. xxxvii; xliv; 15.
61 *Ibid.*, p. 43.
62 *Ibid.*, p. 31.
63 *Forms*, p. 38.
64 *Division*, p. 36.
65 *Philosophy*, p. 66.
66 *Essays*, p. 89.
67 *Rules*, p. 32.
68 *Ibid.*, p. 144.
69 *Ibid.*, p. 146.
70 *Philosophy*, p. 21.
71 *Rules*, p. xxxvii.
72 *Ibid.*, pp. xli; 146; 37; 44.
73 *Essays*, p. 89.
74 *Forms*, p. 38.
75 *Rules*, p. 23.
76 *Ibid.*, pp. 43–4.
77 *Ibid.*, p. 14, emphasis added.
78 *Ibid.*, p. 15.
79 *Ibid.*, p. 144, emphasis added.
80 *Philosophy*, p. 66, emphasis added.
81 *Rules*, p. xlvi.
82 *Ibid.*, p. 34.
83 *Ibid.*, p. xli.
84 *Ibid.*, p. 32.
85 *Suicide*, p. 310.
86 *Division*, p. 36.
87 *Ibid.*, p. 280.
88 *Rules*, p. 34.
89 *Division*, pp. 285–6.
90 *Suicide*, p. 310.
91 *Forms*, p. 42.
92 *Rules*, pp. xxxvii; 34.
93 *Suicide*, p. 310.

 94 *Forms*, p. 41.
 95 *Division*, pp. 285–6.
 96 *Rules*, pp. 33–4.
 97 *Ibid.*, p. 17.
 98 *Ibid.*, p. xlvi.
 99 *Ibid.*, p. 42.
100 *Suicide*, pp. 311–12.
101 'Prefaces', p. 351.
102 *Rules*, pp. xliv; lii, note; 3.
103 *Suicide*, p. 311.
104 *Essays*, p. 136.
105 *Forms*, p. 239.
106 *Rules*, p. 32.
107 *Forms*, p. 41.
108 *Rules*, p. 17.
109 *Ibid.*, p. 29.
110 *Ibid.*, p. xlv.
111 *Education*, p. 119.
112 *Suicide*, pp. 142; 310.
113 *Philosophy*, p. 79.
114 *Ibid.*, p. 33.
115 *Essays*, p. 138.
116 'Sociology', p. 373.
117 *Forms*, pp. 107; 258.
118 *Ibid.*, 14–15; 72; 68; 426–7; 445; 477; 479.
119 *Suicide*, pp. 318; 334–6.
120 *Ibid.*, p. 162.
121 *Division*, p. 285.
122 *Ibid.*, pp. 285–6.
123 *Ethics*, p. 169.
124 *Ibid.*, p. 161.
125 *Forms*, pp. 239–40.
126 *Ibid.*, p. 251.
127 *Suicide*, pp. 325–6.
128 *Ethics*, pp. 161–2.
129 *Rules*, pp. 142–3.
130 *Philosophy*, p. 64.
131 *Rules*, pp. 142–3.
132 *Socialism*, pp. 5–6; 17.
133 *Ibid.*, p. 7.
134 *Ibid.*, pp. 8–9. Durkheim analyzes feminism and racism in similar
    ways. See Lehmann (Forthcoming).

6 COLLECTIVE TRUTH

 1 From *Pragmatisme et Sociologie*, cited in Bellah (1959).
 2 Related to the idea of knowing as seeing is the idea of knowing as
   reading. Thus it is not surprising that Durkheim makes the following

formulation. 'The future is already written for him who knows how to read it.' From *L'Année Sociologique*, cited in Giddens (1971a). Others who recognize and criticize Durkheim's tendency to empiricism, his epistemology of perception or sensation, include: Benton (1977), Keat and Urry (1975) ('positivism'); and Pearce (1989). See especially Hirst (1975) ('realism'). Gane (1988) recognizes this tendency, but supports it. Munch (1988) believes that Durkheim's sociological theory of knowledge emphasizes consensus rather than collective empiricism.

3 *Rules*, p. 23.
4 *Suicide*, p. 279.
5 *Division*, p. 88.
6 *Suicide*, pp. 226–7.
7 *Forms*, p. 482.
8 *Ibid.*
9 *Ibid.*, p. 487.
10 *Rules*, p. xlix.
11 *Ibid.*, p. 1.
12 *Forms*, p. 490.
13 *Ibid.*
14 *Ibid.*, p. 493.
15 *Ibid.*, p. 483, emphasis added.
16 *Ibid.*, p. 492.
17 *Ibid.*, p. 486.
18 *Division*, p. 307.
19 *Ibid.*, p. 379, emphasis added.
20 *Essays*, p. 141.
21 *Rules*, p. xliv.
22 *Classification*, p. 81, emphasis added.
23 *Forms*, p. 270, emphasis added.
24 Lukes (1985) calls particular attention to the fact that Durkheim denies the existence of a split between primitive and modern thought. Fenton (1984) and Gane (1988) find that late Durkheim (*Primitive Classification* and *Forms* versus *Division*) equates primitive and religious thought with modern and scientific thought as social and *conceptual* (as opposed to individual and sensate). Hamnett (1984) and Worsely (1956) find that late Durkheim equates primitive, religious thought with modern, scientific thought as social and *relative* (as opposed to apodictic and objective).
25 *Forms* p. 486, emphasis added.
26 *Suicide*, pp. 335–6.
27 *Division*, pp. 280; 52.
28 *Rules*, p. 14, emphasis added.
29 *Ibid.*, p. 44.
30 *Ibid.*, p. 72, note.
31 *Suicide*, pp. 310–18.
32 *Ibid.*, p. 336, emphasis added.
33 *Division*, p. 280, emphasis added.
34 *Essays*, p. 88.

35 *Ibid.*, p. 137.
36 *Education*, pp. 95–6, emphasis added.
37 For some of the contrasting views on Durkheim's relationship to socialism, see Barnes (1920); Benoit-Smullyan (1948); Benton (1977); Coser (1967); Fenton (1980, 1984); Gane (1984, 1988); Giddens (1971a); Hirst (1973, 1975); Lukes (1985); Mestrovic (1988); Mitchell (1931); Nizan (1971); Parsons (1949); Pearce (1989); Ranulf (1939); Richter (1960); Therborn (1976); Zeitlin (1981).
38 *Socialism*, p. 7.
39 *Ibid.*, pp. 9–10.
40 On Durkheim's theory of religion, see especially Pickering (1984), Poggi (1971) and Lukes (1985).
41 *Forms*, pp. 20–2.
42 *Ibid.*, p. 87.
43 *Ibid.*, p. 107.
44 *Ibid.*, p. 234.
45 *Ibid.*, pp. 251; 258.
46 *Ibid.*, p. 257, emphasis added.
47 *Ibid.*, p. 486.
48 *Ibid.*, p. 257, emphasis added.
49 *Ibid.*, p. 388.
50 *Ibid.*, pp. 408–9.
51 *Ibid.*, pp. 427; emphasis added, 445; 459; 465; 477.
52 *Ibid.*, p. 465, emphasis added.
53 *Ibid.*, p. 239.
54 *Ethics*, p. 160; emphasis added.
55 *Forms*, p. 475.
56 *Ethics*, p. 162.
57 *Formes*, p. 98; *Forms*, p. 87, emphasis added.
58 *Forms*, p. 257, emphasis added.
59 *Ibid.*, p. 464, emphasis added.
60 Mestrovic (1988) recognizes and supports Durkheim's equation of collective with objective knowledge, social knowledge with truth as a matter of method: collective knowledge is rational, and is constrained by standards of truth etc. Hamnett (1984) criticizes Durkheim's identification of collective knowledge and truth as 'legerdemain'. Munch (1988) accepts the collective knowledge/truth equation as a relationship of consensual legitimation.
61 *Forms*, p. 20.
62 *Ibid.*, p. 240.
63 *Ibid.*, pp. 240, 251; *Suicide*, p. 318.
64 *Forms*, pp. 251–8; *Suicide*, p. 335.
65 *Forms*, p. 95.
66 *Ibid.*, p. 261.
67 *Ibid.*, p. 426.
68 *Ibid.*, p. 445.
69 *Ibid.*, p. 465.
70 *Ibid.*, p. 468.
71 *Ibid.*, p. 259.

72 *Ibid.*, p. 465.
73 *Ethics*, pp. 160–1.
74 *Essays*, p. 141.
75 *Forms*, p. 21.
76 *Ibid.*, p. 87.
77 *Ibid.*, p. 22.
78 *Ibid.*, p. 26.
79 *Ibid.*, p. 166.
80 *Ibid.*, p. 40.
81 *Ibid.*, p. 233.
82 *Ibid.*, p. 234.
83 *Ibid.*, pp. 404; 406.
84 *Ibid.*, p. 270.
85 *Ibid.*, p. 365.
86 *Ibid.*, p. 271.
87 *Ibid.*, p. 494.
88 *Ibid.*, p. 477.
89 *Ibid.*, p. 478.
90 *Ibid.*
91 *Ibid.*, p. 479.
92 *Ibid.*, p. 478.
93 *Ibid.*, pp. 478–9.
94 *Ibid.*, p. 25, note, emphasis added.
95 *Ibid.*, p. 271, emphasis added.
96 *Ibid.*, p. 465, emphasis added.
97 *Ibid.*, p. 477, emphasis added.
98 *Ibid.*, p. 271.
99 *Ibid.*, p. 15.
100 *Ibid.*, p. 477, emphasis added.
101 This line of reasoning directly contradicts Parsons (1949) and others who see a fundamental difference between early Durkheim (*The Division of Labor*) and late Durkheim (*The Elementary Forms*), whether the difference is between positivism and voluntarism or between materialism and idealism. Durkheim changes the focus of his attention, and the emphasis of his concerns, from the social body, and the material, economic, individual and problematic sphere of social life; to the social mind, and the ideal/ideational, religious/moral, collective and panacean sphere of social life. He does not change his theoretical system. At the end of his life he looks back to the collective type of society and the unity of the collective consciousness which he would like to dialectically synthesize with modern, specialized, individualized society in a movement of reform and sublation. In the *Forms*, he is merely dealing with matters closer to his heart, and preparing to begin his lifelong dream and most cherished project, a systematic study of morality, by historically examining religion to find its 'essence' and universal function. The *Forms* is a profoundly deterministic book, if anything more so than the *Division* with its deliberate deference to individualism. And the *Forms* is a materialist work, both ontologically

and epistemologically; in the sense that Durkheim, because of his collective body/mind/subject, always combines materialism and idealism. For further indications of the chronological consistency of his thought, oriented around morality, see Giddens (1971a); LaCapra (1985); Lukes (1985); Tiryakian (1978); Wallwork (1972). LaCapra, for example, calls the *Forms* the '*summa*' of Durkheim's work.

102 *Forms*, p. 490.
103 *Ibid.*, p. 487.
104 *Ibid.*, p. 493.
105 *Division*, pp. 287–91.
106 *Ibid.*
107 *Ibid.*
108 *Forms*, p. 477.
109 *Education*, p. 78, emphasis added.
110 'Prefaces', pp. 341–7, emphasis added.
111 *Forms*, p. 493, emphasis added.
112 *Ibid.*, pp. 477–8.
113 *Ibid.*, pp. 41–2, emphasis added.
114 On Durkheim's view of society as subject and object of truth, as totality, see: Mestrovic (1988). Hirst (1975) recognizes Durkheim's view of the ultimate object of truth as society, and the ultimate mechanism of truth as the perception of reality by a subject. However, he understands Durkheim's subject of science as an *individual* subject.
115 *Education*, p. 79. On whether Durkheim's focus is on humanity (internationalist) or society (nationalist), see e.g. Fenton (1980, 1984); Lukes (1985); Mitchell (1931).
116 *Ethics*, pp. 79–80.
117 *Forms*, p. 479.
118 *Education*, p. 119.

Bibliography

Agger, Ben, *Cultural Studies as Critical Theory*, New York: Falmer, 1992.
——, *The Discourse of Domination: From the Frankfurt School to Postmodernism*, Evanston: Northwestern University Press, 1991.
——, *Fast Capitalism: A Critical Theory of Significance*, Urbana: University of Illinois Press, 1989.
——, *Socio(onto)logy*, Chicago: University of Illinois Press, 1989.
Alexander, Jeffrey C., 'Rethinking Durkheim's Intellectual Development I', *International Sociology* 1:1 (March, 1986), 91–107.
Alpert, Harry, 'Emile Durkheim: Enemy of Fixed Psychological Elements', *American Journal of Sociology* 63:6 (May, 1958), 662–4.
——, *Emile Durkheim and His Sociology*, New York: Columbia University Press, 1939.
Althusser, Louis, *Essays in Self-Criticism*, London: New Left Books, 1976.
——, *For Marx*, London: Verso, 1979.
——, *Lenin and Philosophy*, New York: Monthly Review Press, 1971.
——, *Montesquieu, Rousseau, Marx*, London: Verso, 1982.
——, and Etienne Balibar, *Reading Capital*, London: Verso, 1979.
Barnes, Harry, 'Durkheim's Contribution to the Reconstruction of Political Theory', *Political Science Quarterly* 35:2 (1920), 236–54.
Bellah, Robert N., 'Durkheim and History', *American Sociological Review* 24 (August, 1959), 447–60.
——, ed., *Emile Durkheim on Morality and Society*, Chicago: University of Chicago Press, 1983.
Benoit-Smullyan, Emile, 'The Sociologism of Emile Durkheim and His School', in Barnes, Harry, *An Introduction to the History of Sociology*, Chicago: University of Chicago Press, 1948, 499–537.
Benton, Ted, *Philosophical Foundations of the Three Sociologies*, Boston: Routledge & Kegan Paul, 1977.
Besnard, Philippe, 'L'anomie dans la biographie intellectuelle de Durkheim', *Sociologie et Sociétés* xiv:2 (1982), 45–53.
——, ed., *The Sociological Domain: The Durkheimians and the Founding of French Sociology*, New York: Cambridge University Press, 1983.
Bologh, Roslyn W., *Love or Greatness: Max Weber and Masculine Thinking – A Feminist Inquiry*, Boston: Unwin Hyman, 1990.

Bottomore, Tom, 'A Marxist Consideration of Durkheim', *Social Forces* 59:4 (June, 1981), 902–17.

——, and Robert Nisbet, *A History of Sociological Analysis*, New York: Basic Books, 1978.

Brantlinger, Patrick, *Crusoe's Footprints*, New York: Routledge, 1990.

Coser, Lewis A., 'Durkheim's Conservatism and its Implications for Sociological Theory', in Coser, *Continuities in the Study of Social Conflict*, New York: Free Press, 1967.

——, *Masters of Sociological Thought*, New York: Harcourt, Brace, Jovanovich, 1971.

Derrida, Jacques, 'Afterword: Toward an Ethic of Discussion', in *Limited inc.*, Evanston: Northwestern University Press, 1988, 111–60.

Fenton, Steve with Robert Reiner and Ian Hamnett, *Durkheim and Modern Sociology*, Cambridge: Cambridge University Press, 1984.

——, 'Race, Class and Politics in the Work of Emile Durkheim', in UNESCO, *Sociological Theories: Race and Colonialism*, Paris: UNESCO, 1980, 143–81.

Filloux, Jean-Claude, *Durkheim et le Socialisme*, Geneva: Libraire Droz, 1977.

——, 'Il ne Faut pas Oublier que Je Suis Fils de Rabbin', *Revue Française de Sociologie* 17:2 (April, 1976), 259–66.

Gane, Mike, 'Durkheim: The Sacred Language', *Economy and Society* 12:1 (February, 1983a), 1–47.

——, 'Durkheim: Woman as Outsider', *Economy and Society* 12 (1983b) 227–70.

——, 'Institutional Socialism and the Sociological Critique of Communism', *Economy and Society* 13 (1984), 305–30.

——, *On Durkheim's Rules of Sociological Method*, New York: Routledge, 1988.

Giddens, Anthony, *Capitalism and Modern Social Theory*, Cambridge: Cambridge University Press, 1971a.

——, 'Classical Social Theory and the Origins of Modern Sociology', *American Journal of Sociology* 81:4 (1976), 703–29.

——, 'Durkheim as a Review Critic', *Sociological Review* 18:2 (July, 1970), 171–96.

——, 'Durkheim's Political Sociology', *Sociological Review* 19:4 (November, 1971b) 477–519.

——, 'The "Individual" in the Writings of Durkheim', *Archives Européennes de Sociologie* 12:2 (1971c), 210–28.

Gieryn, Thomas, 'Durkheim's Sociology of Scientific Knowledge', *Journal of the History of the Behavioral Sciences* 18:2 (April, 1982), 107–29.

Glock, Charles and Phillip Hammond, *Beyond the Classics*, New York: Harper & Row, 1973.

Gouldner, Alvin, 'Introduction', in Durkheim, *Socialism and Saint-Simon*, Yellow Springs, Ohio: Antioch Press, 1958, pp. v–xxvii.

Hall, Stuart, 'The Hinterland of Science: Ideology and the "Sociology of Knowledge"', *Working Papers in Cultural Studies* 10 (1977), 9–32.

Hamnett, Ian, 'Durkheim and the Study of Religion', in Fenton, Steve with Robert Reiner and Ian Hamnett, *Durkheim and Modern Sociology*, New York: Cambridge University Press, 1984, 202–18.

Hirst, Paul Q., *Durkheim, Bernard and Epistemology*, Boston: Routledge & Kegan Paul, 1975.

——, 'Morphology and Pathology: Biological Analogies and Metaphors in Durkheim's *The Rules of Sociological Method*', *Economy and Society* 2:1 (February, 1973), 1–34.

Jones, Robert, 'On Understanding a Sociological Classic', *American Journal of Sociology* 83:2 (1977), 279–319.

Kaufman-Osborn, Timothy, 'Modernity's Myth of Facts: Emile Durkheim and the Politics of Knowledge', *Theory and Society* 17:1 (January, 1988), 121–45.

Keat, Russell and John Urry, *Social Theory as Science*, Boston: Routledge & Kegan Paul, 1975.

Knapp, Peter, 'Hegel's Universal in Marx, Durkheim and Weber: The Role of Hegelian Ideas in the Origin of Sociology', *Sociological Forum* 1:4 (Fall, 1986), 586–609.

LaCapra, Dominick, *Emile Durkheim: Sociologist and Philosopher*, Chicago: University of Chicago Press, 1985.

Lacroix, Bernard, *Durkheim et la Politique*, Paris: Presses de la Fondation Nationale des Sciences Politiques, 1981.

Larrain, Jorge, 'Durkheim's Concept of Ideology', *The Sociological Review* 28:1 (February, 1980), 129–39.

Lehmann, Jennifer M., *Durkheim and Women: The Problematic Relationship*, Lincoln: The University of Nebraska Press, Forthcoming.

——, 'Durkheim's Response to Feminism: Prescriptions for Women', *Sociological Theory* 8:2 (1990), 163–87.

——, 'Durkheim's Women: The Durkheimian Theory of the Structures and Functions of Sexuality', *Current Perspectives in Social Theory* 11 (1991), 141–67.

——, 'The Undecidability of Derrida/The Premature Demise of Althusser', *Current Perspectives in Social Theory* 13 (1993).

Lukes, Steven, 'Durkheim's "Individualism and the Intellectuals"', *Political Studies* 17:1 (March, 1969), 14–30.

——, *Emile Durkheim: His Life and Work*, Stanford: Stanford University Press, 1985.

Marske, Charles, 'Durkheim's "Cult of the Individual" and the Moral Reconstitution of Society', *Sociological Theory* 5:1 (Spring, 1987), 1–14.

Mestrovic, Stjepan, 'Durkheim's Concept of the Unconscious', *Current Perspectives in Social Theory* 5 (1984), 267–88.

——, 'Durkheim's Renovated Rationalism and the Idea that "Collective Life is Only Made of Representations"', *Current Perspectives in Social Theory* 6 (1985), 199–218.

——, *Emile Durkheim and the Reformation of Sociology*, Totowa, N.J.: Rowman and Littlefield, 1988.

Mitchell, M. Marion, 'Emile Durkheim and the Philosophy of Nationalism', *Political Science Quarterly* 46:1 (1931), 87–106.

Moore, Barrington, 'Strategy in Social Science', in M. Stern and A. Vidich, eds., *Sociology on Trial*, Englewood Cliffs: Prentice Hall, 1963.

Munch, Richard, *Understanding Modernity*, New York: Routledge, 1988.

Nisbet, Robert, 'Conservatism and Sociology', *American Journal of Sociology* 58 (1952), 167–75.

——, *Emile Durkheim*, Englewood Cliffs: Prentice Hall, 1965.

——, *The Sociology of Emile Durkheim*, New York: Oxford University Press, 1975.

Nizan, Paul, *The Watchdogs*, New York: Monthly Review Press, 1971.

Nye, D.A. and C.E. Ashworth, 'Emile Durkheim: Was He a Nominalist or a Realist?' *British Journal of Sociology* 22:2 (June, 1971), 133–48.

Parsons, Talcott, 'Durkheim on Religion Revisited: Another Look at *The Elementary Forms of the Religious Life*', in Glock and Hammond, eds., (1973).

——, *The Structure of Social Action*, Vols. 1 and 2, New York: Free Press, 1949.

Pateman, Carole, *The Sexual Contract*, Stanford: Stanford University Press, 1988.

Pearce, Frank, *The Radical Durkheim*, Boston: Unwin Hyman, 1989.

Pickering, W.S.F., *Durkheim's Sociology of Religion: Themes and Theories*, London: Routledge & Kegan Paul, 1984.

Poggi, Gianfranco, *Images of Society: Essays on the Sociological Theories of Tocqueville, Marx, and Durkheim*, Stanford: Stanford University Press, 1972.

——, 'The Place of Religion in Durkheim's Theory of Institutions', *Archives Européennes de Sociologie* 12:2 (1971), 229–60.

Pope, Whitney, 'Classic on Classic: Parsons' Interpretation of Durkheim', *American Sociological Review* 38:4 (August, 1973), 399–415.

——, 'Durkheim as a Functionalist', *The Sociological Quarterly* 16:3 (Summer, 1975), 361–79.

——, Jere Cohen and Lawrence E. Hazelrigg, 'On the Divergence of Weber and Durkheim: A Critique of Parsons' Convergence Thesis', *American Sociological Review* 40:4 (August, 1975), 417–27.

Ranulf, Svend, 'Scholarly Forerunners of Fascism', *Ethics* 50 (1939), 16–34.

Richter, Melvin, 'Durkheim's Politics and Political Theory', in Wolff (1960), 170–210.

Ritzer, George, *Sociological Theory*, New York: Alfred A. Knopf, 1988.

Schmid, Herman, 'On the Origin of Ideology', *Acta Sociologica* 24:1–2 (1981), 57–73.

Strawbridge, Sheelagh, 'Althusser's Theory of Ideology and Durkheim's Account of Religion: An Examination of Some Striking Parallels', *Sociological Review* 30:1 (1982), 125–140.

Szacki, Jerzy, *History of Sociological Thought*, Westport: Greenwood Press, 1979.

Takla, Tendzin and Whitney Pope, 'The Force Imagery in Durkheim: The Integration of Theory, Metatheory, and Method', *Sociological Theory* 3:1 (Spring, 1985), 74–88.

Therborn, Goran, *Science, Class and Society*, London: New Left Books, 1976.

Tiryakian, Edward, 'Emile Durkheim', in Bottomore and Nisbet (1978).

Wallace, Ruth, 'Emile Durkheim and the Civil Religion Concept', *Review of Religious Research* 18:3 (1977), 287–90.

——, 'The Secular Ethic and the Spirit of Patriotism', *Sociological Analysis* 34:1 (Spring, 1973), 3–11.

Wallwork, Ernest, *Durkheim, Morality and Milieu*, Cambridge: Harvard University Press, 1972.

Willer, Judith, 'The Implications of Durkheim's Philosophy of Science', *Kansas Journal of Sociology* 4:4 (Fall, 1968), 175–190.

Wityak, Nancy and Ruth Wallace, 'Durkheim's Non-Social Facts About Primitives and Women', *Sociological Inquiry* 51 (1981), 61–7.

Wolff, Kurt, ed., *Emile Durkheim*, Columbus: Ohio State University Press, 1960.

Worsley, P.M., 'Emile Durkheim's Theory of Knowledge', *Sociological Review* 4 (1956), 47–62.

Zeitlin, Irving, *Ideology and the Development of Sociological Theory*, Englewood Cliffs: Prentice Hall, 1981.

Bibliography of Durkheim's works

'Contribution', Dagan, Henri, *Enquête sur l'antisemitisme*, Paris: P.V. Stock, 1899, 59–63.

Contributions to L'Année Sociologique, New York: Free Press, 1980, edited by Yash Nandan.

'Cours de science sociale: leçon d'ouverture', *Revue Internationale de l'Enseignement*, xv, 23–48, 1888.

De la Division du Travail Social, Paris: Alcan, 1893.

The Division of Labor in Society, New York: MacMillan, 1933.

'The Dualism of Human Nature', in Wolff (1960), 325–40.

'A Durkheim Fragment: The Conjugal Family', *American Journal of Sociology*, 5, lxx, 527–36.

L'Education Morale, Paris: Alcan, 1925.

The Elementary Forms of the Religious Life, New York: MacMillan, 1915.

Emile Durkheim on Institutional Analysis, Chicago: University of Chicago Press, 1978, edited by Mark Traugott.

Essays on Morals and Education, Boston: Routledge & Kegan Paul, 1979, edited by W.S.F. Pickering.

Les Formes Elémentaires de la Vie Religieuse. Paris: Alcan, 1912.

Incest: The Nature and Origin of the Taboo, New York: Lyle Stuart, 1963.

'Individualism and the Intellectuals', *Political Studies*, xvii, 1969, 14–30.

'Introduction to the Sociology of the Family', in Traugott (1978).

Leçons de Sociologie, Paris: Presses Universitaires de France, 1950.

Moral Education, New York: Free Press of Glencoe, 1961.

'Pragmatism and Sociology' (1913–14) in Wolff (1960), 386–436.

'Prefaces to L'Annéé Sociologique', in Wolff (1960), 341–53.

Primitive Classification, Chicago: University of Chicago Press, 1973. (With Marcel Mauss.)

Professional Ethics and Civic Morals, London: Routledge & Kegan Paul, 1957.

Les Règles de la Méthode Sociologique, Paris: Alcan, 1895.

The Rules of the Sociological Method, Glencoe, Illinois: Free Press of Glencoe, 1938.

Socialism and Saint-Simon, Yellow Springs, Ohio: Antioch Press, 1958.

Le Socialisme, Paris: Presses Universitaires de France, 1928.

'La Sociologie en France au XIXe siècle', *Revue Bleue*, 4e serie, xii, 1900, 609–13.

Sociologie et Philosophie, Paris: Alcan, 1924.

'Sociologie et sciences sociales', *Revue Philosophique de la France et de L'étranger*, lv, 1903, 465–97.

'Sociology', in Wolff (1960), 376–385.

'Sociology and its Scientific Field', in Wolff (1960), 354–75.

Sociology and Philosophy, Glencoe, Illinois: Free Press of Glencoe, 1953.

Le Suicide, Paris: Alcan, 1897.

Suicide, Glencoe, Illinois: Free Press of Glencoe, 1951.

Index